Absolute Beginner's Guide

to

Corel®
WordPerfect® 10

Laura Acklen

201 West 103rd Street,
Indianapolis, Indiana 46290

Absolute Beginner's Guide to Corel® WordPerfect® 10

International Standard Book Number: 0-7897-2921-0

Library of Congress Catalog Card Number: 2002113719

Printed in the United States of America

First Printing: February 2003

06   05   04   03   4   3   2

Trademarks

All terms mentioned in this book that are known to be trademarks or service marks have been appropriately capitalized. Que Publishing cannot attest to the accuracy of this information. Use of a term in this book should not be regarded as affecting the validity of any trademark or service mark.

Corel and WordPerfect are registered trademarks of Corel Corporation.

Warning and Disclaimer

Every effort has been made to make this book as complete and as accurate as possible, but no warranty or fitness is implied. The information provided is on an "as is" basis. The author and the publisher shall have neither liability nor responsibility to any person or entity with respect to any loss or damages arising from the information contained in this book.

Associate Publisher
Greg Wiegand

Acquisitions Editor
Stephanie J. McComb

Development Editor
Laura Norman

Managing Editor
Charlotte Clapp

Project Editor
Tonya Simpson

Copy Editor
Geneil Breeze

Indexer
Erika Millen

Proofreader
Linda Seifert

Technical Editors
Dan Fingerman
Patricia Cardoza

Team Coordinator
Sharry Lee Gregory

Interior Designer
Anne Jones

Cover Designer
Dan Armstrong

Page Layout
Cheryl Lynch

Contents at a Glance

Table of Contents

About the Author

Laura Acklen has been writing books about WordPerfect since 1993 when she wrote her first book, *Oops! What To Do When Things Go Wrong with WordPerfect*. She contributed to three versions of Que's *Special Edition Using WordPerfect* (6, 6.1, and 7) and co-authored Que's *Special Edition Using Corel WordPerfect 9* and *Special Edition Using Corel WordPerfect 10* books with Read Gilgen. She writes articles for Corel's OfficeCommunity.com, is a moderator at WordPerfect Universe (www.wpuniverse.com), and maintains a presence on the Corel newsgroups. She is also the Webmistress of WPWriter.com, a Web site devoted to WordPerfect.

Dedication

To my in-laws, Jim and Mary Alice Acklen, for the gift of a warm, loving, tightly knit, and slightly crazy extended family.

Acknowledgments

My favorite part of a project is having an opportunity to say thank you to everyone who helped bring it to fruition. To begin, I would like to gratefully acknowledge the assistance of Read Gilgen, my favorite writing partner, on the Tables, Lists and Outlines, and Graphics chapters.

I was thrilled to have another opportunity to work with Stephanie McComb. It is such a pleasure to work with someone who is on the author's side. Stephanie really got behind the idea of writing a beginner book that focused on the most frequently used application in a suite—the word processor—rather than trying to cover all the applications in 350 pages. I'm very grateful for her faith in me and in what I wanted to do with this book.

I would also like to thank Corel WordPerfect Product Managers Dan Alder and Julie Anne Leggett. They took time out of their busy days to quickly and thoughtfully respond to our requests for information. I want to thank you both for the support and encouragement. I also want to mention the assistance I received from Cindy Howard, Lead Program Manager, and Wendy Lowe, Program Manager for Corel WordPerfect Office products. Your responsiveness is appreciated!

I would also like to thank my sweet husband and children for their patience with my crazy work schedule.

We Want to Hear from You!

As the reader of this book, *you* are our most important critic and commentator. We value your opinion and want to know what we're doing right, what we could do better, what areas you'd like to see us publish in, and any other words of wisdom you're willing to pass our way.

As an associate publisher for Que Publishing, I welcome your comments. You can email or write me directly to let me know what you did or didn't like about this book—as well as what we can do to make our books better.

Please note that I cannot help you with technical problems related to the *topic* of this book. We do have a User Services group, however, where I will forward specific technical questions related to the book.

When you write, please be sure to include this book's title and author as well as your name, email address, and phone number. I will carefully review your comments and share them with the author and editors who worked on the book.

Email: feedback@quepublishing.com

Mail: Greg Wiegand
        Que Publishing
        201 West 103rd Street
        Indianapolis, IN 46290 USA

For more information about this book or another Que title, visit our Web site at www.quepublishing.com. Type the ISBN (excluding hyphens) or the title of a book in the Search field to find the page you're looking for.

INTRODUCTION

If you are new to WordPerfect 10 or to word processing in general, this is the book for you. With clear, concise explanations and lots of numbered steps, you'll quickly learn everything you need to get the most out of the WordPerfect application. We assume no previous experience with a word processor, so you can start from the very beginning and work up to some pretty advanced features.

If you purchased a Dell, Gateway, or HP computer, you may have received a free copy of Corel's Productivity Pack, which includes WordPerfect 10 and Quattro Pro 10. Certain models of Sony computers come with a copy of the standard edition of Corel's WordPerfect Office 2002, which includes WordPerfect 10, Quattro Pro 10, and Presentations 10.

WordPerfect is classified as a word processor, but in reality, it is much, much more. The majority of users find that even though they have the whole suite of applications to choose from, they spend most of their time in WordPerfect. From writing a simple letter, to creating presentation materials, to using tables to perform calculations, WordPerfect can do it all.

What does this mean to you? Quite simply, that you don't need to learn two or three applications to get your job done. You can do most, if not all, of your tasks in WordPerfect.

For this reason, we decided that we could best serve new users of the Productivity Pack, Family Pack, or WordPerfect Office 2002 suite, by focusing our attention on WordPerfect. There are three bonus appendixes get you up and running in Quattro Pro.

Some Key Terms

To use WordPerfect, you need to know the basic terminology used for common mouse actions:

- **Point**—Move the mouse on the desk to move the pointer onscreen. The tip of the arrow should be on the item to which you are pointing.
- **Click**—Press and release the left mouse button once. You use a click to select commands and toolbar buttons, as well as perform other tasks.
- **Double-click**—Press and release the left mouse button twice in rapid succession.
- **Right-click**—Press and release the right mouse button once. You can right-click to display a QuickMenu just about anywhere in the program.
- **Drag and drop**—Hold down the mouse button and drag the pointer across the screen. Release the mouse button. Dragging is most often used for selecting and moving text and objects.

Things to Keep in Mind

You can customize many features of WordPerfect so that it is set up the way you like to work. That's one of the major benefits of using WordPerfect. For consistency, though, this book makes some assumptions about how you use your computer. When working through steps and especially when viewing the figures in this book, keep in mind the following distinctions:

- WordPerfect gives you many different methods to perform the same task. For example, for commands, you can select a command from a menu, use a shortcut key, use a toolbar button, or use a QuickMenu. This book usually mentions one or two methods (the most common for that particular task) and then includes other methods in a tip.
- Your WordPerfect screen may not look identical to the one used in the figures in this book. For instance, if you use the ruler, you see that. (Most of the figures in this book don't show the ruler.) Don't let these differences distract you; WordPerfect may look different, but it works the same way.
- Your computer setup is most likely different from the one used in the book. Therefore, you will see different programs listed on your Start menu, different fonts in your font list, different folders and documents, and so on. Again, don't be distracted by the differences.

How to Use This Book

This book is divided into six parts, each part focusing on a different theme. The book builds on the skills you need, starting with the basics of formatting and then moving to more complex topics such as templates and macros. You can read the book straight through, look up topics when you have a question, or browse through the contents, reading information that intrigues you. Here is a quick breakdown of the parts.

Part I, "Learning the Basics," covers the essentials for creating and editing documents. Everything you need to know to create, edit, spell check, print, and apply basic formatting is in this section. Chapter 1 has an introduction to WordPerfect 10. Chapter 2 covers creating and saving documents. Chapter 3 focuses on locating and opening documents. In Chapter 4, you learn editing techniques. Chapter 5 covers basic formatting techniques and working in Reveal Codes. Chapter 6 explains how to use the writing tools.

Part II, "Making It Look Nice," explains how to apply formatting to paragraphs (Chapter 7) and pages (Chapter 8). Chapter 9 covers the use of styles for consistency and flexibility when you format your documents.

Part III, "Organizing Information," focuses on ways to organize information. Chapter 10 shows you how to use the Tables feature to organize and format information in columns. Chapter 11 shows you how to quickly create bulleted and numbered lists, and how to organize information in an outline format.

Part IV, "Adding Visuals," explains how to add graphics and other elements to improve the appearance of your documents. Chapter 12 shows you how to add graphic lines and images to your documents. Chapter 13 explains how you can copy or link information from another program into a WordPerfect document.

Part V, "Automating Your Work," covers the tools that you can use to automate repetitive tasks. In Chapter 14, you learn how to use the Merge feature to generate documents, such as form letters with envelopes and labels. In Chapter 15, you learn how to create and manage contact information with the CorelCENTRAL Address Book. Chapter 16 shows you how to use templates to automate the creation of frequently used documents. In Chapter 17, you learn how to create and play macros, which are capable of automating virtually every process in WordPerfect. Finally, Chapter 18 covers the Task Manager included with Corel's Family Pack and several editions of the Corel Productivity Pack.

Part VI contains four appendixes, three of which get you up to speed with Quattro Pro. Appendix A explains how to enter and format data. Appendix B covers formulas and functions, so you'll learn how to create formulas and how to use the built-in functions. Appendix C covers formatting and adjusting the structure of a spreadsheet. Appendix D points out the differences between the different Corel WordPerfect products.

I hope you enjoy your WordPerfect learning experience!

Conventions Used in This Book

You will find cautions, tips, and notes scattered throughout this book. Don't skip over these; they contain some important tidbits to help you along the way.

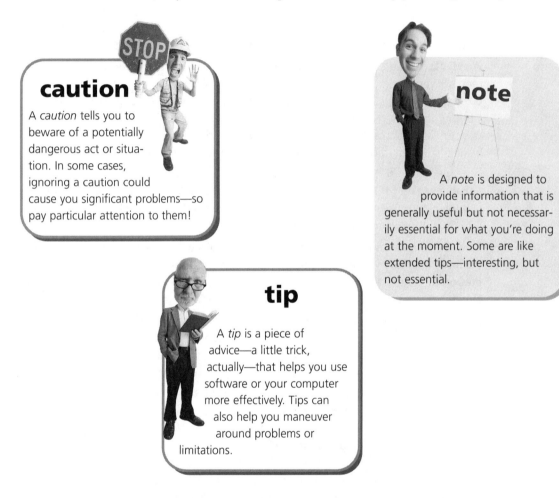

caution

A *caution* tells you to beware of a potentially dangerous act or situation. In some cases, ignoring a caution could cause you significant problems—so pay particular attention to them!

note

A *note* is designed to provide information that is generally useful but not necessarily essential for what you're doing at the moment. Some are like extended tips—interesting, but not essential.

tip

A *tip* is a piece of advice—a little trick, actually—that helps you use software or your computer more effectively. Tips can also help you maneuver around problems or limitations.

There are some other helpful conventions in the book to make your learning experience as smooth as possible. Text that you are going to type looks like this: `type a filename`. Buttons you click, menu commands you select, keys you press, and other action related items are in **bold** in the text to help you locate instructions as you are reading. New terms being defined in the text are in *italic*. Keep these conventions in mind as you read through the text.

PART i

LEARNING THE BASICS

- Get WordPerfect up and running and learn your way around the screen.

- Find out how to work with the toolbars that hold all those buttons.

- Learn about the WordPerfect menus and how to get help if you're stuck.

1

GETTING AROUND AND GETTING HELP IN WORDPERFECT

The *Absolute Beginner's Guide* books are written for new users, so the first section starts at the very beginning. In this chapter, you'll learn how to start and exit WordPerfect and how to recognize different parts of the screen. You'll figure out what a toolbar is, why you want to use it, and how to switch to another toolbar. You'll see how to use the mouse or the keyboard to select from the menus. Finally, you'll discover how you can use the Help system to learn more about the vast collection of features in WordPerfect. After you complete this first section, you'll be ready to jump to whatever chapter interests you.

What Is WordPerfect?

Whether you've just purchased your first computer and found this program called WordPerfect 10 installed, or you know how to use your computer but just purchased WordPerfect 10, this book is for you.

If this is the first time you've ever used WordPerfect, you're in for a real treat. You'll soon see that WordPerfect is the most intuitive software application you've ever used. Whether you are self-employed, work for someone else, or you use WordPerfect at school or at home, you'll be pleasantly surprised at how easy it is to create and edit documents. Here are just a few things you can do with WordPerfect:

- Write a letter or memo
- Create a simple newsletter or brochure
- Write a report, thesis, or resume
- Create a list or outline
- Create tables with built-in calculations
- Prepare a mass mailing with envelopes and labels

If you've been working with computers for a while or have used another word processor before, you can skim through most of this chapter and just pick up what you need to get started.

If you just bought a new computer with WordPerfect preinstalled, and you want to get started in WordPerfect right away, some basic help, such as the steps to start and exit WordPerfect, how to work with your mouse and keyboard to select from menus, and other basic computing techniques are covered—just in case you need them.

Getting WordPerfect Up and Running

The fastest way to start WordPerfect is to double-click the program shortcut on the desktop. If you don't have the shortcut, you can use the Start menu instead by clicking the **Start** button, pointing to **Programs**, and then pointing to **WordPerfect Office 2002** to open the submenu (see Figure 1.1). Click WordPerfect 10 to start the program.

> **note**
>
> If you don't see the WordPerfect Office 2002 folder on your Start menu, the program hasn't been installed on your system yet. Insert the Corel CD in the CD drive. If the Setup program doesn't start in a minute or two, choose **Start**, **Run**; browse to the CD drive; and then double-click setup.exe to start the Setup program.

FIGURE 1.1
You can launch
WordPerfect 10
from the Start
menu with just
two clicks.

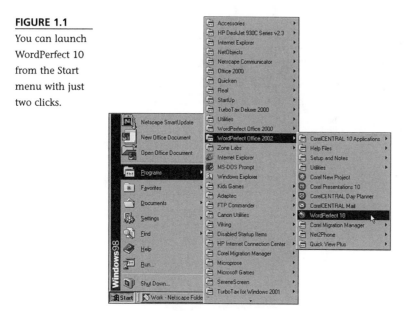

FIGURE 1.1
You can launch
WordPerfect 10
from the Start
menu with just
two clicks.

Getting Acquainted with WordPerfect

You might be new to WordPerfect, but if you've used another Windows program, you'll recognize most of the screen elements. There is always a title bar, menu bar, toolbar, and control buttons. This is one of the nice things about Windows—learning one application puts you ahead of the game when you need to learn another.

When you start WordPerfect, a blank document appears (see Figure 1.2), so you can start typing immediately. The insertion point shows you where the text will appear. The shadow cursor shows you where the insertion point will be if you click the mouse button.

You might see some gray lines on your screen. These are called *guidelines*. They help you see the text area of your page by marking the top, bottom, left, and right margins.

If you find the guidelines distracting, you can turn them off by choosing **View**, **Guidelines** from the menu. In the Guidelines dialog box, remove the check mark next to **Margins**; then click **OK**.

tip

Clicking and dragging the guidelines is a quick way to change the margins.

Insertion point

Title bar   Guidelines   Menu bar   Toolbar   Property bar

FIGURE 1.2

The WordPerfect screen has the same elements that you have seen in other Windows applications.

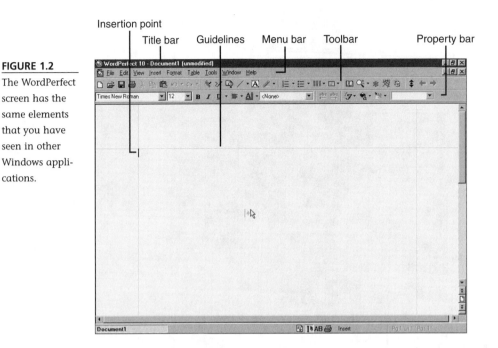

Working with the Property Bar and Toolbars

The property bar is placed right on top of the white workspace. This bar can morph into something else, depending on what you are doing at the time. You might start out with the text property bar, but as soon as you create a table, it switches to the table property bar. When you create an outline, you get the outline property bar, and so on. It's *very* cool. The buttons that you need magically appear, and you get your work done twice as fast because you aren't searching through the menus for a command.

The toolbar is different from the property bar. It doesn't change unless you tell it to. The toolbar you see in Figure 1.2 is called the WordPerfect 10 toolbar and has buttons for general editing tasks. There are 22 other toolbars to choose from, including WordPerfect 7, WordPerfect 8, WordPerfect 9, and Microsoft Word 97 toolbars. Other toolbars contain buttons for working with fonts, outlines, graphics, tables, macros, and so on.

To see a list of toolbars:

1. Right-click the toolbar to open the toolbar QuickMenu (see Figure 1.3). You'll see that the WordPerfect 10 toolbar already has a check mark next to it. If a check mark appears next to the name, it means that the toolbar is already on.

2. Click the toolbar you want to turn on. Clicking an *unchecked* toolbar name turns it on; clicking a *checked* toolbar name turns it off.

3. To see a complete list of available toolbars, click **More**.

4. Click anywhere in the document to clear the toolbar QuickMenu.

If you don't see the toolbar or the property bar, it might have been moved to another part of the screen. Look on the left and right sides of the document window. Also, look at the bottom of the screen, just above the status bar. If you don't see the bars at all, they've probably been turned off. Choose **View**, **Toolbars**. Place a check mark in the box next to **Property Bar** and/or **WordPerfect 10**.

FIGURE 1.3
Right-click a toolbar to open the QuickMenu, where you can switch to another toolbar or turn off the toolbar(s).

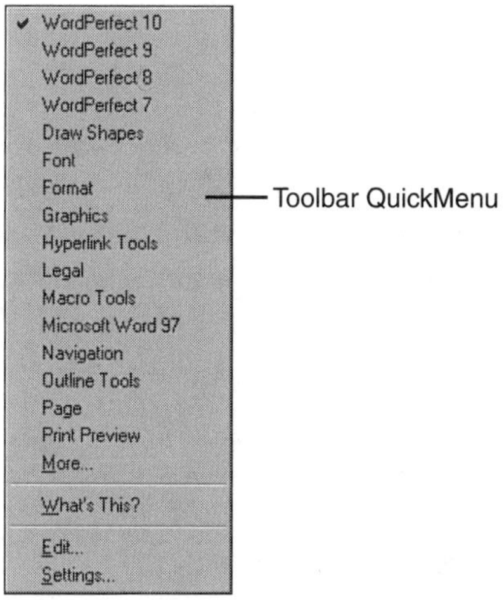

Toolbar QuickMenu

- WordPerfect 10
- WordPerfect 9
- WordPerfect 8
- WordPerfect 7
- Draw Shapes
- Font
- Format
- Graphics
- Hyperlink Tools
- Legal
- Macro Tools
- Microsoft Word 97
- Navigation
- Outline Tools
- Page
- Print Preview
- More...
- What's This?
- Edit...
- Settings...

Using the Menus

The menus in WordPerfect work the same way as in any other Windows program, so if you've been working with a computer for more than a few days, you've probably already figured out this part. However, you might have just purchased your first computer, and because you might need a little help with this, I'm including a short section.

They are called *pull-down menus* because when you open a menu, it cascades down into the window. In WordPerfect, they open up into the white workspace. You can use the mouse or the keyboard to select from the menus.

Working with the mouse:

- To open a menu with the mouse, click the menu name.
- To open a submenu, point to an item with an arrow next to it.
- To select an item, click it.

Working with the keyboard:

- To open a menu with the keyboard, hold down **Alt**, and then press the underlined letter. For example, to open the File menu, press **Alt+F**.
- To open a submenu or select an item, press the underlined letter (this time, without the Alt key).
- To move around in the menus, use the arrow keys. Press **Enter** to choose a highlighted command.

Getting Help

WordPerfect 10 offers an amazing amount of support to get you up and running as quickly as possible. Even if you're not sure exactly what you're looking for, you can still find the help you need. After you've found the information that you need, you can quickly get right back to where you were and continue working.

Getting "Quick and Easy" Help

The best place to start is with techniques that give you just enough help to get you started. Sometimes all you need is a little hint to get you pointed in the right direction. The first two items show you how to display QuickTips for screen elements and menu items. This is a great way to get acquainted with the toolbars and menu commands.

- You can find out the name of a toolbar button by pointing to it with the mouse and pausing. A QuickTip appears and tells you either the name or a brief description of the button. You can use this on all types of screen elements, not just toolbar buttons.
- You can get descriptions of menu commands by pointing to the command and pausing. A QuickTip appears with a description.

■ You can press **Shift+F1** to change the mouse pointer into a What's This pointer. Click on a screen element for a description.

■ In dialog boxes, click the **What's This** button, and then click the dialog box option on which you want help. A QuickTip appears with a description for that option (see Figure 1.4). For more help, click the **Help** button in the lower-right corner. This opens a Help window with the help topic for that dialog box or feature.

What's This button

FIGURE 1.4

Most dialog boxes have a What's This button next to the Close button.

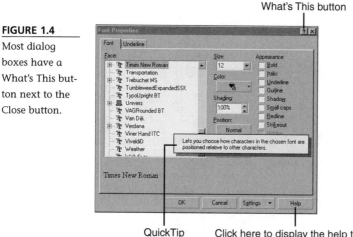

QuickTip   Click here to display the help topic.

Accessing the Help Topics

Help topics are great when you need a little push in the right direction. For more details, including many numbered steps and links to related items, go to the Help Topics:

■ Choose **Help**, **Help Topics**. Click the **Contents** tab. The Contents section is more task-oriented, so you'll find the features organized into projects, such as adding images to your documents or using Internet tools. Double-click the book icons to open up the category. Help topics have a question mark icon next to them (see Figure 1.5). Double-click these icons to display a help topic.

■ Choose **Help**, **Help Topics**. Click the **Index** tab. The Index is great when you want to search for a subject and get a list of help topics to choose from. Type a keyword (or just the first few letters) to jump down through the index (see Figure 1.6). Double-click an index entry to display the help topic, or in some cases, a list of possible help topics to choose from.

Double-click this icon to display a help topic.

FIGURE 1.5

The Contents tab of the Help Topics dialog box organizes help topics using a book-and-chapter model.

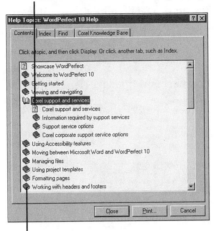

Double-click the book icon to open more topics.

Type a keyword here.

FIGURE 1.6

The Index tab of the Help Topics dialog box displays the help topics alphabetically.

Double-click an entry.

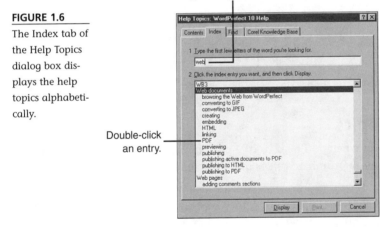

Getting Help on the Web

If you have an Internet connection, there are several ways to access Corel Web sites for support:

- The first method is through Corel Connector, which gives you access to Corel Web sites through Internet Explorer. Choose **Help**, **Corel Connector** to open a window with a list of Corel sites. Click an item in the list to launch Internet Explorer and visit the site. *(Note: You must have Internet Explorer installed on your system to use Corel Connector.)*

■ The second method uses your default Windows browser (which may or may not be Internet Explorer). Choose **Help**, **Corel on the Web**; then choose an item from the list. WordPerfect launches the default browser and then takes you to the selected page. Figure 1.7 shows Corel's Office Community Web page, where you'll find articles, tutorials, tips and tricks, downloads, links, and resources.

FIGURE 1.7

The Corel Web Site option on the Help menu takes you to OfficeCommunity. com, Corel's WordPerfect Office Web site.

■ Corel also maintains an online searchable knowledge base. Choose **Help**, **Help Topics**; then click the Corel Knowledge Base tab. Type in a keyword, and then click **Search** to search through thousands of technical information documents (TIDs) created by Corel's Technical Support department. You can also go directly to the knowledge base at http://kb.corel.com.

Helping Microsoft Word Users Make the Transition

For those making the transition from Microsoft Word, there is a special help section just for you. Choose **Help**, **Microsoft Word Help**. In this section of help topics, you'll learn how to

■ Open Microsoft Word documents in WordPerfect.

■ Save documents in Microsoft Word format so you can easily share documents with clients and associates who use Word.

■ Turn on the Microsoft Word toolbar so you can find familiar buttons.

- Compare the Word shortcut keys to WordPerfect shortcut keys so you can see the differences. A link takes you to a help topic that explains how to customize the shortcut keys to reflect Microsoft Word or WordPerfect settings.

- Compare WordPerfect and Word features so you can match up similar features.

THE ABSOLUTE MINIMUM

- Learn how to start WordPerfect with a desktop shortcut or through the Start menu.

- Get acquainted with all the elements on the screen and learn what they do.

- Learn how to use the toolbars and property bar. There are more than 20 different toolbars to pick from, including a toolbar that has the same buttons as the toolbar in Microsoft Word.

- Use the mouse or the keyboard to choose commands from the menus.

- When you get stuck, you can get help right away in the Help Topics and on the Web. They're all inside WordPerfect, so you don't have to stop and launch another program.

- Identify WordPerfect's default settings for all new documents.

- Learn how to insert and delete text as you edit a document. Use the mouse and keyboard to move around and to reposition the insertion point.

- Learn how to save and print a completed document.

- Discover how to save documents in a different format so they can be opened in other programs.

2

CREATING AND EDITING DOCUMENTS

In Chapter 1, you learned how to start the program and how to use the toolbars and menus. You also learned how easy it is to get help if you get stuck on something. This chapter shows you how to create and print documents, so you're about to go "hands on." You'll see that you can start typing as soon as you start the program. You can use the mouse or the keyboard to move around and make changes. When you're satisfied, you can print and save the document.

Creating Documents

When you start WordPerfect, you can immediately start typing in the blank document. The new document that you are creating comes with standard settings already in place. Table 2.1 lists some of these settings.

TABLE 2.1   WordPerfect's Default Settings

Element	Default Setting
Font	Times New Roman 12 point
Margins	1 inch at the top, bottom, left, and right
Line spacing	Single-spaced
Tabs	Every 1/2 inch
Paper size	8 1/2 inches × 11 inches
Automatic backup	Every 10 minutes

Typing Text

One of the many features built into WordPerfect 10 as a result of user feedback is the click-and-type feature. Quite simply, you click anywhere in a document window and start typing. You don't have to press Enter to insert blank lines, or Tab to move over on the line.

To type text in a document:

1. Click anywhere in the document window (the white page). The insertion point moves to the new place (see Figure 2.1).

2. Begin typing text.

3. When you are ready to start a new paragraph or insert a blank line, press **Enter**.

As you type along, you might notice that things happen automatically. For example, if you forget to capitalize the first word in a sentence, WordPerfect corrects it for you. This is the Format-As-You-Go feature working for you. Format-As-You-Go fixes common mistakes as you type.

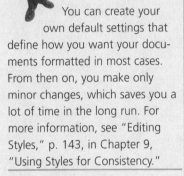

note

You can create your own default settings that define how you want your documents formatted in most cases. From then on, you make only minor changes, which saves you a lot of time in the long run. For more information, see "Editing Styles," p. 143, in Chapter 9, "Using Styles for Consistency."

If you're working in one document and you want to create a new document, click the **New Blank Document** button on the toolbar. You can also choose **File**, **New** (**Ctrl+N**).

caution

It's important that you do not press Enter at the end of every line as you would with a manual typewriter. This causes all sorts of formatting problems when you edit the text or change the formatting.

For more information on customizing Format-As-You-Go, see Chapter 6, "Using the Writing Tools."

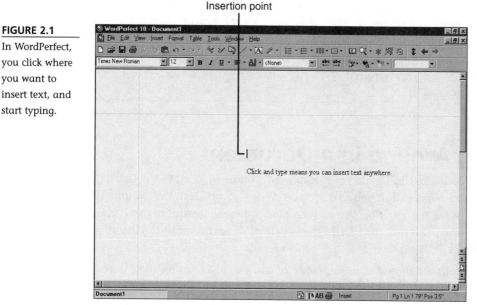

FIGURE 2.1

In WordPerfect, you click where you want to insert text, and start typing.

Erasing Text

The beauty of using a word processor is that no matter how many mistakes you make when you type, you can correct them all before anyone else sees the document. There are several ways to erase text; you are probably familiar with some of them.

- The Backspace key is the most popular method because most mistakes are seen right away. Backspace moves backward, deleting text as long as you hold down the key.

- If you happen to be in front of the problem, click right before the text you want to delete, and then press **Delete**. If you hold down the key, you can delete bigger chunks of text. The longer you hold down the key, the faster the text disappears.

- Select the text with either the mouse or the keyboard, and then press **Delete**.

caution

Be careful with Backspace and Delete! It's easy to get in a hurry and delete more text than you intended. If it's too late and you've deleted too much text, you can bring it back with Undo. You can either click the **Undo** icon, or choose **Edit**, **Undo** (**Ctrl+Z**).

INSERTING TODAY'S DATE

If you stop and think about it, you might be surprised at the number of times a day you type in the date. In WordPerfect, you can insert the current date in just one keystroke. Simply click in the document where you want the date to appear and press **Ctrl+D**. Choose **Insert**, **Date/Time** if you want to customize the date or insert the time instead.

WordPerfect gets the current date and time from Windows. If the date or time that you insert is wrong, you need to reset the Windows date/time. Double-click the time on your taskbar to open the Date/Time Properties dialog box, where you can make the necessary changes.

Moving Around in a Document

To make changes to your document, you have to move the insertion point to the section of text that you want to edit. When you click in the document window, you move the insertion point to the place where you want to insert text. The same thing is true for text that you want to delete. You must move the insertion point to that text to remove it.

Both the mouse and the keyboard can be used to move the insertion point in a document. I'll cover the mouse first because it's a bit more straightforward.

Using the Mouse to Get Around

To move the insertion point with the mouse:

- **Point and click**—Point to the location in the text where you want to place the insertion point, and then click.

- **Scrollbars**—All Windows applications use scrollbars, so you might have seen these before. Click the **up** and **down** arrows on either end of the vertical scrollbar to scroll a line at a time. To scroll faster, click and drag the scroll box on the vertical scrollbar. When you drag the scroll box, WordPerfect displays a QuickTip with a page number to show you where you are in the document. The horizontal scrollbar appears only if the document is too wide to fit in the document window. To scroll from side to side, click the **scroll arrows** or click and drag the scroll box.

If you have any experience with a computer, the information in the next couple of sections will be completely familiar to you, and you can skip to the next major section on printing. For those who might be starting out with their first computer, the information is provided as a reference.

■ **Browse buttons**—These buttons are located at the bottom of the vertical scrollbar (see Figure 2.2). They allow you to jump back and forth between specific items. By default, you browse by page, so you click the **double up arrow** to go to the previous page, and click the **double down arrow** to go to the next page. To switch to another method of browsing, click the **Browse By** button, located between the double up and down arrows.

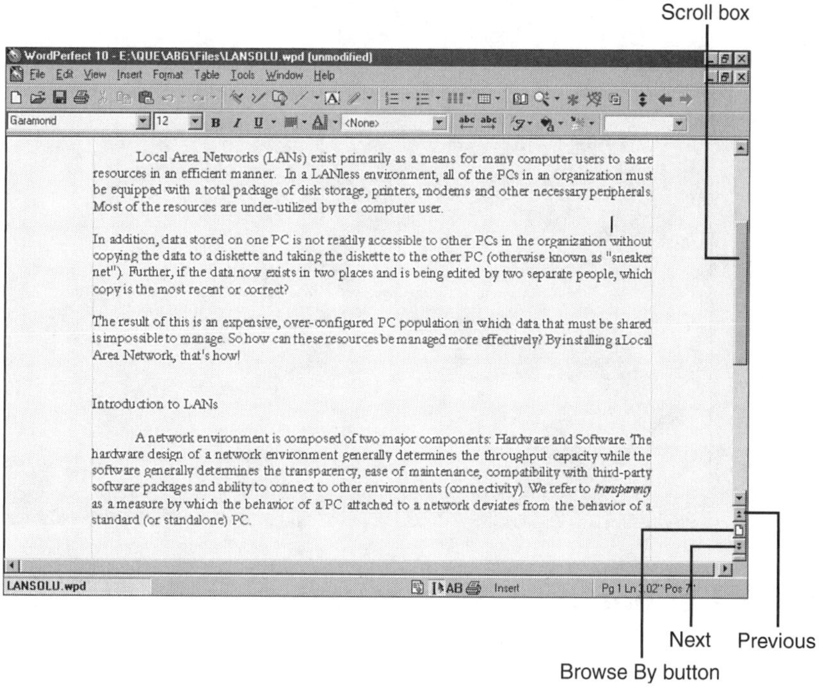

Scroll box

FIGURE 2.2

You can scroll through a document by pages, headings, footnotes, and other elements by using the Browse buttons.

Next   Previous

Browse By button

 ■ **Back and Forward buttons**—These two buttons are located on the right side of the toolbar. The **Back** button takes you backward through a list of previous insertion point locations. The **Forward** button moves you forward through the list of insertion point locations. If the Back button isn't available, you haven't moved the insertion point yet. If the Forward button isn't active, you haven't used the Back button to go back to a previous location yet.

 ■ **Autoscroll button**—The Autoscroll button is located right next to the Back button. Click the **Autoscroll** button on the toolbar to turn on "automatic scrolling." The cursor shows up in the middle of the screen and changes to a dot with up and down arrows (see Figure 2.3). To scroll upward, move the mouse up; the pointer changes to a dot with an upward arrow.

To scroll downward, move the mouse down; the pointer changes to a dot with a downward arrow. To speed up scrolling, move the mouse pointer to the left or right side of the screen. Move back toward the center to slow down. To turn off Autoscroll, click in the document window or click the Autoscroll button.

FIGURE 2.3

The Autoscroll feature is helpful when you're working in lengthy documents.

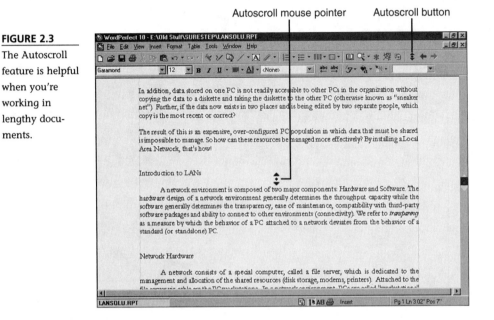

Autoscroll mouse pointer   Autoscroll button

Using the Keyboard to Get Around

If you prefer to keep your hands on the keyboard, there are quite a few ways to move around in a document. Some people feel that moving the insertion point with the keyboard is quicker and more accurate. Table 2.2 contains a list of WordPerfect 10 keyboard shortcuts.

TABLE 2.2 WordPerfect's Keyboard Shortcuts

Keystroke(s)	Insertion Point Moves
Right arrow	One character to the right
Left arrow	One character to the left

tip

The list of keyboard shortcuts might look a bit intimidating, but don't worry. There are only a couple of different ways to move around; it's just that each method can be used in more than one direction (that is, up, down, left, right). Try one or two at first; then add others as you become more comfortable.

Keystroke(s)	Insertion Point Moves
Down arrow	One line down
Up arrow	One line up
Ctrl+Right arrow	One word to the right
Ctrl+Left arrow	One word to the left
Ctrl+Down arrow	One paragraph down
Ctrl+Up arrow	One paragraph up
Home	To beginning of current line
End	To end of current line
Page Down (PgDn)	To bottom of current screen
Page Up (PgUp)	To top of current screen
Alt+Page Down	To top of next physical page
Alt+Page Up	To top of previous physical page
Ctrl+Home	To beginning of document
Ctrl+End	To end of document

Printing a Document

When you're ready to print, it can be done in as little as two keystrokes. This shortcut works only if you want to print the entire document and you don't need to switch to a different printer.

To quickly print the entire document, press **Ctrl+P** and press **Enter**.

The Print dialog box shown in Figure 2.4 has options to change the number of copies, switch to a different printer, print only specific pages, and much more. Choose **File**, **Print** (**Ctrl+P**) to open the Print dialog box. Make your choices, and then click **Print**.

tip

WordPerfect has a Print Preview feature that allows you to see exactly how your document will look when it is printed. You can fine-tune the formatting and double-check for consistency without printing a copy that might be discarded. Choose **File**, **Print Preview** to open the Print Preview window and display the Print Preview toolbar.

Click to switch to a different printer

FIGURE 2.4

The Print dialog box is bypassed with the quick print (Ctrl+P, Enter) method.

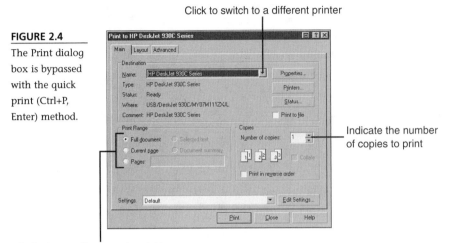

Indicate the number of copies to print

Indicate specific pages to print here

Saving Documents

Electronic copies of documents have virtually replaced paper copies, so even if you don't expect to work with a document again, it's a good idea to save it on disk so that you have a record of it. Bear in mind that because fewer paper copies are kept, the electronic copies need more protection. It's very important that you back up your important files regularly.

Saving and Closing Documents

Until you save your document, it is stored in memory. Memory is a temporary storage location because when you turn off your computer, the memory space is cleared. If a storm comes up and the power is interrupted, or if your system locks up, you'll lose everything that you haven't saved.

One of the new features in WordPerfect 10 is called Auto-Suggest Filename. The first time you save a document, WordPerfect automatically inserts a suggested filename in the File Name text box. You can either accept this name or type your own.

Follow these steps to save a document:

1. Click the **Save** button or choose **File**, **Save** (**Ctrl+S**).

   ■ If you've already named this document, it will seem like nothing has happened. Because the document has already been named, WordPerfect saves the changes without any intervention from you. The only difference you'll see is (unmodified) after the filename in the title bar—this is how you know a document has been saved.

■ If you haven't named the document yet, the Save As dialog box appears (see Figure 2.5).

This is where the file will be saved.

FIGURE 2.5
The Save As dialog box is used when you need to save a new document.

Auto-suggest filename

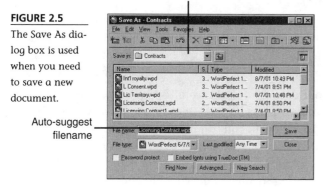

2. Type a filename and press **Enter** (or click the **Save** button).

■ Filenames can be up to 255 characters long and can contain letters, numbers, and spaces. Some symbols can be used, but not others, so to avoid problems, stick with dashes (–) and underscores (_).

■ You can include the name of the drive and the folder where you want the document to be saved when you type the filename. For example, typing d:\financials\fy2002 saves the document fy2002 to drive d: in the financials folder.

■ When you type a filename without selecting a location, the document is saved in the default folder, which is the folder that WordPerfect is currently pointing to.

BACKING UP YOUR WORK AUTOMATICALLY
WordPerfect has a Timed Document Backup feature that automatically makes a backup copy of your document while you work. It's already turned on and set to make a backup every 10 minutes. You can adjust the interval and take a look at where your backup files are created in the Files Settings dialog box. Choose **Tools**, **Settings**, **Files**. If necessary, click the **Document** tab. You can adjust the Timed Document Backup interval by typing a new value in the **Timed Document Backup** text box or by clicking the spinner arrows next to the text box.

Saving to a Different File Format

Let's face it—Microsoft Word users outnumber WordPerfect users. Even though WordPerfect is more flexible, easier to use, and much more powerful, Microsoft products continue to dominate the market.

You probably have friends and business associates who use Microsoft Word for their word processing. You might be thinking that because you use WordPerfect and they use Word, you can't collaborate on documents. Not a problem! WordPerfect 10 has the most complete conversion filters for Microsoft Word products available today.

All you have to do is save your documents in Microsoft Word format. Your friends and associates can open your documents in Word, make their changes, save the file in Word format, and send it back to you. You can then open the document in WordPerfect without losing anything. You can choose to save the document back to WordPerfect format, or you can keep the file in Word format. Either way, you can continue to use WordPerfect without sacrificing the capability to share documents with Word users.

To save a file in a different format:

1. Choose **File**, **Save As**.
2. In the Save As dialog box, click the **File type** drop-down list arrow to open the list of file types.
3. Scroll through the list to locate the file format that you want to use (see Figure 2.6). As you can see, WordPerfect can save to many different Word formats.

FIGURE 2.6

The Save As dialog box is used when you need to save a document to a different file format.

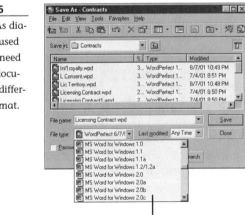

Select the file type here.

4. Select the format from the **File type** drop-down list.

5. If necessary, type a filename and select a location for the file.

6. Click **Save**.

Closing Documents

When you're finished with a document, you clear it off your screen by closing the document window. If you haven't saved it yet, you'll get a chance to do that.

To close a document:

1. Click the **Close** button on the menu bar.

   If you haven't made any changes since the last time you saved, WordPerfect closes the document. If you *have* made some changes, you'll be prompted to save the document (see Figure 2.7).

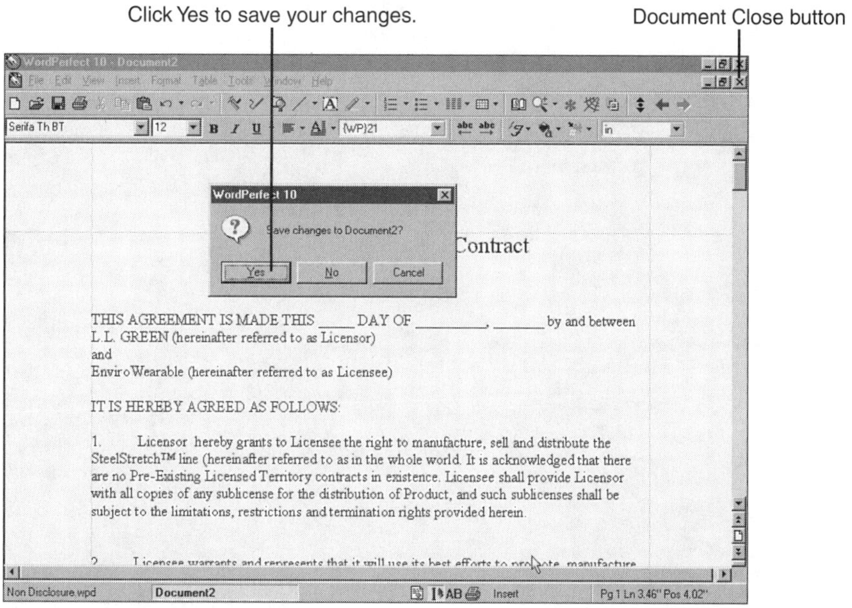

Click Yes to save your changes.   Document Close button

FIGURE 2.7

When you click the Close button, WordPerfect prompts you to save your changes before clearing the document off the screen.

2. Click **Yes** if you want to save your work; click **No** if you want to close the document without saving.

   If you click **Yes** and you haven't yet given this document a name, the Save As dialog box appears (refer to Figure 2.6). This is where you can type a name and location for the file. Otherwise, WordPerfect saves and closes the document.

3. Type the filename and press **Enter**.

THE ABSOLUTE MINIMUM

■ You learned how to create a new document and how to move around in a document so you can edit the text.

■ When you're finished editing, you save your changes, and if you want a copy, you send the document to the printer.

■ It's easy to save documents in a different format so that you can collaborate on documents with people who use other programs.

■ When you are ready to move on to something else, you can close a document and clear it off the screen.

- Learn how to get around in the Open File dialog box.

- See how to navigate through drives and folders and display the files in other folders.

- Learn how to search for a file when you can't remember the name or where it is located.

- Convert documents from a different format so you can work with documents created in other programs.

- Learn how to organize your files into folders so you can locate them later.

- Learn how files can be moved, copied, renamed, and deleted—all from within the file management dialog boxes.

3

FINDING AND OPENING DOCUMENTS

In Chapter 2, "Creating and Editing Documents," you learned how to create a document from scratch and save it to disk. In many cases, you can use an existing document to help get you started on a new document. One of the most common word processing tasks is editing an existing document to create a new and unique document. For example, suppose that you create a newsletter for your company for the month of June. When July rolls around, you probably won't create another newsletter from scratch. You'll open the June newsletter, revise it, and save it as the July newsletter.

Getting Familiar with the Open File Dialog Box

When you're ready to open a file, you'll use the Open File dialog box. It's important to spend a few minutes getting familiar with this dialog box because you will spend more time in it than in any other dialog box in WordPerfect.

To display the Open File dialog box:

1. Click the **Open** button, or choose **File**, **Open** (**Ctrl+O**). The Open File dialog box appears (see Figure 3.1).

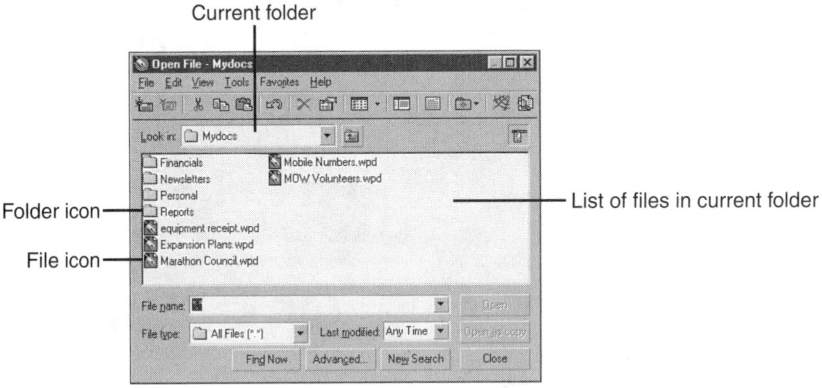

FIGURE 3.1
Use WordPerfect's Open File dialog box to locate and open documents.

Current folder

Folder icon

File icon

List of files in current folder

Opening a File

When you open the Open File dialog box, WordPerfect automatically displays the contents of the default, or the most recently used folder. The section "Navigating Through Drives and Folders" covers switching to a different drive and/or folder.

To open a file:

1. Click the file you want to open.

2. Click **Open**. You can also double-click the file to select and open at the same time.

Customizing the View

There are several different ways to display files and folders in the Open File dialog box. It could be personal preference, or it could be that a different view makes it easier to locate a file.

> **tip**
>
> WordPerfect maintains a list of the previous nine documents that you've opened. They appear at the bottom of the File menu. To choose one of these documents, open the **File** menu and either click the filename or press the underlined number next to the filename. WordPerfect opens the file into a new document window, and you are ready to go.

Whatever the reason, it's a snap to switch to a different view with the View button.

You can click the **View** button to cycle through the different views, or you can click the **drop-down arrow** to the right of the View button to choose from the following options:

- **Large Icons**—Displays the folders and files with large icons

- **Small Icons**—Displays the folders and files with small icons, so more files can be seen at once

- **List**—Displays the folders and files with small icons

- **Details**—Displays the folders and files with small icons along with the size, type, and creation/modification date and time (see Figure 3.2)

tip

In WordPerfect, you can open as many as nine documents at once. To select more than one document, click the first document, and hold down the **Ctrl** key as you click the others. When you're finished selecting files, click **Open**.

FIGURE 3.2
The Details view provides the most information about the files and folders.

Views button

List of files in Details view

You can enlarge the Open File dialog box and display more files and folders at one time. This is especially helpful when you are using the Details view. Point to a side or corner of the dialog box and wait for the two-sided arrow. Click and drag the dialog box border. Release the mouse button when you're satisfied with the new size.

note

Different types of files have different file icons. For example, a WordPerfect document has an icon of a pen on a blue background. The icon for a Word document has blue W on a white page. Application files usually have a smaller version of the icon that appears on the desktop. The icons can help you zero in on the file you want.

Rearranging the File List

The Details view has an added advantage. You can sort the file list by the creation/modification date, the size, or the type. For example, you might arrange the file list by the creation/modification date to locate a file that you edited on a specific date (see Figure 3.3).

To rearrange the file list:

1. Click a column heading that you want to sort by, such as **Type**.

2. Click the column heading again to arrange the list in reverse order.

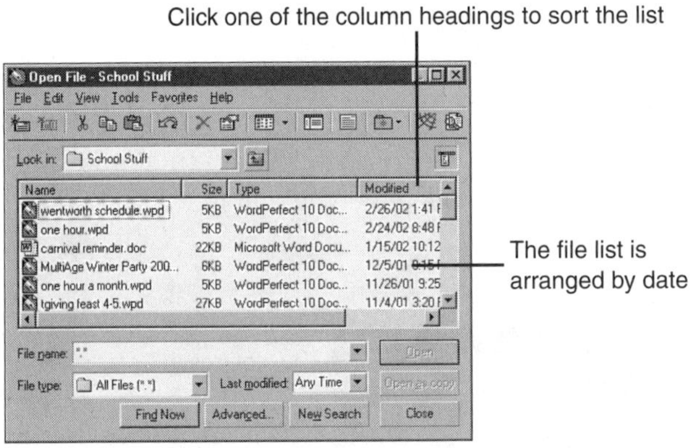

Click one of the column headings to sort the list

FIGURE 3.3

Arranging the file list by date or by type can help you locate a specific file.

The file list is arranged by date

Navigating Through Drives and Folders

At first, you might choose to save all your documents in the same folder. It's easier when you are just starting out to keep everything in one place. However, the more documents you create, the more difficult it becomes to locate the one you want. The "Organizing Files in Folders" section, later in this chapter, covers file management strategies to help you get your files organized.

Moving around in the drives or folders on your system is easily done thanks to the tools in the Open File dialog box. Try these techniques to look through the drives and folders:

- Double-click a folder icon to open the folder and display the list of files and folders in that folder.

- Click the **Go Back One Folder Level** button (see Figure 3.4) to move up a level in the folder list, or to move back to the previous folder.

- Click the **Look in** drop-down list arrow and choose another drive.

Folders button

FIGURE 3.4

Arranging the
file list by date
or by type can
help you locate
a specific file.

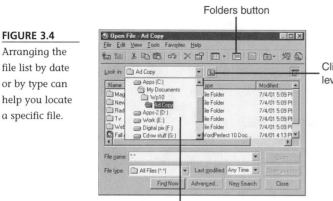

Click here to move up a
level in the folder list.

Choose another drive from the Look In drop-down list.

If you like the way the Windows Explorer looks, you
can make the WordPerfect Open File dialog box
look just like it. Click the Folders button (refer to
Figure 3.4) to split the file list in two. The left side
(or pane) has a list of drives and folders. The right
side doesn't change. It still has the list of folders
and files in the current folder.

Searching for a File

With the size of the hard drives installed in computers today, you could store literally thousands of files
on one disk. Even with the best file management
system, locating a single file can be daunting.
Learning how to use the tools that help you locate
files is one of the most important skills you can master. WordPerfect has a nice collection of tools to help you locate files so you don't have to start another program to
do a search.

note

When you open a dif-
ferent folder in the Open
File dialog box, that folder
becomes the new default folder.
The next time you open the Open
File dialog box, you'll see the list
of files in that folder.

Listing Files by Type

When you have a lot of different types of files in a folder, limiting the number of
files in the list can be a big help. One way to accomplish this is to display only a
specific type of file in the list. For example, if you display only WordPerfect documents in the list, it's easier to find the file you are looking for.

By default, the file type is set to All Files, so you will see every file saved in that folder, whether or not you can work with that file in WordPerfect.

To display only a particular type of file:

1. Click the **File type** drop-down list arrow to display the list of file types (see Figure 3.5).

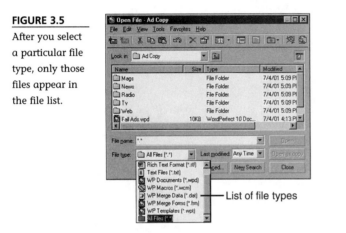

List of file types

2. Choose the type of file you want displayed in the list, such as WP Documents (*.wpd) or Word Documents (*.doc).

3. When you are ready to see all the files again, select **All Files (*.*)** from the **File type** drop-down list.

Listing Files by Modification Date

One of most popular methods is grouping files by modification date. Most people can remember *when* they worked on a document faster than they can remember the name of the file. The fact that you don't have to be exact about the time frame helps. The list of options includes This Week, This Month, Last Week, Last Month, and so on.

To display a list of files by modification date:

1. Click the **Last modified** drop-down list arrow to display a list of general time frames (see Figure 3.6).

2. Either type a specific date in the **Last modified** text box, or select an option from the list.

FIGURE 3.6

Grouping files by modification date is a popular way to locate files.

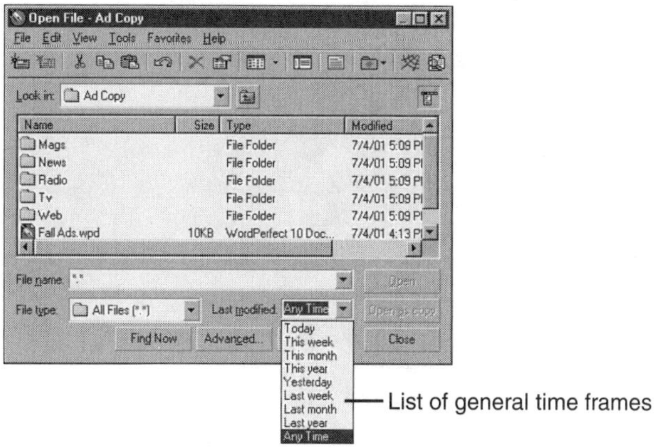

List of general time frames

3. When you are ready to display the complete list of files again, open the **Last modified** drop-down list and select **Any Time**.

BACK UP IMPORTANT FILES REGULARLY

If you have ever suffered through a hard disk crash, you don't need to be told how important it is to back up your data. Imagine how you would feel if all of a sudden, you couldn't get to any of the files on your computer. Avoid a potential disaster by backing up your important files on a regular basis. Use the **Last modified** option in the Open File dialog box to display only those files that you have modified within a certain time frame, and then copy those files onto a floppy disk or CD for safekeeping.

Searching by Filename or Content

Last, but certainly not least, is the capability to search for files by the filename or by the file's contents. Some of us can remember a filename, or at least a part of the filename, but almost everyone can remember something about the contents of a file. Whether it's a client name, a project name, a technical term, or a phone number, all you need is a piece of information that can be found in the file.

To search for files by filename:

1. Type the filename, or a portion of the filename, in the **File name** text box.

2. Click **Find Now**. WordPerfect searches through the files and builds a new list based on the search. When the search is complete, the Find Now button changes to a Back button (see Figure 3.7).

3. When you are ready to switch back to the full list of files, or if you want to start another search, click **Back**.

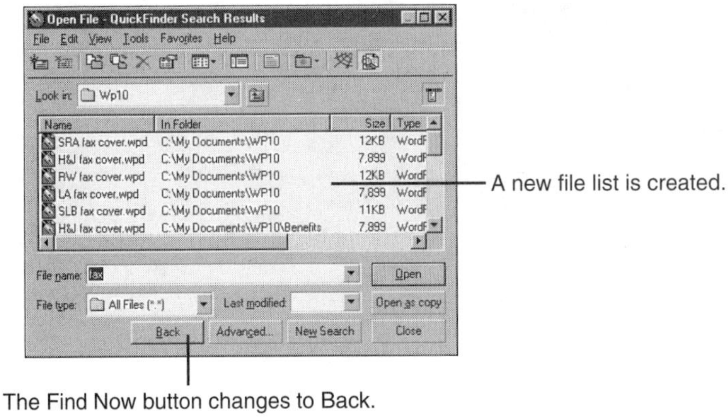

FIGURE 3.7

When you
search for files,
WordPerfect
builds a new list
of files that fit
the search
criteria.

A new file list is created.

The Find Now button changes to Back.

To search for files by content:

1. Type a piece of information that can be found in the text of the file you are searching for in the **File name** text box.

2. Click **Find Now**. WordPerfect searches through the files and builds a new list based on the search.

3. When you are ready to switch back to the full list of files, or if you want to start another search, click **Back**.

If you start a search in a particular folder, WordPerfect searches through the files and the subfolders in that folder. This is especially helpful when you can't remember exactly where you stored a file.

Converting Documents on Open

It's no secret that a substantial chunk of the word processing users on the planet use Microsoft Word. Although that might change now that the Department of Justice has ruled against Microsoft, in the short term, you are likely to share documents with Word users. Thankfully, WordPerfect 10 has developed the most comprehensive set of conversion filters available for Microsoft Word documents.

You might also be surprised at how many WordPerfect users are still using older versions of the program. Some companies are resistant to change, and others are limited by the computing power of their systems. Thousands, if not millions, of local government employees are quite happily using WordPerfect 7 and 8.

Thank goodness for WordPerfect's built-in file conversion feature that enables you to open nearly every kind of word processing document. All you have to do is open the file and let WordPerfect's conversion filters do all the work. Bear in mind that if your copy of WordPerfect was free with an HP, Dell, or Sony computer, you might not have the full-blown set of filters found in the Standard, Professional, or Academic version of the Corel WordPerfect Office 2002 suite.

When you save a converted document, WordPerfect asks whether you want to save it in the latest WordPerfect format (WordPerfect 6/7/8/9/10) or in the original format from which it was converted. If you are returning the document to someone who isn't using WordPerfect, select the original format and click **OK**.

If you get an "Invalid format" error message when you try to open a file in a different format, you might need to install additional conversion filters. The complete set of filters is not installed with the suite, due to space considerations. The Family Pack and Productivity Pack versions install everything by default.

> **tip**
>
> You don't need to worry about converting your WordPerfect files from an earlier version when you upgrade to WordPerfect 10. The file format for WordPerfect files hasn't changed since version 6.0.

To install additional conversion filters:

1. Insert the CD in the drive.
2. When the Setup program starts, click **Custom Setup**.
3. Move past the options until you get to **Conversion Filters**; place a check mark in the box.
4. Click **Next** until the install starts.

When the install is finished, the new filters are integrated into WordPerfect, and they are now ready to use.

Organizing Files in Folders

One nice thing about WordPerfect is that you can do all your file management tasks from within the program. You don't have to start Windows Explorer to create new folders and move files around. Also, you can work with virtually any file on your system, not just WordPerfect files.

The file management tools are available in every file-related dialog box, such as Save As, Insert File, Insert Image, and Select File. Because the Open File dialog box is used more often, it is used here in the examples.

Creating New Folders

Setting up an electronic filing system is just like setting up a filing system for your printed documents. Just as you take out a manila folder and attach a label to it, you can create a folder on your hard disk and give it a name. Organizing files into folders by account, subject, project, or client helps you locate the files you need quickly and easily.

To create a new folder:

1. Open the drive or folder where you want to create the new folder.

2. Right-click in the file list and choose **New**, **Folder**. You can also choose **File**, **New**, **Folder**. A new folder icon appears in the file list with a temporary name of New Folder (see Figure 3.8).

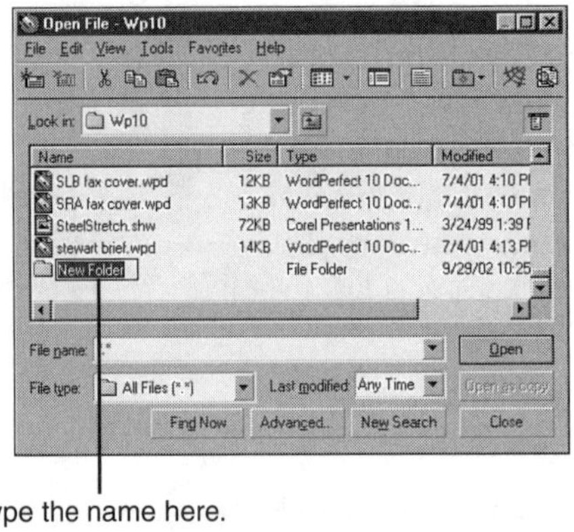

FIGURE 3.8

When you create a new folder, you replace the temporary name of New Folder with a name you choose.

Type the name here.

3. Type a name for the folder. Because the temporary name New Folder is selected, the name that you type automatically replaces it.

Moving and Copying Files

If you accidentally save a file to the wrong folder, it's not a disaster. You can always move it to another folder later. Be sure to *move* the file rather than copy it because you don't want two copies in two different places. Things can get pretty confusing when you are trying to figure out which copy is the most recent.

On the other hand, there are good reasons why you would want to copy a file rather than move it. Backups come to mind. If you've been working on an important document all day, make a copy of the file onto a floppy disk or CD when you're finished. You'll sleep better at night knowing that you have a backup copy in case something happens to the original. Likewise, if you want to share a file with a co-worker on your network, you want to copy the file to his folder on the network. This way, you still have your original, and he has a copy that he can freely edit.

Remember, if you want to move or copy more than one file, you need to click the first file to select it. Then hold down the **Ctrl** key and click the others. Continue to hold down the **Ctrl** key until you are finished selecting the other files.

To move files:

1. Select the file(s) that you want to move.
2. Click the **Cut** button, or choose **Edit**, **Cut**.
3. Navigate to the folder where you want to store the files.
4. Click the **Paste** button, or choose **Edit**, **Paste**.

To copy files:

1. Select the file(s) that you want to copy.
2. Click the **Copy** button, or choose **Edit**, **Copy**.
3. Switch to the folder where you want to store the files.
4. Click the **Paste** button, or choose **Edit**, **Paste**.

The instructions to move and copy files work on folders, too, so if you want to work with all the files in a folder, you don't have to select them all. Just select the folder and work with it instead.

Renaming Files

When you save a file (or create a folder), you try to give it a descriptive name. Later, however, that name might no longer seem appropriate. It could be as simple as a misspelling in the name, or a case where the content of the file changes and the name needs to reflect that change. Regardless of the reason, you can quickly rename a file or folder in just two steps.

To rename a file or folder:

1. Click the file or folder that you want to rename.
2. Wait a second and click the file or folder name again. An outline appears around the file or folder name, and the name is selected (see Figure 3.9).
3. Edit the name as necessary.
4. Either press **Enter** or click in the file list when you are finished.

tip

Clicking, pausing, and clicking again can be a little tricky, especially if you inadvertently move the mouse between clicks. You might find it easier to choose **File**, **Rename** to rename a file.

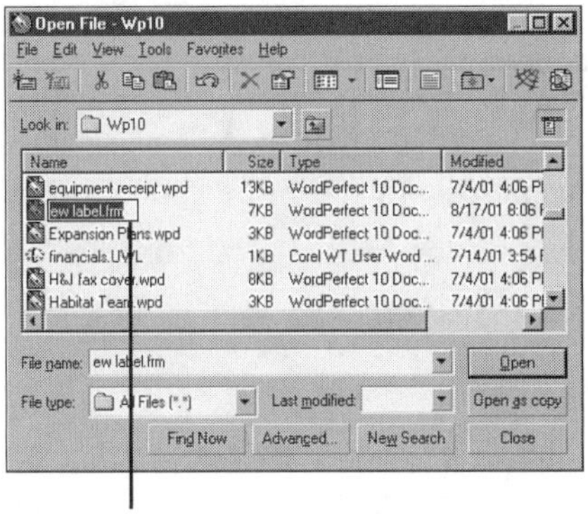

FIGURE 3.9
When an out-line appears around the file-name and the text is selected, you can edit the name.

An outline appears around the name.

Deleting Files and Folders

If you decide that you no longer need a folder, you can delete it. Before you do, open the folder and make sure that there are no folders or files that you need to keep. Deleting a folder automatically deletes the contents.

To delete a file or folder:

1. Select the file or folder.

2. Click the **Delete** button or choose **File**, **Delete**.

Mistakes can happen to anyone, which is why we all love the Undo Delete feature. If you accidentally delete a file or folder, you can quickly restore it by clicking the **Undo Delete** button (see Figure 3.10).

FIGURE 3.10
The Open File dialog box has a Delete and an Undo Delete button.

Undo Delete button

Delete button

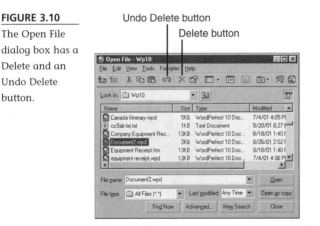

THE ABSOLUTE MINIMUM

- You learned how to use the Open File dialog box, so you can now comfortably work in all the file management dialog boxes in WordPerfect.

- You became skilled at navigating through the drives and folders on your system so you can work with files in another folder.

- Searching for a file is easy, even if you don't remember the name or where the file is located.

- Converting documents from a different format is as easy as opening them in WordPerfect. The built-in conversion filters do all the work for you.

- Anything you can do in Windows Explorer, you can do in WordPerfect. You saw how to move, copy, rename, and delete files from within a file management dialog box.

IN THIS CHAPTER

- Learn how to select text, and move and copy selected text so you can quickly move things around as you edit your documents.

- Bail yourself out of trouble with the Undo feature.

- Adjust the zoom setting to make it easier to inspect small details in a document.

- Open multiple documents at the same time and preview a document before printing.

- Learn how to fax a document directly from WordPerfect, and use your email program to attach a document to an email message.

4

REVISING DOCUMENTS

This chapter focuses on the techniques you will need to revise your documents. The single most common action you'll take on your documents is selecting text. After you've selected a portion of your document, you can take action on that portion without affecting the rest of the document. You'll learn how to move and copy selected text in this chapter; other actions that you can take on selected text are covered in later chapters.

In the second half of the chapter, you learn how to use the Zoom feature to adjust the size of the document onscreen. You'll learn how to open multiple documents and how to switch back and forth between open documents. Finally, you'll learn how to use Print Preview and how to set the options in the Print dialog box.

Selecting Text

The Select feature is a powerful tool. Whenever you just want to work with a section of text, you can select that portion and work on it independently from the rest of the document. Selecting text is flexible, and, because of the visual nature, it's easy to comprehend. When you edit documents, you'll do a lot of selecting, so it's worth a few minutes to learn some shortcuts.

Selecting Text with the Keyboard

You can use either the mouse or the keyboard to select text. Let's look at selecting text using the keyboard first. You might want to review the navigation techniques in Table 2.2 because you'll use those same techniques to select text with the keyboard.

To select a portion of text:

1. Position the insertion point at the beginning of the area you want to select.

2. Hold down the **Shift** key.

3. Use the arrow keys, or any of the navigation shortcuts that you learned about in Chapter 2, to move to the end of the selection. For example, to select text a word at a time, hold down the **Shift** key while pressing **Ctrl+right arrow**. To select everything from the cursor to the end of the line, hold down the **Shift** key and press **End**.

WordPerfect shows the selection with a different background color (see Figure 4.1). You can now work with this area of the document as a single unit.

FIGURE 4.1

Selected text is displayed with a different background color.

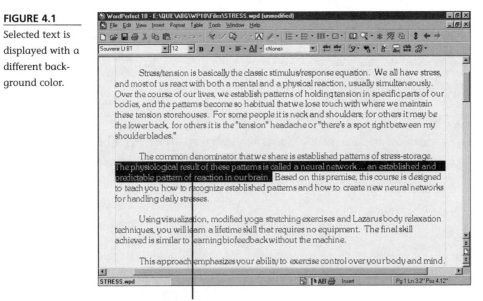

Selected text

Selecting Text with the Mouse

Selecting text with the mouse is also easy, although it might take a bit of practice before you get really good at it. Table 4.1 shows several methods of using the mouse to select text.

TABLE 4.1 Selecting Text with the Mouse

Mouse Action	What It Selects
Drag across text	One whole word at a time
Double-click	Entire word
Triple-click	Entire sentence
Quadruple-click	Entire paragraph
Single-click in left margin	Entire sentence
Double-click in left margin	Entire paragraph

note

Notice that when you move the mouse pointer into the left margin the pointer reverses direction and points to the right (instead of the regular left-facing pointer). When you see this special pointer, you can click to select a line, or double-click to select a paragraph.

Moving and Copying Text

Now that you have text selected, you're probably wondering what to do with it. As you read through this book, you'll learn dozens of things that you can do with selected text. One of the most basic functions is to move or copy text. If you move the text, deleting it from the original location, you are *cutting and pasting* text. When you make a copy of the text, leaving a copy in the original location, you are *copying and pasting* text.

One thing that makes WordPerfect unique is that you can choose from a number of different methods to accomplish the same result. The program conforms to your working style, not the other way around. There are several different ways to cut/copy and paste selected text. The different alternatives are listed here. Generally, the steps to move and copy are

1. Select the text you want to copy or move.
2. Copy (or cut) the selected text.
3. Reposition the insertion point at the target location.
4. Paste the text you copied (or cut).

Some methods for copying, cutting, and pasting text work better in certain situations. For example, if your hands are already on the keyboard, the keyboard methods might be more convenient. Others prefer to use the mouse. Experiment with the different methods and find your favorites.

To copy selected text:

- Click the **Copy** button.
- Choose **Edit**, **Copy**.
- Right-click the selected text and choose **Copy**.
- Press **Ctrl+C**.
- Press **Ctrl+Insert**.

To cut selected text:

- Click the **Cut** button.
- Choose **Edit**, **Cut**.
- Right-click the selection and choose **Cut**.
- Press **Ctrl+X**.
- Press **Shift+Delete**.

To paste selected text:

- Click the **Paste** button.
- Choose **Edit**, **Paste**.
- Right-click in the document and choose **Paste**.
- Press **Ctrl+V**.
- Press **Shift+Insert**.

If you prefer, you can also use the mouse to drag selected text from one location and drop it in another. The drag-and-drop method works best when you are moving or copying text within the document window. When you have to scroll up or down, things get a little tricky.

To drag and drop text:

1. Select the text you want to move or copy.

2. Position the mouse pointer on the high-lighted text. The pointer changes to an arrow.

3. If you want to move the text, click and hold down the mouse button; if you want to copy the text, hold down the **Ctrl** key before you click and hold down the mouse button.

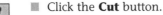

tip

If you can remember the Shift key, you can use a series of keyboard shortcuts to move and copy text. Shift+arrow keys to select the text, Shift+Delete to cut the text, and then Shift+Insert to paste the text. Practice this technique and see how much time you save!

4. Drag the mouse to the target location. The mouse pointer changes to an arrow along with a small rectangular box (see Figure 4.2). An insertion point also appears showing you exactly where the text will be inserted when you release the mouse button.

FIGURE 4.2

You can use the mouse to quickly drag and drop text.

Move/copy mouse pointer

Insertion point shows where the pasted text will appear.

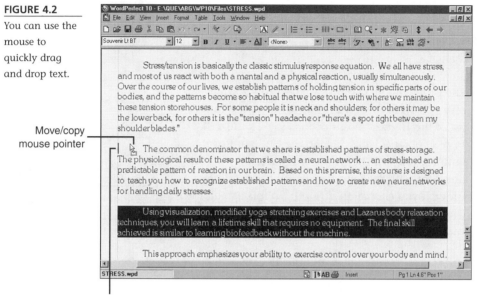

5. Release the mouse button.

6. The text is still selected, so if you didn't get the text right where you wanted it, click and drag it again.

7. When you have the selection where you want it, click in the document window to deselect the text.

Using Undo to Fix Your Mistakes

WordPerfect has the ultimate "oops" fixer, and it's called Undo. Essentially, Undo reverses the last action taken on a document. For example, if you delete selected text, Undo brings it back. If you change the margins, Undo puts them back the way they were. It's as if you never took the action.

Undo has a twin feature called Redo. Redo reverses the last Undo action. If you accidentally Undo too many things, Redo puts them back.

To use the Undo feature:

- Click the **Undo** button on the toolbar.
- Choose **Edit**, **Undo**.
- Press **Ctrl+Z**.

To use the Redo feature:

- Click the **Redo** icon on the toolbar.
- Choose **Edit**, **Redo**.

The Undo and Redo buttons have drop-down arrows next to them. Click the arrow to display a list of the 10 most recent actions (see Figure 4.3). Instead of repeatedly clicking the Undo or Redo buttons, you can choose an action from one of the lists. Stay with me now, because this gets a little tricky. If you choose an action from this list, all the actions up to, and including that selected action, will be reversed, not just the selected action.

> **note**
>
> By default, WordPerfect remembers the last 10 actions you took on the document. You can increase this amount to a maximum of 300 actions. Choose **Edit**, **Undo/Redo History**, **Options**, and change the Number of Undo/Redo Items.

Click here to open the Redo history list.

Undo history list

FIGURE 4.3

Use the Undo and Redo history lists to select which action to undo/redo.

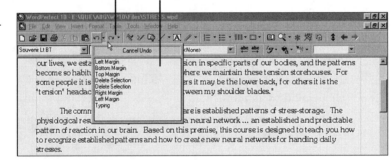

Using the Zoom Feature

Zoom controls the magnification of the document onscreen. It doesn't affect the printed copy, so you can freely use whatever zoom setting you prefer. By default, WordPerfect displays documents at a zoom ratio of 100%, which displays the text and graphics in the same size that they will be when printed. A zoom setting of 50% displays the document at half the printed size. A zoom setting of 200% displays the document twice as large as the printed copy.

To adjust the zoom setting:

1. Click the drop-down arrow next to the **Zoom** button on the toolbar (or on the Print Preview toolbar). A pop-up menu of zoom settings appears (see Figure 4.4).

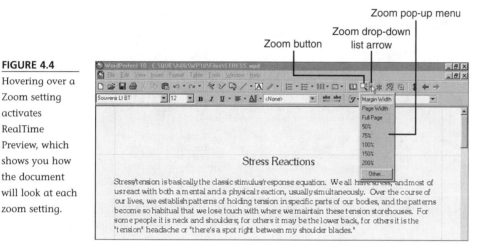

FIGURE 4.4

Hovering over a Zoom setting activates RealTime Preview, which shows you how the document will look at each zoom setting.

2. Select a zoom setting.

RealTime Preview can show you a preview of each zoom setting before you choose it. Simply point to and hover over any of the zoom settings. This activates RealTime Preview, which shows you how each setting will look. As you read through the book, you'll see other ways that RealTime Preview helps you make decisions.

If you have a Microsoft IntelliMouse or other type of mouse with a scroll wheel, you can adjust the zoom ratio by holding down the **Ctrl** key and rotating the wheel. Notice that the wheel has small notches. WordPerfect zooms in or out at intervals of 10% for each notch on the wheel.

You might decide that you don't like any of the preset zoom settings. If so, choose **Other** from the Zoom pop-up menu, or choose **View**, **Zoom**. This opens the Zoom dialog box, where you can type the preferred zoom ratio.

Zooming In with the Mouse

The Zoom feature can be turned on, and you can zoom in and out of a document by clicking the left and right mouse buttons. This method works well when you're going back over a document and you need to be able to zoom in on small details and then zoom back out to scroll down.

To zoom in and out with the mouse:

1. Click the **Zoom** button on the toolbar. The mouse pointer changes to a magnifying glass (see Figure 4.5).

Zoom button

FIGURE 4.5

The Zoom feature can be turned on, and you can zoom in and out with the mouse.

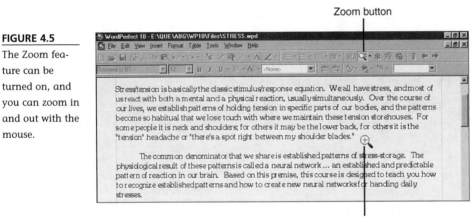

Magnifying glass pointer

2. Click in the document window to start zooming in.

3. Continue clicking the left mouse button to zoom in on the document.

4. Click the right mouse button to zoom out.

5. Continue clicking the right mouse button to zoom all the way out.

Zooming In on a Specific Area

There are times when you will want to zoom in and out of a specific area of a document. For example, if you are working with lots of graphics and graphics captions, you might want to zoom in on each graphic so that you can proofread the caption.

To magnify a specific section of a document:

1. Click the **Zoom** button on the toolbar. The mouse pointer changes to a magnifying glass.

2. Click and drag the area of the document you want to magnify (see Figure 4.6). WordPerfect adjusts the zoom ratio to display the selected text as large as possible.

3. Click the **Zoom** button again to turn off the magnification feature.

4. If necessary, click the **Zoom** button drop-down arrow and choose a normal zoom ratio once again.

FIGURE 4.6

Using the Zoom pointer, you can click and drag across an area to enlarge it.

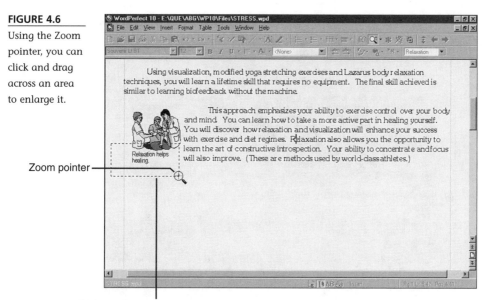

Zoom pointer

Click and drag the area to enlarge.

Working with More Than One Document

Think of how you use your computer. On a typical day, you probably have two or three applications running at once—WordPerfect, your email application, several Web browser windows, a scanner or digital camera program, and so on. Your taskbar has buttons for every program that you are running so that you can quickly switch back and forth between programs.

In that same spirit, WordPerfect lets you work on up to nine document windows at once. Each document has a button on the application bar (at the bottom of the screen), so you can quickly switch back and forth between documents (see Figure 4.7).

You already know how to open a document. You might not realize that when you open a document, WordPerfect automatically places it in a new document window. So, if you are already working on something, you can open other documents without disturbing anything. Also, you can open more than one file at a time while you're in the Open File dialog box. Simply click the first file, and then hold down the **Ctrl** key to click the other files.

To start a new document, you need a blank document in a new document window. Click the **New Blank Document** icon on the toolbar; choose **File**, **New**; or press **Ctrl+N**.

FIGURE 4.7

Each open document has a button on the application bar.

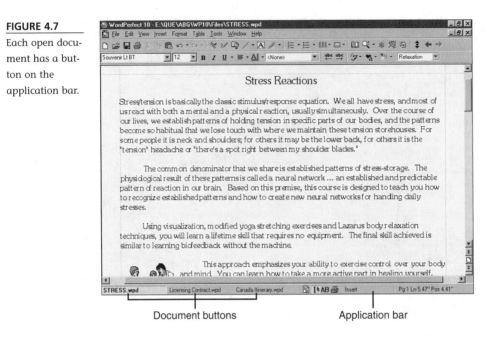

Document buttons   Application bar

You can switch from one document to another with any of the following methods:

- On the application bar, click the name of the document you want to work on.
- Open the **Window** menu and click the document you want.
- Press **Ctrl+F6** (Previous Window) repeatedly until WordPerfect displays the document you want to work on.

Multiple document windows make it a snap to cut, copy, and paste between documents. Simply cut or copy while viewing one document, and then switch to another document and paste.

Previewing and Printing Documents

In Chapter 2, "Creating and Editing Documents," you learned how to do a quick print of a document. With the quick print method, you skip over the Print dialog box and send the entire document to the default printer.

What if you want to print to a different printer? Or maybe you need five copies of a document. Let's cover some of the most frequently used options. You can tackle the rest when a situation arises, and you need the other tools.

Switching to Print Preview

The Print Preview feature shows you exactly what your document will look like when you print it. Use it as often as possible. You'll save time, paper, printer resources, and frustration.

Earlier versions of WordPerfect included a Print Preview feature, but you couldn't make any changes while in it. In WordPerfect 10, you can freely edit the text, reposition graphics, change the margins, and so on.

Using buttons on the Print Preview toolbar, you can switch to a Two Page view, or you can use the Zoom feature to adjust the size of the page. Other buttons give you access to the Spell Checker, the Make It Fit feature, and both the Page Setup and the Print dialog boxes.

To use the Print Preview feature:

1. Choose **File**, **Print Preview** from the menu. The current page is displayed (see Figure 4.8).

2. Make any necessary adjustments.

3. When you are finished, click the **Print Preview** button to switch back to the document window.

FIGURE 4.8

Print Preview displays a fully editable representation of how the document will look when printed.

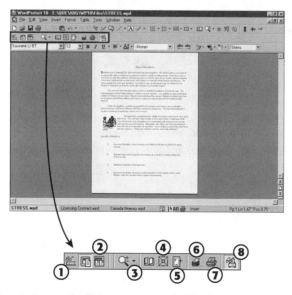

1. Click here to turn on the Ruler.
2. Click here to switch to Two Page view.
3. Click here to adjust the zoom setting.
4. Click here to use Make It Fit.
5. Click here to open the Page Setup dialog box.
6. Click here to open the Print dialog box.
7. Click here to print the document.
8. Click here to switch back to the document window.

Changing the Number of Copies

The cost of printing multiple copies on a laser printer is virtually identical to the cost of running copies on a copier. It's much faster just to print three copies of a document than it is to print a copy, walk to the copier, punch in your account number, figure out which buttons to press to get three copies, and wait for them to be finished.

To change the number of copies:

1. Click the **Print** button (**Ctrl+P**) to display the Print dialog box (see Figure 4.9).

2. Change the number in the **N̲umber of copies** text box.

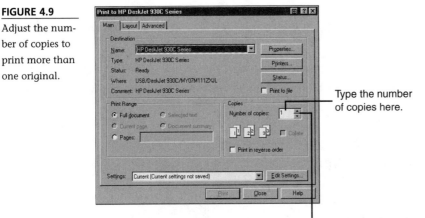

FIGURE 4.9

Adjust the number of copies to print more than one original.

Type the number of copies here.

Click the spinner arrows to change the number of copies.

If you choose to print more than one copy, WordPerfect groups the copies as illustrated in the Copies area of the dialog box. You can collate the copies by enabling the **Col̲late** check box.

Printing Specific Pages

When you're revising a multipage document, it doesn't make sense to print the whole thing when you need to check only a few pages. Save trees and print just the pages that you need to proofread.

- To print the current page, choose **Current P̲age**.
- To print multiple pages, type the page numbers that you want to print in the **Pages** text box. For example, if you need to print pages 3 through 9, type **3-9**.

If you also want to print page 15, type **3-9, 15** in the text box. Finally, if you type a page number followed by a dash, WordPerfect prints from that page number to the end of the document. For example, **13-** prints page 13 and everything that follows it.

- To print selected text, select the text before you open the Print dialog box. Then click **Selected Text**.

If you click the **Advanced** tab of the Print dialog box, you see options for printing multiple pages or labels, secondary pages, chapters, and volumes. However, under the Main tab you can indicate only page numbers.

> **caution**
>
> The numbers you enter in the **Pages** text box must be in numeric order; otherwise, all the pages might not print. For example, if you specify **12-15, 4**, only pages 12–15 print. To print these specific pages, you must enter **4, 12-15**.

When you choose to print selected text, the text appears on the printed page in the same location in which it would have appeared had you printed the surrounding text. For example, if you select the last paragraph on the page, the paragraph prints by itself at the bottom of the page.

Faxing Documents from WordPerfect

How many times have you printed a document, fed it into a fax machine, and then put the printout in the recycle bin? You can save some time, paper, and printing resources by faxing directly from WordPerfect. You must have several items in place first:

- A fax board must be installed in your computer (or connected to your network). Most modems come with faxing capabilities built in, so if you have a modem, you probably already have the hardware needed to fax. Check your modem manual for more information.

- A Windows-based fax program must be installed on your computer. When fax software is installed, a fax printer is added to your list of available printers. You can check this by opening the Print dialog box in WordPerfect and looking at the Name drop-down list. Many modems also ship with fax software. Check your modem documentation for more information.

- The person to whom you send the fax must have a fax machine or a computer-based fax program and a fax/modem to receive the fax.

To send a fax from WordPerfect:

1. With the document that you want to fax in the active window, click the **Print** button or choose **File**, **Print**.

2. On the Main tab, click the **Name** drop-down list arrow and choose the fax printer from the list.

3. Make other changes to the print setup as desired (for example, which pages to print).

4. Click **Fax** to fax the document. WordPerfect prepares the document and hands it off to the fax software.

5. Your fax software displays a dialog box that enables you to designate where to send the fax. If the dialog box doesn't appear, click the fax software icon on the Windows taskbar.

6. Fill in the destination information in the fax program's dialog box and then send the fax.

After the document is scheduled for sending, you can use the fax program's software to monitor the fax status, check the fax logs, or even cancel the fax if it hasn't been sent yet.

Sending Documents via Email

If you can send an email message, you can send documents via email. There are two options: A selected portion of the document can be sent as a part of a message, or the entire document can be sent as an attachment to the message.

To determine whether your mail program has been installed and is integrated with WordPerfect, choose **File**, **Send To**. Supported mail programs are listed on the menu, as is a Mail Recipient option (see Figure 4.10).

To send the current document as an email attachment, choose **File**, **Send To**, **Mail Recipient**. Windows switches to your email program, which then adds the document as an attachment and enables you to send a message with the attachment (see Figure 4.11).

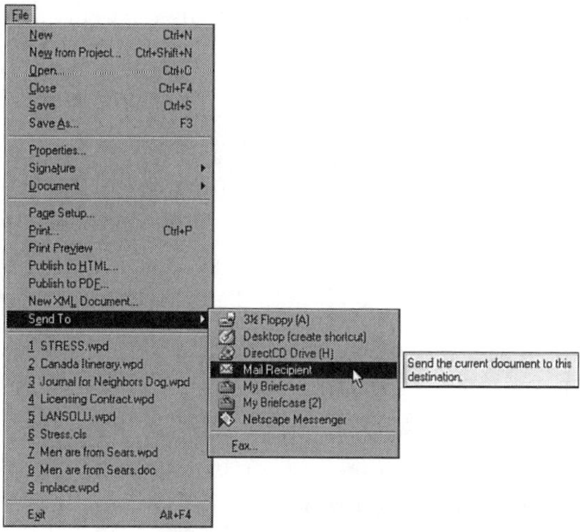

FIGURE 4.10

If your mail program is installed and recognized by WordPerfect, it appears on the File, Send To menu.

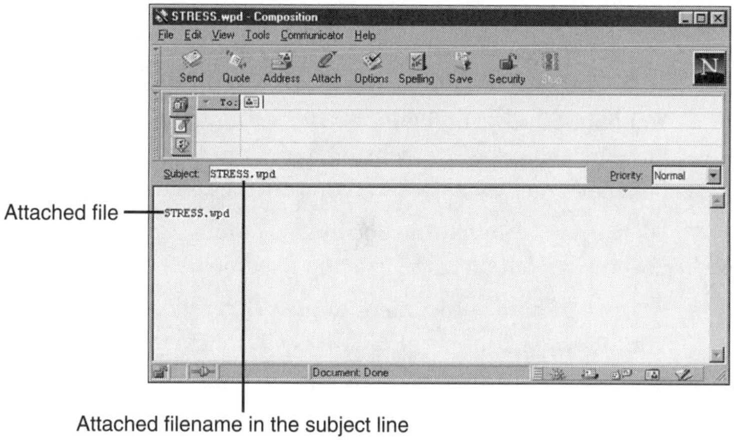

FIGURE 4.11

If you send your document as an attachment, the receiver can then download the attachment and open it in WordPerfect.

Attached file ——— STRESS.wpd

Attached filename in the subject line

You can also send just a portion of the document as part of the body of your message. In WordPerfect, select the text you want to mail; choose **File**, **Send To**, **Mail Recipient**. The mail program is launched, and the selected text is added to the body of the message. You provide an address, edit the text, and send the message.

If your email program does not appear on the WordPerfect File, Send To menu, you still have these options:

- You can save the document and open your mail program separately. Compose a message and attach the document.

- You can copy text from a WordPerfect document and paste it in the body of the mail message. Bear in mind that this method removes most, if not all, of WordPerfect's formatting.

THE ABSOLUTE MINIMUM

- Selecting text is one of those skills that you'll use over and over again. After you learn how to select text, you can use the same techniques to select items in other applications. From rearranging a list to using an already formatted heading to create a new one, you'll move and copy text frequently in your documents.

- The Undo feature is the ultimate "oops" fixer. Even if you've just accidentally selected the entire document and deleted it, Undo can bring it back.

- You might find your favorite zoom setting and leave it alone from then on, but when you need to read some tiny print or check a detailed graphic, you'll be able to quickly switch to a different setting and then back again.

- You can open up to nine documents at once, so you can easily create a new document from pieces of existing documents.

- Before you send a document to the printer, take a minute to preview it in Print Preview. You might be surprised at how many mistakes you can catch.

- Printing and mailing documents are still done, but more frequently, users are faxing and emailing documents directly from WordPerfect.

In This Chapter

- Learn how to use bold, italic, and underline to emphasize important text.

- Select different fonts and font sizes to improve the appearance of your documents.

- Change the margin settings to squeeze more text on a page.

- Create an envelope with the mailing address automatically inserted for you.

- Choose from more than 1,500 symbols and special characters that can be inserted into a document.

- Turn on Reveal Codes and learn how to edit or remove codes.

5

Basic Formatting

Now that you've created, edited, and printed documents, the next step is to learn how to use some basic formatting techniques. This chapter shows you how to apply emphasis to words using tools such as bold and underline. You'll also learn how to choose a new font or change a font size and how to change the page margins, which is especially helpful when printing on letterhead. And if you're going to print a letter, you're probably going to need an envelope to go with it. Special characters and symbols serve a lot of purposes, whether you are inserting a happy face or the copyright symbol.

Last, but certainly not least, the Reveal Codes feature is explained. Reveal Codes is WordPerfect's secret weapon, so don't miss this discussion.

Emphasizing Important Text

In an oral presentation, you use different intonations for emphasis. To get an important point across, you might raise your voice and pronounce each word slowly and clearly. Speaking in a monotone will either bore your audience to tears or put them to sleep. Using a different tone of voice and pausing before important points helps to hold your audience's attention.

You can do the same thing with a printed document. Judicious use of bold, italic, underline, and other effects can guide a reader through the text and draw attention to key points.

To apply bold, italic, or underline:

1. Select the text.

2. Click the **Bold**, **Italic**, or **Underline** button on the property bar (or any combination of the three).

When bold, italic, or underline has been applied to a section of text, the buttons on the property bar appear "pushed in" (see Figure 5.1).

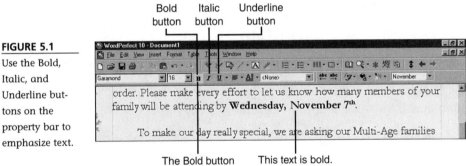

FIGURE 5.1

Use the Bold, Italic, and Underline buttons on the property bar to emphasize text.

Choosing the Right Font

Choosing a font can be intimidating, especially because there are now thousands of fonts to choose from. It's worth the time and effort, though, because the right font can improve the appearance of a document and make it easier to read. Attractive fonts generate interest in your subject. Titles and headings should be larger than the body text so that they stand out a bit. It takes only a few minutes to select the fonts in a document, and the results are well worth your effort.

INSTALLING THE BONUS FONTS

Corel offers more than 1,000 fonts with WordPerfect Office 2002. Of these, 24 are the character set fonts, which contain the symbols and foreign language alphabets. During a typical installation, a default set of 77 fonts is installed. The rest can be installed separately, using either the Corel Setup Wizard or the Fonts folder.

You can open the Fonts folder from the Control Panel. Click **Start**, point to **Settings**, and click **Control Panel**. Double-click the **Fonts** icon. In the Fonts folder, choose **File**, **Install New Font**, and then follow the instructions. You'll need to have the WordPerfect Office 2002 CD #2 ready to insert.

Selecting Fonts and Font Sizes

The quickest way to choose a different font is to click the **Font Face** drop-down arrow on the property bar. A drop-down list of fonts appears, and a large preview window pops up at the top of the document (see Figure 5.2). As you point to a font in the list, the sample text in the preview window changes into that font.

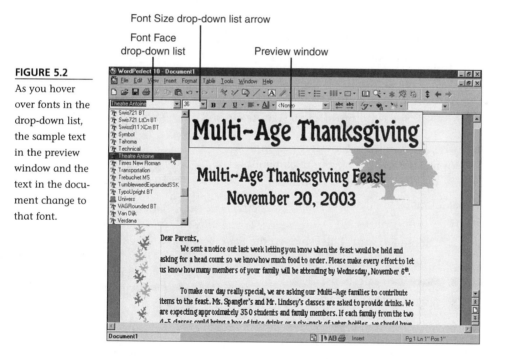

FIGURE 5.2

As you hover over fonts in the drop-down list, the sample text in the preview window and the text in the document change to that font.

Thanks to Corel's RealTime Preview, the text in the document does the same thing. You don't have to play guessing games, trying to figure out how a font will look from a tiny piece of sample text—you can see how a whole page of text will look. When you find the font that you want, click it.

Choosing a different font size works essentially the same way as choosing a different font. Click the **Font Size** drop-down arrow on the property bar to open a drop-down list of sizes. If you click the scroll arrows, you'll see that the list has sizes ranging from 6 points to 72 points. A preview window with sample text opens next to the list. As you move the mouse down through the list, the sample text and the document text expand and contract to show the new size.

caution

As you format your document, remember to always position the insertion point first. As a general rule, your changes take effect at the insertion point, which may or may not be where you want them. You can always click **Undo** if you make a mistake.

When you've decided which font you want to use for the body text, set that as the default font for the document.

To set a font as the default font for a document:

1. Choose **Format**, **Font** to open the Font Properties dialog box.
2. Make your selections.
3. Click **Settings**.
4. Click **Set Face and Point Size As Default for This Document**.

Likewise, if you select a font that you want to use for most, if not all, of your documents, set that as the default for all *new* documents.

To set a font as the default for all new documents:

1. Choose **Format**, **Font** to open the Font Properties dialog box.
2. Make your selections.
3. Click **Settings**.
4. Click **Set Face and Point Size As Default for All Documents**.

tip

If you want to use a font size that isn't shown in the list, click the **Font Size** box (to select the current size), and then type the size you want.

SAVING THE FONTS WITH THE DOCUMENT

Have you ever tried to make last-minute changes to a document on a machine that didn't have the same fonts installed? It can be a nightmare. Thanks to font-embedding technology, you can save fonts with a document so that they go where the document goes. When you save a file, choose **Embed fonts using TrueDoc (TM)** in the Save File dialog box. WordPerfect compresses the fonts and saves them with the file.

Choosing a Font from the QuickFonts List

Let's say you just finished revising the text in your resume. You're ready to polish the appearance. You're finished experimenting, so you know which fonts you want to use for your headings and job titles. Even with the Font Face and Font Size drop-down lists, reselecting the same fonts and sizes over and over can be tedious.

Thank goodness for the QuickFonts feature, which maintains a running list of the last 10 fonts (with sizes and effects) that you selected. Click the **QuickFonts** button on the property bar (see Figure 5.3), and then click the font you want to reuse. In case you're wondering, RealTime Preview doesn't work here.

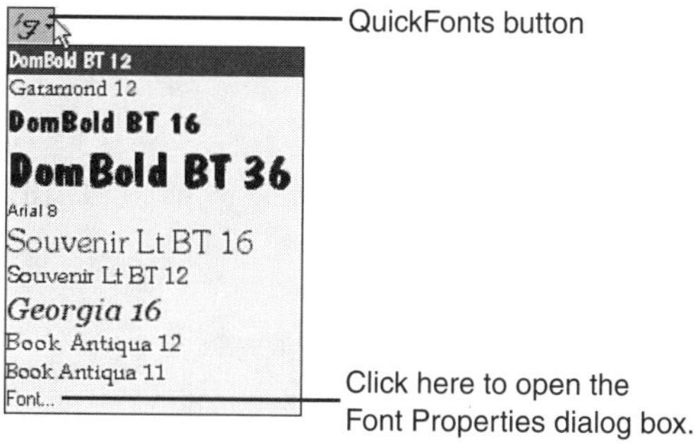

FIGURE 5.3
Click the **QuickFonts** button to select from the 10 most recently used fonts.

QuickFonts button

DomBold BT 12
Garamond 12
DomBold BT 16
DomBold BT 36
Arial 8
Souvenir Lt BT 16
Souvenir Lt BT 12
Georgia 16
Book Antiqua 12
Book Antiqua 11
Font...

Click here to open the Font Properties dialog box.

Some good rules of thumb: Don't use more than three or four fonts on a page, don't apply bold *and* italic *and* underline (all at once), don't use a bunch of different font sizes, and do choose an attractive font that suits the subject matter. Figure 5.4 shows the text from two newsletters. The newsletter on the left uses decorative fonts, but they are difficult to read. Also the combination of bold, underline, and italic on the date is too "busy." The newsletter text on the right uses an attractive font, the use of bold or italic alone, and a smaller type size. The use of bullets in the list of items also helps the reader to follow along.

FIGURE 5.4

The newsletter on the right illustrates how different font selections can improve the appearance of the text.

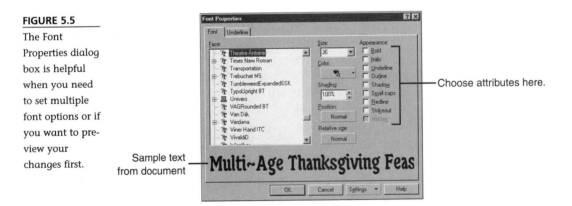

Using Other Font Effects

Bold, italic, and underline all have buttons on the property bar, so they are the most accessible font effects. The other effects, also called *attributes*, are found in the Font Properties dialog box.

To use the other font effects:

1. Position the insertion point where you want the effects to start (or select some existing text).

2. Choose **Font** from the **Format** menu (**F9**) or from the **Quickmenu** to open the Font Properties dialog box (see Figure 5.5).

FIGURE 5.5

The Font Properties dialog box is helpful when you need to set multiple font options or if you want to pre-view your changes first.

Sample text from document

Choose attributes here.

3. Click **OK** when you're finished choosing effects.

The font attributes are listed in the Appearance section. As you select attributes, the sample text in the lower-left corner shows you how the attributes will look when applied to the text. The RealTime Preview feature pops up again here—WordPerfect pulls in a short section of text from your document and uses it as the sample text. (If you're working in a blank document, the sample text is the name of the currently selected font.)

Use the Font Properties dialog box anytime you need to set more than a couple of font options at once. For example, if you need to choose a different font and size, and apply bold and italic, it's faster to do it all at once in the Font Properties dialog box than to choose each one separately from the property bar.

ADDING FONT ATTRIBUTE BUTTONS TO THE TOOLBAR

If you use font attributes a lot, consider adding buttons for them to the toolbar. Or create a new Fonts toolbar and add *all* your favorite buttons to it.

Choose **Tools**, **Settings**, **Customize**. If necessary, click the Toolbars tab. You can add to an existing toolbar, or you can create a new toolbar. To add a button to an existing toolbar, select the toolbar, and then choose **Edit**. Open the **Feature Categories** drop-down list and choose **Format**. Select the feature in the list, and then click **Add Button**. To create a new toolbar, click **Create**, type a name for the toolbar, and then click **OK**. Add buttons as previously described.

Changing Margins

It's not something you think about every day, but you can actually make your document easier to read by adjusting the margins. A wider margin creates more white space around the text and keeps the number of words on a line down. And remember, the shorter the line, the less likely the reader is to lose her place.

On the other hand, if you're trying to keep down the number of pages, you might want to make the margins smaller so that you can fit more on a page. When you use headers and footers, for example, you might want to cut down the top and bottom margins to 1/2 inch. In WordPerfect, the margins are set to 1 inch on all sides by default. This differs from Microsoft Word, where the default left and right margins are 1.25 inch and the top and bottom margins are 1 inch.

There are several different ways to adjust the margins. Using the mouse, you can click and drag the guidelines in or out, or click and drag the margin indicators on the ruler. Or, you can open the Margins dialog box and change the settings there.

Using the Guidelines

Using the guidelines is a popular choice because most of us leave the guidelines turned on. They don't take up any space in the document window, unlike the ruler.

To adjust the margins with the guidelines:

1. Position the mouse pointer over a guideline and wait until the pointer changes to a double-arrow.

   - To adjust the top margin, position the mouse pointer over the horizontal guideline at the top of the document window.

> **caution**
>
> If you don't see the guidelines (as shown in Figure 5.6), someone might have turned them off on your system. Choose **View**, **Guidelines**; place a check mark next to **Margins**; and then click **OK**.

   - To adjust the left margin, position the pointer over the vertical line on the left side of the document window.

   - To adjust the right margin, position the pointer over the vertical line on the right side of the document window.

   - To adjust the bottom margin, position the pointer over the horizontal guideline at the bottom of the document window.

2. Click and drag the guideline. When you click and drag, a dotted guideline and a bubble appear. The dotted guideline shows you where the new margin will be, and the bubble tells you what the new margin will be (in inches) when you release the mouse button (see Figure 5.6).

Adjusting the Left and Right Margins Using the Ruler

The ruler is a nice feature for people who use tabs a lot in their documents. With the ruler displayed, it's a snap to add, move, or delete tabs. For more information on setting tabs with the ruler, see Chapter 7, "Working with Paragraphs."

Margin indicators on the ruler show what the current margins are. You can click and drag these indicators to adjust the left and right margins.

To adjust the left and right margins with the ruler:

1. If necessary, display the ruler by choosing **View**, **Ruler**. The ruler appears under the property bar.

2. Position the cursor over the left or right edge of the margin indicator and wait for the double arrow.

3. Click and drag the margin indicator to the left or right to adjust the margin (see Figure 5.7).

FIGURE 5.6

Clicking and dragging guide-lines is a quick way to adjust the margins.

The bubble shows the new margin setting.

Margin guideline

The dotted guideline marks the new margin.

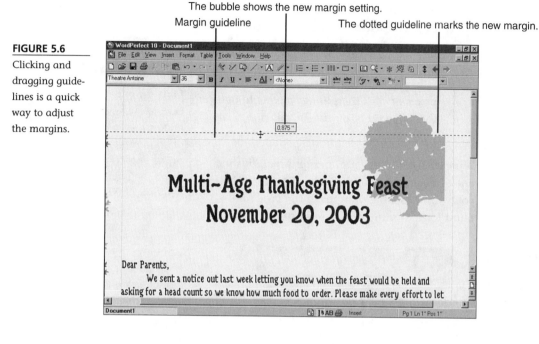

FIGURE 5.7

It's easy to adjust the left and right mar-gins with the ruler.

Left margin indicator

The bubble indicates the new margin setting.

Ruler   Right margin indicator

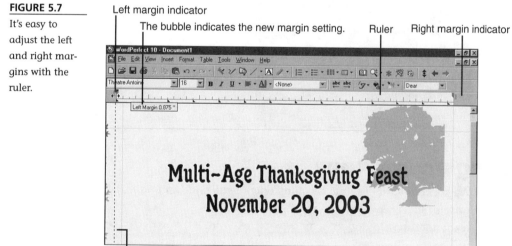

The dotted guideline marks the new margin.

Using the Page Setup Dialog Box

If you're not comfortable with clicking and dragging, or if you just want to be more precise, you can make your changes in the Page Setup dialog box.

To set the margins in the Page Setup dialog box:

1. Choose **Format**, **Margins** (**Ctrl+F8**) to open the Page Setup dialog box (see Figure 5.8).

2. Either type the measurements in the text boxes or click the spinner arrows to bump the value up or down—in this case, 0.1 inch at a time.

You can quickly set equal margins by adjusting one of the margins and clicking **Equal**. Also, if you want to set the margins to the bare minimum for that printer, click **Minimum**.

caution

Certain types of printers (such as inkjet and laser printers) are not capable of printing to the edge of the paper. This area is called the *unprintable zone*. The size of this zone varies from printer to printer, so the information is kept in the printer's setup.

If you try to set a margin within the unprintable zone, WordPerfect automatically adjusts it to the printer's minimum margin setting.

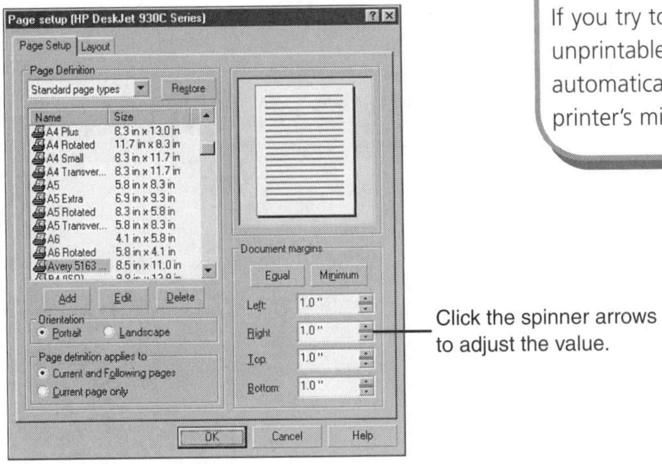

FIGURE 5.8

Use the Page Setup dialog box to adjust the margin settings.

Click the spinner arrows to adjust the value.

Creating an Envelope

We spend a lot more time emailing documents back and forth, and we don't need to print as many envelopes as we used to. Still, it's fast and easy, so the next time you reach for a pen to address an envelope, why not let WordPerfect do the work?

WordPerfect figures out where the mailing address is in the document and pulls it into the envelope dialog box, so you don't even have to retype it. You may wonder how this is done. The program looks for three to six short lines of text followed by a blank line. If two address blocks are in a letter, such as a return address followed by a mailing address, WordPerfect uses the second address.

To create an envelope:

1. Choose **Format**, **Envelope** to display the Envelope dialog box (see Figure 5.9).

ENTERING YOUR PERSONAL INFORMATION

You might see the following message (instead of the Envelope dialog box): "The Template feature allows you to enter information about yourself that will personalize your templates. You need only enter this once." Creating an envelope is one area in the program where your personal information is used.

You have a choice: You can either create a record in the Address Book with your personal information now, in which case WordPerfect automatically inserts your return address, or you can skip this step and type your return address in the envelope manually. Keep in mind that if you skip the step of entering your personal information, you'll be prompted to do it every time you try to do something that involves a template or your personal information.

FIGURE 5.9

WordPerfect locates the mailing address and inserts it in the Envelope dialog box so that you don't have to type it twice.

If the return address does not appear, type it here.

WordPerfect inserts the mailing address.

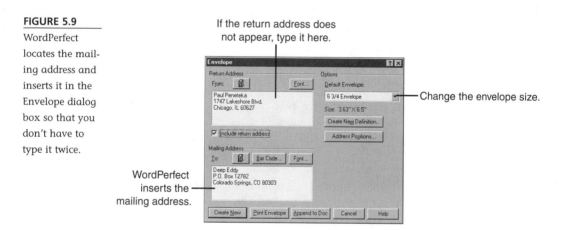

Change the envelope size.

2. If there isn't a return address in the **From** text box, or if you want to revise the address, you have a couple options:

   ■ Click in the **From** text box and enter the information.

   ■ Click the **Address Book** icon if you want to select an address from one of the available address books. (The type and number of address books that you have available will vary depending on your email capabilities.)

3. If necessary, you can do the following:

   ■ You can either manually replace the mailing address or click the **Address Book** icon and choose a mailing address from one of the available address books.

- Click the **Font** button to change the font and/or font size for the return address and mailing address.

- Click the **Bar Code** button; then type the recipient's ZIP code and choose a position for the bar code.

- Click the **Address Positions** button and then adjust the placement of the return and mailing addresses.

- Click the **Default Envelope** drop-down list arrow, and then choose a size from the pop-up list.

4. When you're finished, choose from the following:

- Click the **Create New** button if you want to place the envelope in a new document.

- Click the **Print Envelope** button to send the envelope directly to the printer.

- Click the **Append to Doc** button if you want to place the envelope at the bottom of the current document.

caution

Some printers have a large unprintable zone on the left side, which interferes with printing the return address on the envelope. A macro that comes with WordPerfect 10, called `flipenv`, is used to create an envelope that is rotated 180 degrees (the text is upside down) so that you can get around the problem. See Chapter 17, "Creating and Playing Macros."

Inserting Symbols

The capability to insert symbols is one area in which WordPerfect stands head and shoulders above the competition. WordPerfect Office 2002 comes with fonts for more than 1,500 special characters and symbols, including entire foreign language alphabets. You can insert the characters anywhere in your document.

Using the Symbols Dialog Box

The Symbols dialog box has a complete list of all the character sets and all the special characters. You can switch to a different character set and quickly insert any symbol from the list.

note

Not all special characters are available in every font. Depending on the font you have selected, you might see empty boxes instead of special characters, which means those characters aren't available. On the other hand, certain fonts, such as Wingdings, are composed entirely of special characters.

To insert special characters with the Symbols dialog box:

1. Click in the document where you want the special character to appear.

2. Choose **Insert**, **Symbols (Ctrl+W)** to open the Symbols dialog box (see Figure 5.10). You might need to scroll down to see the symbol you want.

Click here to switch to another character set.

FIGURE 5.10

Through the Symbols dialog box, you can insert more than 1,500 symbols and characters from foreign language alphabets.

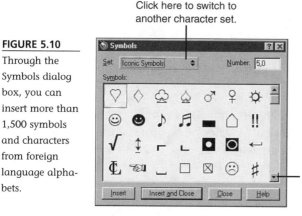

Click here to scroll down through the symbols available in this set.

3. If you don't see the character you need, click the **Set** button and select a different character set from the list.

4. Select the symbol, and then click **Insert**, or double-click a symbol in the list to insert it. The dialog box stays open to make it easier for you to insert other symbols. If you only need to insert one symbol, click **Insert and Close** instead.

5. Click **Close** when you are finished.

Using the Symbols Toolbar Button

You can use the Symbols button on the toolbar to open a palette of 16 common symbols. Using the mouse, you can insert one of the symbols in just two clicks.

To select a symbol from the palette:

1. Click the **Symbols** button on the property bar to open the palette (see Figure 5.11).

tip

WordPerfect has a great shortcut for inserting special characters. The next time you select a symbol, jot down the two numbers in the **Number** text box. The next time you need to insert the character, press **Ctrl+W**, type the two numbers (separated by a space or a comma), and then press **Enter**. For example, to insert the smiley face shown in Figure 5.10, press **Ctrl+W**, type **5,7**, and then press **Enter**.

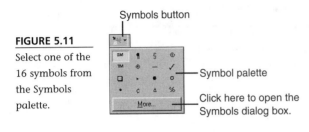

Symbols button

FIGURE 5.11

Select one of the 16 symbols from the Symbols palette.

Symbol palette

Click here to open the Symbols dialog box.

2. Click the symbol that you want to insert.

3. If you don't see the symbol that you want, click **More** to open the Symbols dialog box.

The symbol palette changes as you insert symbols into your documents, remembering up to the last 16 symbols you've used. After you've inserted the symbols that you use most often, they appear on the palette and can be easily inserted with the Symbols button.

Using QuickCorrect

The QuickCorrect feature is designed to automatically correct common spelling errors and typos while you type. There are five common symbols that you can insert with QuickCorrect (see Table 5.1).

TABLE 5.1   Inserting Symbols with QuickCorrect

To Insert This Symbol	Type This
Copyright symbol (©)	(c)
Registered trademark symbol (®)	(r)
One half (½)	1/2
en dash (–)	-- or n-
em dash (—)	--- or m-

If you don't want QuickCorrect to make these automatic replacements, you can take these symbols out of the list. Choose **Tools**, **QuickCorrect**. Select the symbol you want to remove and then click **Delete Entry**.

Turning on Reveal Codes

Opening up the Reveal Codes window is a lot like raising the hood of a car. You're going under the hood of a document to see exactly how formatting codes control the appearance. There is no comparable feature in Microsoft Word.

This is where WordPerfect distinguishes itself from the competition. No other application gives you the same power and flexibility.

When you turn on Reveal Codes, the document window is split in half. The Reveal Codes window takes up the lower half of the screen (see Figure 5.12). What you see in this window is a duplicate of the text in the document window with the codes displayed.

The placement of the codes controls the appearance. You read through the codes just like you read a book—from left to right. A code takes effect where it is placed and remains in effect until another matching code is reached. For example, if you change the top margin, the change stays in effect until the end of the document, or until another top margin code is found.

There are two types of codes: paired and open. *Paired* codes have an On code and an Off code. The On code is at the beginning of the affected text; the Off code is at the end. For example, if you boldface a title, you'll see a Bold On code at the beginning of the title and a Bold Off code at the end. An open code, such as a margin change or a hard return, stands alone. If you want to make changes, you simply edit the codes, or delete them altogether.

FIGURE 5.12

The Reveal Codes window displays the document text and the formatting codes.

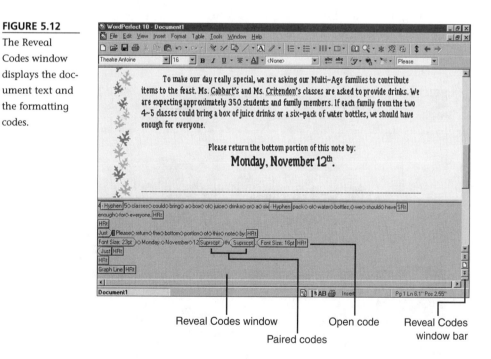

You can use any of the following methods to turn on Reveal Codes:

- Right-click the document window and choose **Reveal Codes** from the QuickMenu.
- Choose **View**, **Reveal Codes**.
- Press **Alt+F3**.
- Drag the **Reveal Codes window bar** located at the bottom of the vertical scrollbar (refer to Figure 5.12).

Formatting codes appear in the Reveal Codes screen as buttons mixed in with the text. The insertion point is shown as a small red box. You can click in the Reveal Codes window to move the insertion point, or you can use the arrow keys.

To edit or delete a code:

- You can delete codes by clicking and dragging them out of the Reveal Codes screen (see Figure 5.13).

note

Be especially careful when you edit a document with Reveal Codes on. If the Reveal Codes window is open, WordPerfect assumes that you see the codes and that you intend to delete them when you use Delete or Backspace.

If you accidentally delete a formatting code, use Undo to restore it. Click the **Undo** button on the toolbar, or press **Ctrl+Z**.

FIGURE 5.13

The quickest way to delete a code is to click and drag it out of the Reveal Codes window.

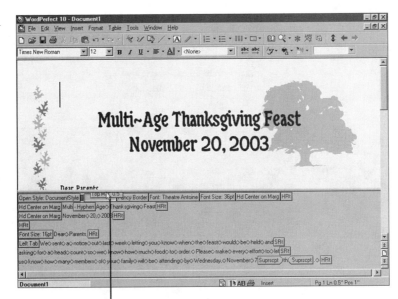

Click and drag a code out to delete it.

■ The quickest way to make formatting adjustments is to edit the code. Simply double-click the code in the Reveal Codes window. This opens the corresponding dialog box, where you can make the necessary changes. When you close the dialog box, your changes are saved.

As you work through these chapters, turn on Reveal Codes now and then so you can see that the selections you make in dialog boxes result in the insertion of codes that control the formatting of a document. The order of the codes is important. If you are having trouble figuring out why something is happening, the first thing you should do is turn on Reveal Codes and check the order of the codes. In many cases, all you need to do is rearrange the order of the codes, or delete the codes causing trouble. Incidentally, you can select and move or copy codes in the Reveal Codes window using the same techniques that you learned in Chapter 4, "Revising Documents."

THE ABSOLUTE MINIMUM

In this chapter, you learned how to perform basic formatting tasks. You learned how to select fonts, apply attributes, change the margins, create envelopes, and insert symbols.

■ You learned the importance of using good judgment when selecting fonts and font attributes to emphasize important sections of text and to improve the appearance and readability of your document.

■ There are several methods for changing the margins, and you got a chance to try them all.

■ You learned how to create and print an envelope.

■ You now know about WordPerfect's unique special character sets. You can insert characters from foreign alphabets, and a huge variety of symbols and other special characters.

■ Understanding the role of codes helps you maintain total control over the formatting.

In the next chapter, you'll learn how to use WordPerfect's writing tools to improve accuracy and ensure consistency in your documents.

IN THIS CHAPTER

- Learn how to run a spell check and use Grammatik to check documents for grammatical errors.

- Use the 30,000-word dictionary to look up definitions.

- Learn how to switch to a different set of writing tools for other languages.

- Learn how to search (and replace) text, codes, or a combination of both.

- Use QuickCorrect, QuickWords, and Format-As-You-Go to make your typing efficient and accurate.

6

USING THE WRITING TOOLS

Word processors have evolved from glorified typewriters to document production engines. At the same time, the type of worker using word processors has evolved. Not everyone has the luxury of an assistant—most of us produce our own materials. People who have never typed their own documents are learning how to use spelling and grammatical checkers to improve the readability and credibility of their work. WordPerfect has an exceptional collection of productivity tools to help automate many common tasks performed by today's office workers.

Recognizing WordPerfect's Automatic Proofreading Features

You might notice that as you type a document, red underlines appear under some words. This is the Spell-As-You-Go feature working for you. Spell-As-You-Go has marked these words as possible misspellings.

Spell-As-You-Go is one of the two automatic proofreading features in WordPerfect—the other is Grammar-As-You-Go, which checks for grammatical errors. The theory behind these two features is that it's faster to correct errors while you are typing than to go back and fix them later. If Grammar-As-You-Go is activated rather than Spell-As-You-Go, you might see blue dashes in the text as well.

To correct a word with Spell-As-You-Go:

1. Right-click a red underlined word to open a list of suggested replacement words that you can choose from (see Figure 6.1).

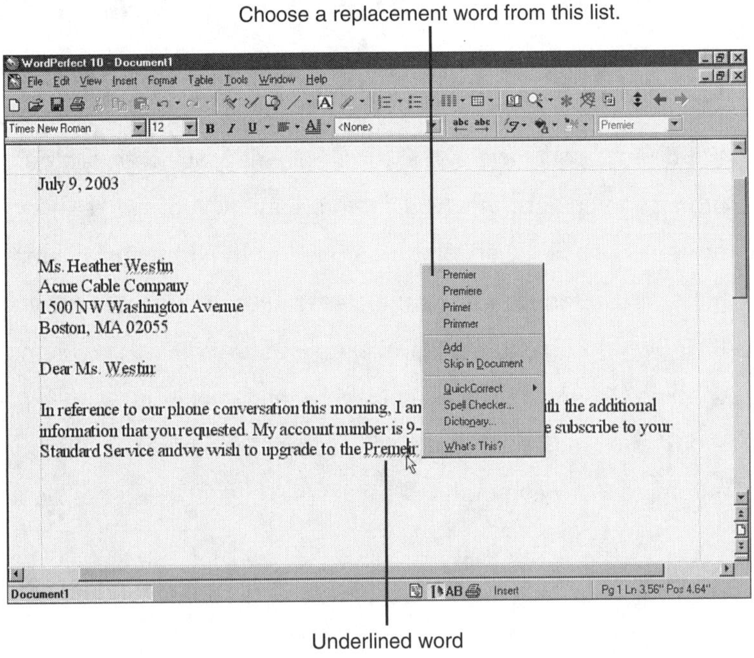

Choose a replacement word from this list.

FIGURE 6.1

When you right-click a red underlined word, a list of suggested replacements appears.

Underlined word

2. Click the correctly spelled word in the list.

That's it—you just corrected the misspelled word. Selecting a word from this list automatically replaces the underlined word with the word you chose.

If you find these proofing marks distracting, you can disable the Spell-As-You-Go and Grammar-As-You-Go features.

To disable the automatic proofing features:

1. Choose **Tools**, **Proofread**. Notice that Spell-As-You-Go has a bullet next to it—this means that it's turned on (see Figure 6.2). Grammar-As-You-Go includes the Spell-As-You-Go feature, so you can select either Spell-As-You-Go only or select Grammar-As-You-Go, but you cannot select both from the Proofread submenu at the same time.

FIGURE 6.2

Choosing Grammar-As-You-Go activates both Grammar-As-You-Go and Spell-As-You-Go.

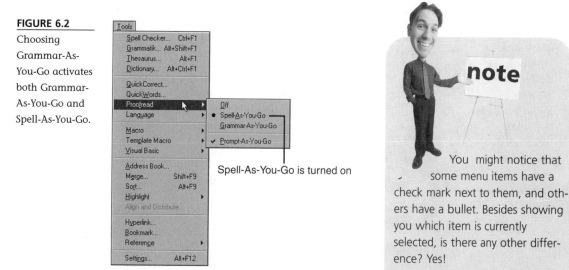

Spell-As-You-Go is turned on

> **note**
>
> You might notice that some menu items have a check mark next to them, and others have a bullet. Besides showing you which item is currently selected, is there any other difference? Yes!
>
> Bullets tell you that only one of the options in that group can be selected at one time. Check marks tell you that more than one option in that group can be selected at one time.

2. Click **Off** to turn off both Spell-As-You-Go and Grammar-As-You-Go.

Spell Checking a Document

Who would have thought something as simple as a few misspelled words could undermine all your hard work? They can, and they will. Like it or not, readers will question the credibility of a writer if they find typos in the text. Save yourself the potential embarrassment by running Spell Checker on every document, no matter how short it is, before you send it off.

Develop a habit of saving documents before you run any of the writing tools such as the Spell Checker. This way, if you make some changes that you decide you don't want to keep, you can always revert to the saved copy. Occasionally, the writing tools will freeze up your system, so it's especially important that you have a good backup that you can revert to after you restart.

To start Spell Checker and correct mistakes in your document:

1. Choose **Tools**, **Spell Checker** or click the **Spell Checker** button on the toolbar. The writing tools dialog box with tabs for Spell Checker, Grammatik, Thesaurus, and the Dictionary appears (see Figure 6.3). Spell Checker immediately begins checking the document. A potential error is highlighted, and suggested replacement words appear in the **Replacements** list box.

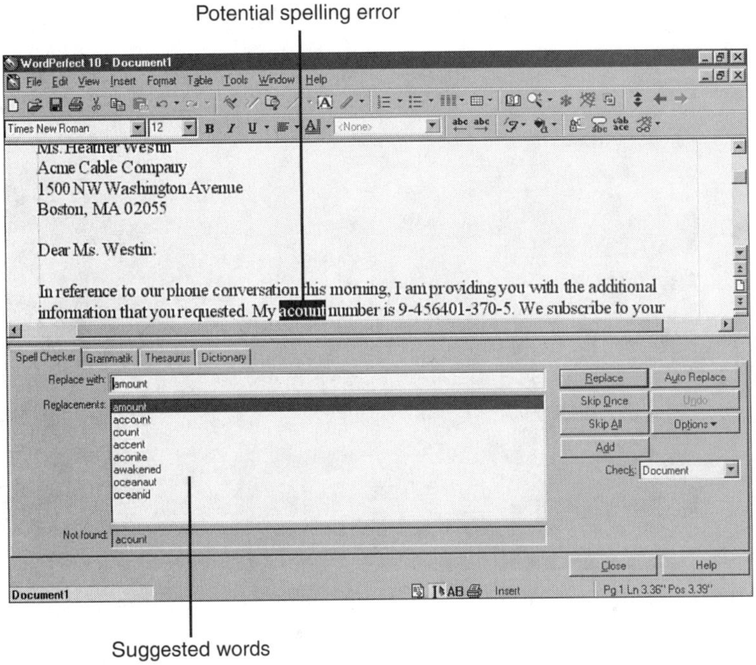

Potential spelling error

FIGURE 6.3

Spell Checker, Grammatik, Thesaurus, and the Dictionary are all integrated into the same dialog box. Click the appropriate tab to switch to another writing tool.

Suggested words

2. Choose from the following options to correct the misspelled word, add the word to the dictionary, or skip the word:

   ■ To correct a misspelled word manually, click in the document window, correct the problem, and then click **Resume** to continue spell checking.

   ■ To replace a misspelled word with the correctly spelled word, select the correctly spelled word in the **Replacements** list box and click **Replace**. In the case of duplicate words and irregular capitalization, select the single word, or the word with correct capitalization, in the **Replacements** list box.

- If this is a frequently misspelled word, select the correct spelling in the **Replacements** list box, and then click **Auto Replace** to add the combination to the QuickCorrect list. (See "Adding and Deleting QuickCorrect Entries" later in this chapter for more information.)

- If the correct spelling doesn't appear in the **Replacements** list, edit the word manually in the **Replace with** box, and then click **Replace**.

- To skip the word here but have Spell Checker stop if it finds it again, click **Skip Once**.

- To skip the word here and for the rest of the document, click **Skip All**.

- To add this word to the active user word list, click **Add**.

- If you accidentally replace the misspelled word with the wrong replacement word, click **Undo**.

note

Choosing **Skip All** adds the word to the document word list, which is saved with the document and doesn't affect other documents. The strength of this feature becomes clear when you work with documents that are full of complex or technical terms. It takes only a few mouse clicks, and once you've built the list, Spell Checker runs faster because it isn't stopping on those terms anymore.

By default, Spell Checker checks the entire document. If you don't want to check the whole document, select the portion that you want to check first. Also, you can specify which portion of the document you want checked by selecting an option on the **Check** drop-down list.

Checking for Grammatical Errors

Grammatik is WordPerfect's grammar checker. A grammar checker proofs documents for correct grammar, style, punctuation, and word use, and thus catches many errors that get by most spell checkers. Interestingly, Spell Checker is integrated into Grammatik, so you only need to run Grammatik to run both.

Grammatik uses grammatical rules when checking a document for problems. Many good writers, however, often bend these rules to make a point. You shouldn't feel compelled to fix every problem or accept every suggested solution if it changes the meaning of your words.

To start Grammatik and check your document:

1. Choose **Tools**, **Grammatik**, or if you already have the writing tools dialog box open, just click the **Grammatik** tab. Grammatik immediately starts checking the document and, like Spell Checker, stops and highlights a potential error (see Figure 6.4).

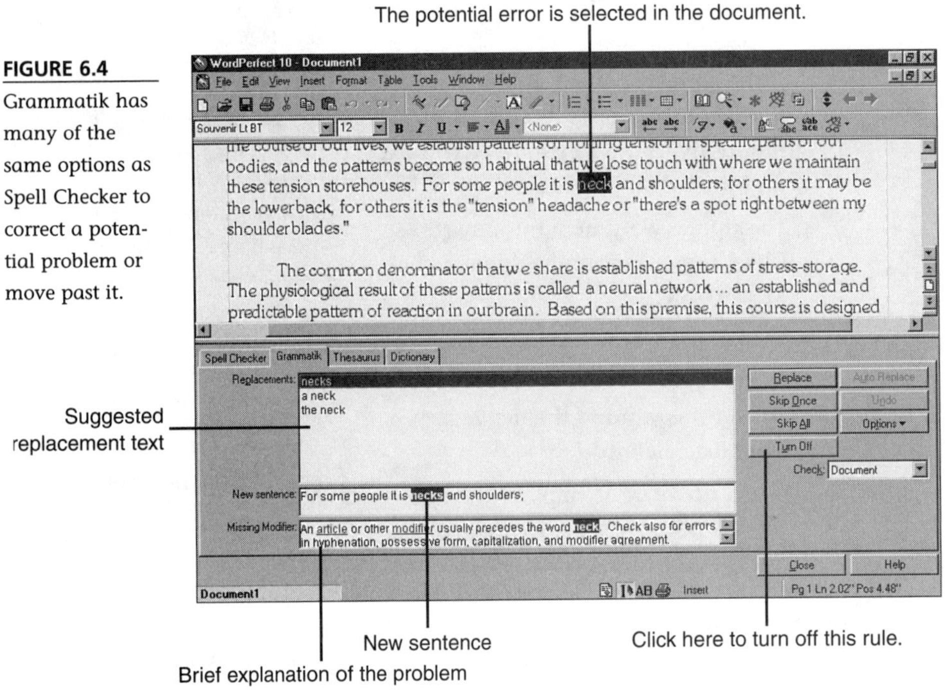

The potential error is selected in the document.

FIGURE 6.4

Grammatik has many of the same options as Spell Checker to correct a potential problem or move past it.

Suggested replacement text

New sentence

Brief explanation of the problem

Click here to turn off this rule.

2. Choose from the following options to correct the error, skip the error, or turn off the rule:

   ■ To correct a writing error manually, click in the document window, correct the problem, and then click **Resume** to continue the grammar check.

   ■ To fix a writing error, select one of the suggestions in the **Replacements** list box and then click **Replace**.

   ■ To skip the writing error here but have Grammatik stop if it finds the error again, click **Skip Once**.

   ■ To skip the writing error here and for the rest of the document, click **Skip All**.

■ The rules by which Grammatik checks your document are organized into *rule classes*. To disable a particular rule class, click **Turn Off**. This change is temporary, so when you run Grammatik again, the rule will be turned back on.

■ If you correct a problem and then change your mind, click **Undo** to reverse the last action taken by Grammatik.

By default, Grammatik checks the entire document. If you want to check only a portion of the document, click the **Check** drop-down list arrow and select an option.

> **note**
>
> Because Spell Checker is integrated into Grammatik, when you run Grammatik, you will also correct errors found by Spell Checker.

Depending on the type of document you are working on, you might want to use a different set of grammatical rules to check your document. Grammatik offers 11 predefined checking styles, and if you're really motivated, you can create your own.

By default, Grammatik uses the Quick Check style to check your documents. It's pretty simple to switch to one of the other checking styles.

To select a different checking style:

1. Choose **Tools, Grammatik** to open the writing tools dialog box.

2. In the Grammatik tab, choose **Options, Checking Styles** to display the Checking Styles dialog box (see Figure 6.5).

FIGURE 6.5

Choose from one of the 11 predefined checking styles in the Checking Styles dialog box.

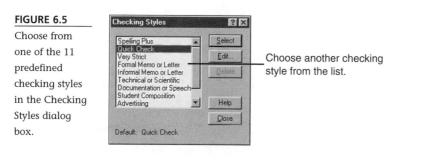

Choose another checking style from the list.

3. To choose a checking style, select it in the list, and then click **Select**. Checking styles remain in effect until you choose another.

Looking Up Words in the Thesaurus

A thesaurus helps you find the just the right word to describe something. Some concepts are more complex than others, and ideas can be expressed in a number of ways. Using the right words enables you to convey exactly the message you want to the reader.

WordPerfect's Thesaurus looks up synonyms (that is, words with similar meanings), antonyms, and related words. You can start the Thesaurus from a blank screen, but if you click on a word first, the Thesaurus looks up that word.

To look up a word in the Thesaurus:

1. Select the word that you want to look up.

2. Choose **Tools**, **Thesaurus** (**Alt+F1**), or, if you already have the writing tools dialog box open, click the **Thesaurus** tab. The Thesaurus looks up the word and, by default, displays a list of synonyms, and, if available, a list of antonyms and related words (see Figure 6.6).

Click here to replace the word in the text.

Click here to see the history.

FIGURE 6.6

The Thesaurus helps you improve your writing by showing you alternate words to use.

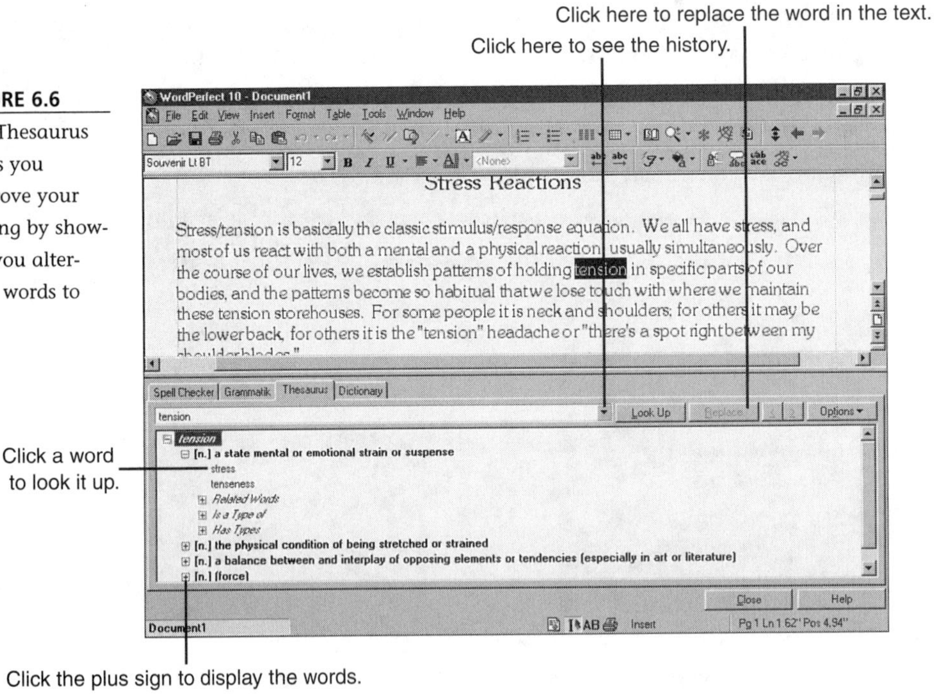

Click a word to look it up.

Click the plus sign to display the words.

3. Choose from the following options to look up words in the Thesaurus:

■ If you selected a word in step 1, the Thesaurus looks up the word and displays the results in the window. Otherwise, you need to type the word you want to look up in the text box and then click **Look Up**.

■ To see a list of words within a category, double-click the category, or click the plus sign in the box. The left and right arrows on your keyboard can also be used to open and close categories.

■ To look up one of the words in the list, double-click the word. A new window opens up for that word. If you double-click a word in the second window, a third window opens. When you fill up three windows, more windows are created (to the right). Click the scroll arrows to move one window to the left or right (see Figure 6.7).

Click here to move one window to the right.
Click here to move one window to the left.

FIGURE 6.7

If you fill up more than three windows, use the scroll arrows to move back and forth in the windows.

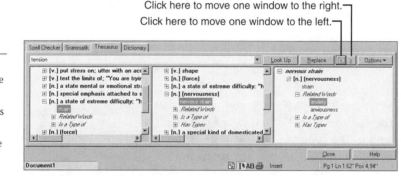

■ To replace the word in the document with the word from the Thesaurus, select the word, and then click **Replace**.

■ If you change your mind about replacing a word, click the **Undo** button, or choose **Edit, Undo** (in the document window) to reverse the change.

■ The Thesaurus has a history list so you can jump back to a word that you noticed earlier. Click the drop-down list arrow next to the **Look Up** button to select from the history list.

Using the Dictionary

WordPerfect 10 includes an integrated version of the *Pocket Oxford Dictionary*, which contains more than 30,000 words. You can look up the definition of a selected word in your document, or you can just type in a word.

To look up a word in the Dictionary:

1. Select the word in your document.

2. Choose **Tools**, **Dictionary** (**Alt+Ctrl+F1**). Or, if you already have the writing tools dialog box open, click the **Dictionary** tab to display the Dictionary dialog box (see Figure 6.8).

Type the word you want to look up here.

FIGURE 6.8

The built-in *Oxford English Pocket Dictionary* contains definitions for more than 30,000 words.

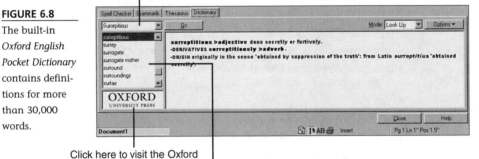

Click here to visit the Oxford University Press Web site.

Select from this list to display other definitions.

With a printed dictionary, you need to have *some* idea of how to spell the word, or you won't be able to find it. The beauty of an electronic dictionary is that you can locate words by searching through the definitions. For example, you can locate all the terms that have the word "flower" in the definition. Also, if you know how to spell a part of the word, you have a much greater chance of locating it with an electronic search.

To search through the dictionary:

1. With the Dictionary dialog box displayed, open the **Mode** drop-down list and click **Search**.

2. Type the word that you want to search for in the text box underneath the writing tools tabs.

3. Click **Go**. A list of terms that contain the search word in the definition appears in the window (see Figure 6.9).

note

The built-in Oxford English Pocket Dictionary can be upgraded to the Oxford English Concise Dictionary, which contains 70,000 definitions. An item on the Options menu takes you to the Corel Store Web page where you can download the upgrade for a nominal charge.

Type the word you want to search for here.

Click here to search through the definitions.

FIGURE 6.9

With an electronic version of a dictionary, it's simple to locate words by searching through their definitions.

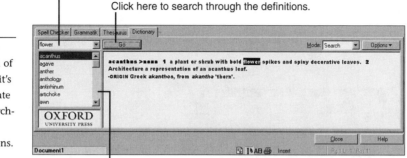

Scroll down through the list to see the rest of the search results.

Switching to a Different Language

We are truly working in a global marketplace. It's not unusual to carry on business with companies located all across the globe. When you write in a different language, you must be able to do more than just enter, display, and print the non-English characters. You also need to be able to correct spelling, check grammar, and look up terms in the Thesaurus, in addition to using the proper date conventions and currency symbols. WordPerfect supports multiple languages in three ways:

■ You can purchase WordPerfect in a different language so that the menus, prompts, messages, dictionaries, and thesauri are all in that language.

■ You can mark sections of a document as being in one of the more than 30 languages supported by WordPerfect. Additional language modules can be installed that support the Spell Checker, Grammatik, Thesaurus, Dictionary, and Hyphenation.

■ A Language Resource File (LRS file), which comes with the program and each language module, contains the information for formatting numbers and footnote-continued messages, among other things. You can edit this file to customize these options.

To switch to a different language:

1. If you want to mark only a section of text, select it first. Otherwise, click in the text where you want to switch to a different language

2. Choose **Tools**, **Language**, **Settings**. The Language dialog box appears, with a list of available language modules (see Figure 6.10).

3. Scroll through the list and double-click the language you want.

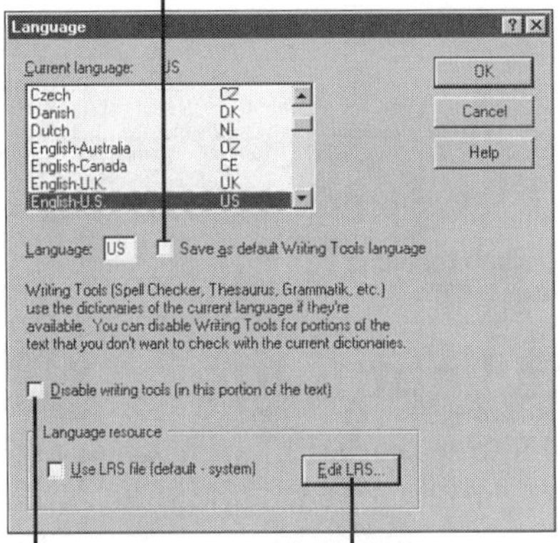

Make this the default writing tools language.

FIGURE 6.10

You can disable the writing tools for sections of text that need to be checked in a different language.

Disable writing tools.

Edit the LRS file.

If you frequently switch back and forth between languages, you'll love this feature—new in WordPerfect 10. You can now display the current language in the application bar. Right-click the application bar (at the bottom of the screen) and click **Settings**. Scroll down through the list, enable the check box next to **Language**, and click **OK**. A new Language button appears on the far-right side of the application bar. Click this button to open the Language dialog box.

You can switch to a different language when you're using any of the writing tools. In the Spell Checker, Grammatik, or the Thesaurus, choose **Options**, **Language** to open the Select Language dialog box (see Figure 6.11). Click **Show Available Languages Only** to display only those languages supported by the current writing tool. Select the language you want and then click **OK**.

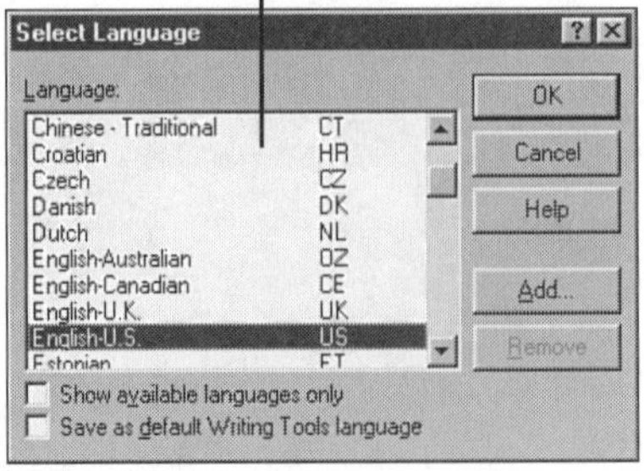

List of available languages

FIGURE 6.11

Use the Select Language dialog box to switch to a different language when you're using the writing tools.

If you purchase additional language modules, you can add them in the Select Language dialog box. Click the **Add** button to add a language. Click **Save as default Writing Tools language** if you want the setting to be permanent.

Searching and Replacing Text and Codes

The Find feature can locate a snippet of text, or a specific code in your document, in just a few seconds. The Replace feature takes the process a step further by allowing you to substitute something else for the search item.

Here's an example of how you might use the Replace feature with Find: Let's say you accidentally misspelled someone's name throughout a long document. You can search for all occurrences and replace them with the correct spelling. The same thing goes for codes. If you decide you want to search for a particular font and replace it with another one, you can do it with Find and Replace by searching for the code for the unwanted font and replacing it with the code of the desired font.

Searching for Text

Searching for text is fairly straightforward. You can do broad searches by searching for the first several characters in a word, or you can be very specific by searching for a particular sentence or phrase.

For the most part, I use Find to quickly jump to the section of text that I need to work on. It's faster than scrolling through a document to find the place where I need to start. That said; don't underestimate the Replace side of the Find and Replace feature. When it comes to making a global change throughout a document, nothing beats it for speed and accuracy.

To search for (and replace) text:

1. Choose **Edit**, **Find and Replace** (**F2**) to open the Find and Replace dialog box (see Figure 6.12).

Type the text you want to search here.

FIGURE 6.12

With Find and Replace, you can quickly locate a section of text and, optionally, replace it with something else.

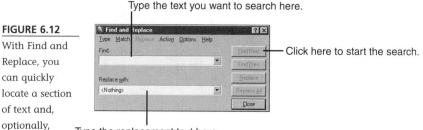

Click here to start the search.

Type the replacement text here.

2. Type the text you want to search for in the **Find text** box. This might be a complete or partial word, phrase, or number.

3. (Optional) Type the replacement text in the **Replace with** text box. The replacement text must be exact because it will be inserted in the document exactly as it appears in the text box.

4. Click **Find Next** to start the search.

If you want to delete selected instances of the search text, leave <Nothing> in the **Replace with** text box (or leave it blank). As you go through the search, you can selectively replace the search text with nothing, deleting it from the document.

When WordPerfect locates the search text, you have the following options:

- Click **Find Next** to continue the search.

- Click **Find Prev** to move back to the previous instance.

- Click **Replace** to replace the search text with the replacement text.

- Click **Replace All** to replace all the rest of the occurrences without further confirmation from you.

- Click **Close** if you're just using Find to locate your place in a document and you want to get to work.

Searching for Codes

You can extend a search into the document codes to either locate a particular code so that you can edit or delete it, or so that you can replace the code with another one. For example, if you often work with converted documents, Find and Replace can be your best friend. After you identify the codes you want to get rid of, you can search for the codes and delete them. Some documents are so poorly formatted that it's quicker to clean out the codes and start over.

---

tip

You can search for a symbol and replace it with another symbol. Click in the **Find** text box and press **Ctrl+W**. Select the symbol from any of the character sets; then click **Insert and Close**. Click in the **Replace with** text box and press **Ctrl+W**. Select the symbol from any of the character sets; then click **Insert and Close**. Click **Find Next**. When WordPerfect stops, click **Replace All** to do a global replacement.

---

note

If you've already closed the Find and Replace dialog box, but you need to continue searching, you can use two shortcuts. You can use the QuickFind buttons on the property bar to move to the next or previous instance of the search text. You can also press **Ctrl+Alt+N** to find the next occurrence and **Ctrl+Alt+P** to find the previous occurrence.

Although this might take numerous find and replace operations, it's still faster than manually deleting each code.

To search for a code:

1. Choose **Edit**, **Find and Replace** (**F2**) to open the Find and Replace dialog box.

2. Choose **Match**, **Codes** from the menu in the Find and Replace dialog box. This opens the Codes dialog box (see Figure 6.13).

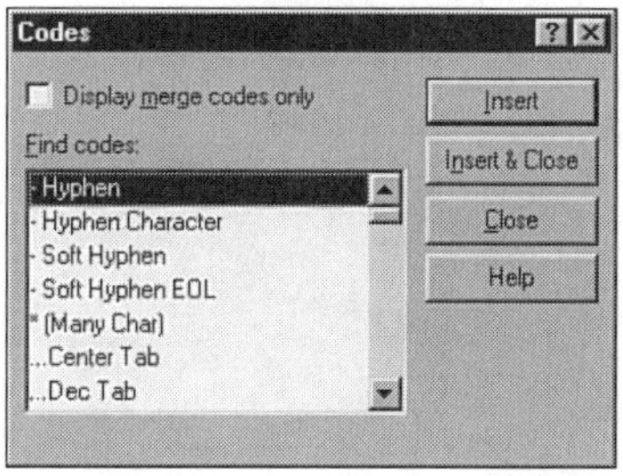

FIGURE 6.13

Using Find and Replace, you can search for virtually any code in a document.

3. When you find the code you want to search for, select it and click **Insert & Close**.

4. Click **Find Next**. When WordPerfect stops, close the Find and Replace dialog box and then turn on **Reveal Codes** (**View**, **Reveal Codes**). The insertion point will be positioned right after the code.

   ▪ To delete the code, press **Backspace** or click and drag it out of the Reveal Codes window.

   ▪ To edit a code, double-click it.

To find and replace a code, follow these steps:

1. Repeat the preceding steps 1–3.

2. Select the **Replace with** text box.

3. Choose **Replace**, **Codes**. The same Codes dialog box shown in Figure 6.13 opens. This time, only the codes that can replace the code you are searching for are available. All the others are grayed out. For example, you can't replace a Center Tab code with a Date Format code.

4. When you find the code you want, select it and then click **Insert & Close**.

5. Click **Find Next**. When WordPerfect stops, click **Replace** to replace this code and move on to the next one; click **Replace All** to replace the rest of the codes without further confirmation.

I mentioned earlier that you could search for a specific font and replace it with another. This is an example of searching for codes with a specific setting. Margin codes also have specific settings, as do line spacing and styles.

To find and replace codes with specific settings:

1. Choose **Edit**, **Find and Replace**, or press **F2** to open the Find and Replace dialog box.

2. Choose **Type**, **Specific Codes** to open the Specific Codes dialog box (see Figure 6.14).

tip

You might not have thought of this yet, but you can combine text and codes in the **Find** text box to look for text followed (or preceded) by a certain code.

FIGURE 6.14

To search for a code with a specific setting, select the code from the Specific Codes dialog box.

3. Select a code from the list and click **OK**. Based on your selection, a modified Find and Replace dialog box appears, with options for you to select the setting that you are searching for. Figure 6.15 shows the dialog box you get after choosing the Font code.

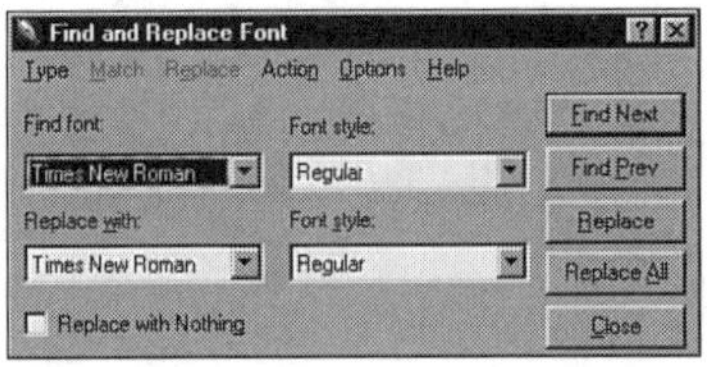

FIGURE 6.15

When you select Font from the Specific Codes dialog box, you get a Find and Replace Font dialog box.

4. Use the Find and Replace Font dialog box options to specify exactly what you want to find (and replace). For example, you could search for Arial Bold and replace it with Technical, or you could search for all the 14-point text and replace it with 16-point text. The possibilities are endless.

5. Click **Find Next** to start the search.

Discovering the Power of QuickCorrect

> **tip**
>
> In the modified Find and Replace dialog box, put a check mark in the **Replace with Nothing** check box if you want to replace the code with nothing, thus deleting it from the document.

The QuickCorrect feature is designed to correct common mistakes automatically, without any intervention from you. Microsoft Word has a similar feature called AutoCorrect. QuickCorrect cleans up extra spaces between words, fixes capitalization errors, corrects common spelling mistakes and typos, inserts special symbols, and replaces regular straight quotation marks with typeset-quality curly quotation marks. It also helps you create graphic lines; bulleted lists; ordinal numbers; and hyperlinks to Internet or intranet addresses, files on your network, or files on a local hard drive. QuickCorrect has a lot to offer, so take a few minutes and learn what it can do for you.

Choose **Tools**, **QuickCorrect** to open the QuickCorrect dialog box (see Figure 6.16). There are tabs for all the different features that fall under the QuickCorrect umbrella.

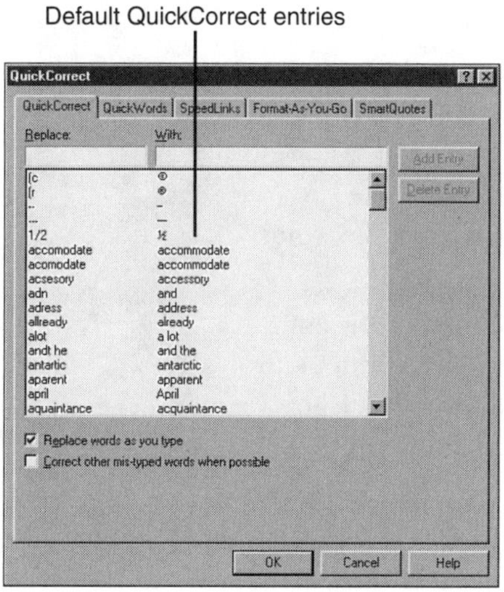

Default QuickCorrect entries

FIGURE 6.16

In the QuickCorrect dialog box, you can add, delete, and edit the QuickCorrect entries. You also can disable QuickCorrect so that it won't correct words while you type.

Adding and Deleting QuickCorrect Entries

QuickCorrect comes with a long list of frequently misspelled words and typos. After you add your own common typing mistakes to the QuickCorrect list, you'll spend a lot less time proofing your documents.

To add words or phrases to QuickCorrect:

1. Choose **Tools**, **QuickCorrect** to open the QuickCorrect dialog box.

2. Type the word or phrase in the **Replace** text box.

3. Type the replacement word or phrase in the **With** text box (see Figure 6.17).

4. Click **Add Entry**.

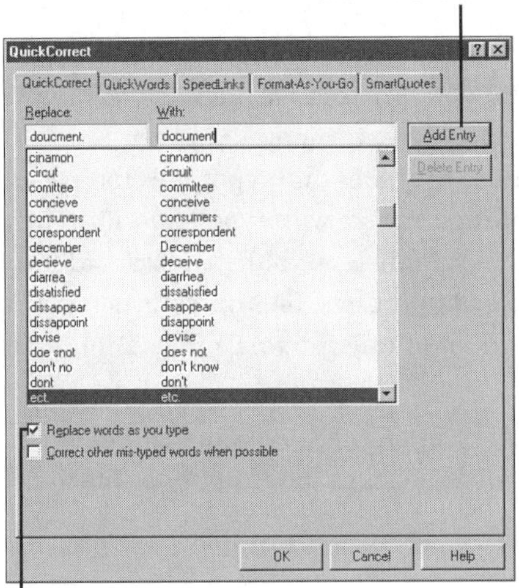

Click here to add the entry.

FIGURE 6.17

You can add your frequent misspellings and typos to the QuickCorrect list and let WordPerfect fix your mistakes automatically.

Click here to turn off QuickCorrect.

If you would prefer not to use the QuickCorrect feature, you can turn it off completely. Choose **Tools**, **QuickCorrect**, and deselect the **Replace words as you type** check box (that is, remove the check mark).

A better solution might be to remove the entries that you don't like so that you can continue to take advantage of those that are helpful. To remove an entry, select it in the list and click **Delete Entry**, **Yes**.

tip

Think of ways you can use QuickCorrect to insert long or hard-to-type words when you type a few characters. For example, you could add an entry to replace "wp2002" with "Corel WordPerfect Office 2002" or "ta7" with "7th period Technology Apps."

Customizing Format-As-You-Go

The Format-As-You-Go feature is designed to keep sentence structure accurate by cleaning up extra spaces and incorrect capitalization. There also are shortcuts for creating lists, graphic lines, ordinal numbers, and symbols.

To customize the Format-As-You-Go feature:

1. Choose **Tools**, **QuickCorrect** to open the QuickCorrect dialog box.
2. Click the **Format-As-You-Go** tab. By default, all the options in the Sentence corrections section are selected, and End of sentence corrections is set to None (see Figure 6.18).

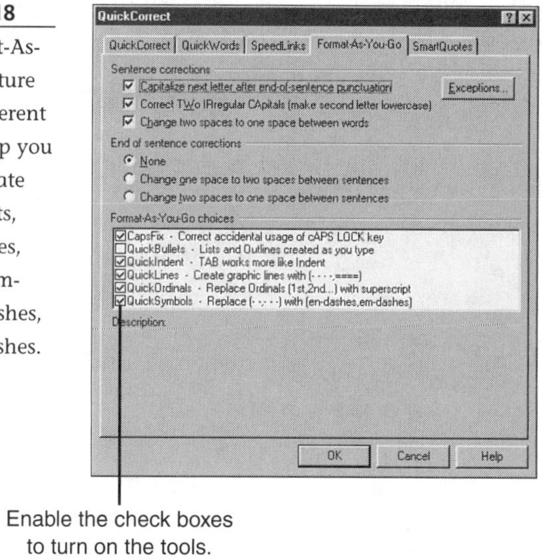

FIGURE 6.18

The Format-As-You-Go feature has six different tools to help you quickly create bulleted lists, graphic lines, ordinal numbers, en dashes, and em dashes.

Enable the check boxes
to turn on the tools.

In addition to the sentence structure corrections, Format-As-You-Go has a variety of shortcuts for creating lists, lines, and ordinal numbers. A check mark in the box indicates that a tool is enabled. You can turn these tools on and off by enabling (add check mark) and disabling (remove check mark) the check boxes.

Select from the following options:

- **CapsFix**—Fixes problems with capitalization when Caps Lock is on by mistake and you hold down the Shift key to capitalize the first letter (such as tHIS). CapsFix works only if Caps Lock is on.

- **QuickBullets**—Helps you quickly create bulleted lists. To quickly create a bulleted list or numbered list, you simply type a letter, number, or bullet character, followed by a Tab. Search for "QuickBullets" in the Help topics for a list of bullet characters.

- **QuickIndent**—Pressing **Tab** at the beginning of the first and second lines of a paragraph creates a left indent for that paragraph.

- **QuickLines**—Typing four dashes and then pressing **Enter** creates a single horizontal line from the left to the right margin; typing four equal signs and then pressing **Enter** creates a double horizontal line from the left to the right margin.

- **QuickOrdinals**—Typing ordinal text after a number converts the ordinal text to superscript when you press the spacebar. As a reminder, superscript text is smaller and set higher than the adjacent text.

- **QuickSymbols**—Typing two hyphens followed by a space inserts an en dash; typing three hyphens followed by a space inserts an em dash.

> **caution**
>
> The QuickBullets feature can be a problem for some users. Not everyone wants a numbered list turned into a code-oriented automatically updated numbered list! It's easy enough to turn off, though—just remove the check mark next to it.

Inserting SpeedLinks

The SpeedLinks feature is designed to automatically generate a hyperlink whenever you type the beginning of an Internet address, such as www, ftp, http, or mailto. You can then give that hyperlink a friendlier name. For example, when you type the URL `http://kb.corel.com`, SpeedLinks creates the hyperlink to the Web page. This also works for email addresses such as *yourname@isp.com*.

To create SpeedLinks:

1. Choose **Tools**, **QuickCorrect**; then click the **SpeedLinks** tab to display the SpeedLink settings (see Figure 6.19).

2. Type the friendlier name that you want to use to activate the hyperlink in the **Link Word** text box (the @ symbol is inserted automatically).

3. Type the location to link it to in the **Location to link to** text box. If necessary, click the **Files** icon to browse your system (or the network) and select a drive, folder, or file.

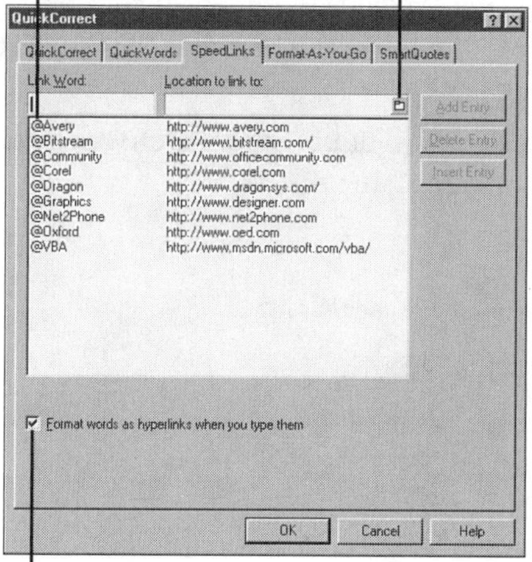

All link words begin with an @.

Click here to browse your system or network.

FIGURE 6.19

Using SpeedLinks, you can create a link word that automatically creates a hyperlink to a Web page, email address, document, folder, or drive.

Click here to deselect automatic hyperlinks.

To insert a SpeedLinks entry in a document, type the @ symbol followed by the link word. When you press the spacebar or Enter, WordPerfect creates the hyperlink for you.

Creating QuickWord Entries

As you can see, QuickCorrect is really a collection of powerful features that help you automate your repetitive tasks. The QuickWords feature is the hidden jewel of QuickCorrect tools. If you are involved in heavy document production (and who isn't), you really need to take a look at this feature.

Here's how it works:

- You assign an abbreviation to a word or phrase.
- You use the abbreviation when typing the document.
- You expand the abbreviation(s), either as you type or all at once.

QuickWords aren't limited to words or phrases. You can create QuickWord text with formatting codes, such as font attributes, or graphics that you would use for logos.

You can assign entire paragraphs to a QuickWords entry and then use them to quickly build documents that consist of form paragraphs (such as wills, leases, contracts, and so on).

To create a QuickWord entry:

1. Select the text or graphic you want to assign to QuickWords. If you want to insert a graphic or logo with a QuickWords entry, turn on Reveal Codes and position the red cursor to the left of the box code. Press **Shift+right arrow** to select the box code.

2. Choose **Tools**, **QuickWords** to display the **QuickWords** tab of the QuickCorrect dialog box (see Figure 6.20).

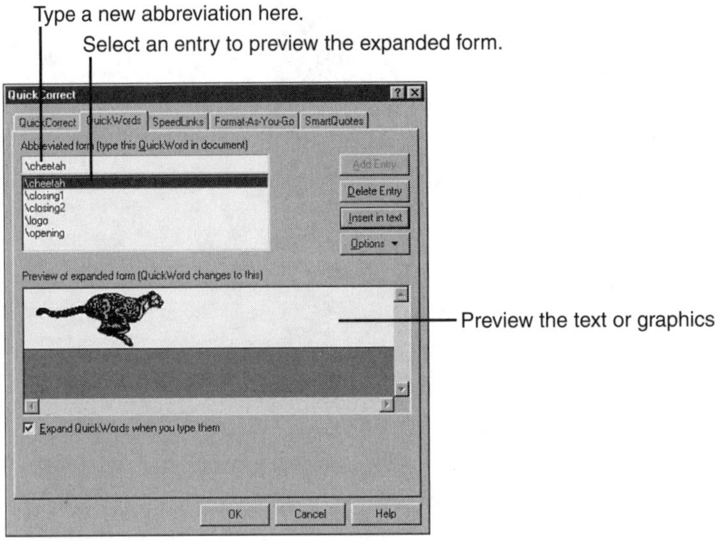

FIGURE 6.20

With QuickWords, you can assign an abbreviation to text or graphics, and then simply type the abbreviation to insert it into a document.

Type a new abbreviation here.

Select an entry to preview the expanded form.

Preview the text or graphics

3. Type the abbreviation you want to use in the **Abbreviated form** text box. The abbreviation can be a few letters or a one- or two-word phrase.

4. Click **Add Entry**.

Use one of the following methods to insert QuickWords in a document:

- Type the abbreviation; then press the **spacebar**, **Tab**, or **Enter** key. If this method doesn't work, the **Expand QuickWords when you type them** option (in the QuickWords tab of the QuickCorrect dialog box) has been disabled. You can manually expand a QuickWord by pressing **Ctrl+Shift+A**.

- Open the QuickWords dialog box, select a QuickWord from the list, and then click **Insert in text**.

It's easy to update a QuickWords entry when the form text changes (in the case of form paragraphs) or if you want to insert a different graphic image with a certain QuickWords entry. To replace a QuickWords entry, follow these steps:

1. Select the text or graphic.

2. Choose **Tools**, **QuickWords**.

3. Select from the list the QuickWords entry that you want to assign to the selected text or graphic.

4. Click the **Options** button and click **Replace Entry**.

5. Click **Yes** in the confirmation message box.

If you change the content of a QuickWord, it makes sense that you would want to assign a new QuickWord name.

To rename a QuickWord entry:

1. Choose **Tools**, **QuickWords**.

2. Select the QuickWords entry.

3. Choose **Options**, **Rename Entry**.

4. Type the new name; then click **OK**.

Every now and then, it's a good idea to go through the QuickWords entries and remove the ones you aren't using anymore.

To delete a QuickWords entry:

1. Choose **Tools**, **QuickWords**.

2. Select the QuickWords entry.

3. Click **Delete Entry**.

Finally, you can turn off QuickWords if you don't want to expand the QuickWords as you type. In the QuickWords dialog box, deselect **Expand QuickWords when you type them**.

caution

Be sure you use words that won't normally come up in your documents for QuickWords abbreviations. For example, you could use "compadd" to expand your company address, "clogo" for the company logo, or "sigblock" for your signature block. If you accidentally use a word or phrase that comes up naturally, QuickWords will expand the abbreviation and insert information in the wrong places.

note

If you're creating a QuickWords entry for a graphic image, be sure that **Expand As Text with Formatting** is selected on the **Options** menu. Otherwise, the graphic won't appear in the document.

THE ABSOLUTE MINIMUM

This chapter focused on the features that help support the job of writing material.

- You learned how to check your documents for spelling and grammatical errors.

- You saw how fast and easy it is to use an electronic Thesaurus and Dictionary.

- Searching and replacing text or codes can save you from long hours of repetitive editing.

- You saw how to incorporate text in other languages into your documents.

- You learned how to take advantage of all the tools in the QuickCorrect collection.

In the next section of the book, you'll learn how to make your document look nice through a variety of formatting options.

PART II

MAKING IT LOOK NICE (FORMATTING)

IN THIS CHAPTER

- Learn how to use center and flush right to align text.

- Use the Justification feature to align paragraphs.

- Learn how to work with tabs and how to indent text.

- Adjust the spacing between lines and paragraphs to make long passages of text easier to read.

7

WORKING WITH PARAGRAPHS

Because this chapter discusses how to format paragraphs, it's a good time to clarify the definition of a paragraph as WordPerfect sees it. At first glance, you might think of a paragraph as several lines of text all together in one chunk. You're right—that is a paragraph, but so is a single line. In fact, anything that ends with a hard return is considered to be a paragraph. (As a reminder, a hard return is inserted into the document each time you press the Enter key.) The hard return ends the current line and moves the insertion point down to the next line.

Aligning Text

One of the most common formatting tasks is centering a line. When you center text on a line, WordPerfect does the math and makes sure that there is an equal amount of space on either side of the text. If you add or remove text, WordPerfect automatically adjusts the position of the text so that it is at the exact center of the page. Flush right is a little less common, but it still has an important place, especially in legal documents. Text that is flush right is aligned against the right margin, so it extends out to the left.

The Justification feature is also used to align text. In addition to Center and Flush Right, you can also justify text so that the left and right margins are smooth. Justification is used in situations where a series of paragraphs needs to be aligned to either the left margin, the right margin, or both margins (full justification).

Using Center and Flush Right

When you issue the command to center or flush right text, the command works for only a single line. Pressing Enter after you type the text turns Center or Flush Right off, so the next line is aligned against the left margin. For this reason, the Center and Flush Right commands are well suited for aligning one or two lines at a time. If you need to align multiple lines or several paragraphs, you're better off using the Justification feature, which is discussed next.

- To center a line of text, press **Shift+F7** and type the text. If you've already typed the text, click at the beginning of the line, and then press **Shift+F7**.
- To align text against the right margin (flush right), press **Alt+F7**, and then type the text. If you've already typed the text, click at the beginning of the line, and then press **Alt+F7**.
- To center or flush right more than one line of existing text, select the text first; then press **Shift+F7** for center or **Alt+F7** for flush right.

You can also find Center and Flush Right commands in the menus. Choose **Format**, **Line** (see Figure 7.1). Note the keyboard shortcuts listed next to the commands.

Justifying Text

Justification controls how text flows between the left and right margins. The Justification feature continues to center or flush right text, even after you press Enter. For this reason, it's a better choice when you need to align multiple paragraphs. To use Justification, you turn it on at a specific point in the document. It stays in effect until the end of the document, or until you switch to a different justification setting.

FIGURE 7.1

The Line menu has commands to make lines of text centered and flush right.

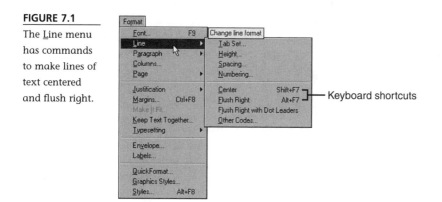

Keyboard shortcuts

The default setting in WordPerfect is left justification, which creates a smooth left margin and a ragged right margin. The result is an open, informal appearance that is accessible and easy to read. For that reason, this book has been formatted with left justification.

There are four other justification options that you might be interested in, especially if you work with columns, newsletters, and formal documents (see Figure 7.2).

WordPerfect offers the following justification options:

- **Left**—Text is aligned against the left margin so that the left margin is smooth and the right is ragged. It's suitable for almost every type of document, especially those with long passages of text. To apply left justification, choose **Format**, **Justification**, **Left** (**Ctrl+L**).

- **Right**—Text is aligned against the right margin so that the right side is smooth and the left is ragged. The unique placement draws attention, but because it's difficult to read, you might not want to use it on more than three or four lines. To apply right justification, choose **Format**, **Justification**, **Right** (**Ctrl+R**).

note

What's the difference between Center and Justify Center? When you change the justification to Center, every line you create from then on is centered, until you change the justification to something else. This works great for title pages, where you have an entire page of centered text. It's not the most efficient option for one or two lines. In this situation, the Center feature is the best choice.

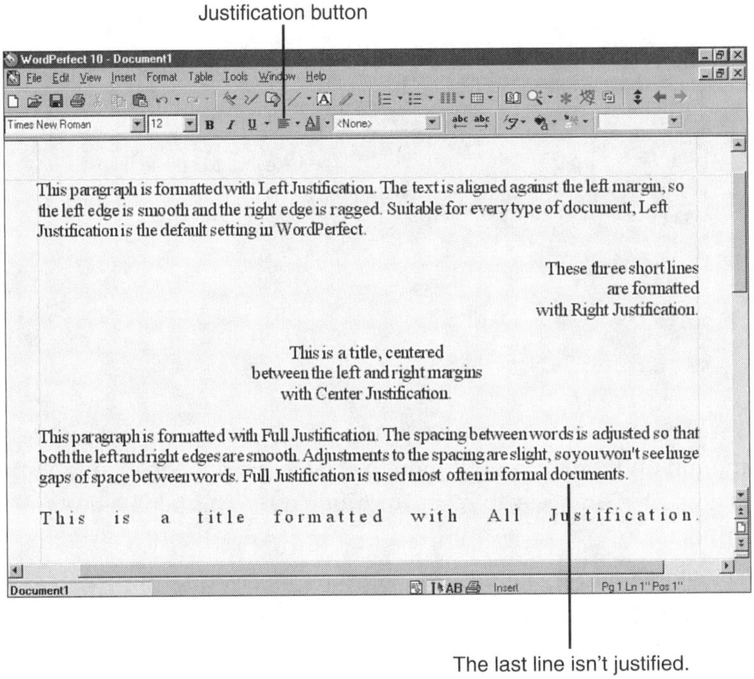

Justification button

FIGURE 7.2
This sample document illustrates the different justification settings.

> This paragraph is formatted with Left Justification. The text is aligned against the left margin, so the left edge is smooth and the right edge is ragged. Suitable for every type of document, Left Justification is the default setting in WordPerfect.
>
> These three short lines
> are formatted
> with Right Justification.
>
> This is a title, centered
> between the left and right margins
> with Center Justification.
>
> This paragraph is formatted with Full Justification. The spacing between words is adjusted so that both the left and right edges are smooth. Adjustments to the spacing are slight, so you won't see huge gaps of space between words. Full Justification is used most often in formal documents.
>
> This is a title formatted with All Justification.

The last line isn't justified.

- **Center**—Text is centered between the left and right margins. To apply center justification, choose **Format**, **Justification**, **Center** (**Ctrl+E**).

- **Full**—Text is aligned against the left and right margins, so both edges are smooth. Full justification gives documents a more formal and organized appearance. To apply full justification, choose **Format**, **Justification**, **Full**, or press **Ctrl+J**.

- **All**—This type of justification stretches lines of text between the left and right margins, regardless of their length. Whereas full justification adjusts the spacing between words, all justification adjusts the spacing between letters as well. This setting is used for letterhead, informal titles and headings, and special effects. To apply all justification, choose **Format**, **Justification**, **All**.

note

You might be wondering how full justification (a smooth left and right margin) is accomplished. WordPerfect makes slight adjustments to the spacing between words so that each line extends from the left to the right margin. Adjustments to the spacing are slight, so you won't see huge gaps of space between words as you can with all justification.

Before you choose which type of justification you want to use in your document, decide where you want the justification to take effect and then move the insertion point there. This might be at the top of the document, the top of a column, or the beginning of a paragraph. If you want to apply justification to a section of text, such as a multiline title, select the text first.

Instead of using the menus, you can click the **Justification** button on the property bar and then choose the justification setting from the pop-up list. This method offers an advantage over the others in that you get a RealTime Preview of each justification setting when you hover over it.

note

With justification set to Full, the last line in a paragraph won't be justified if it doesn't extend to the right margin (or pretty close to it). Refer to Figure 7.2 for an example of how this looks.

Setting Tabs

Tabs may be one of the most misunderstood features in a word processor. Most of us press the Tab key without really thinking about it. We want to move over a bit, and Tab does that for us. What most people don't realize is that there is a lot more to the Tab feature than moving over to the right a little.

There are four types of tabs:

- **Left Align**—Text flows from the right side of the tab stop. This is the "normal" tab.
- **Center**—Text is centered over the tab stop.
- **Right Align**—Text flows from the left side of the tab stop.
- **Decimal Align**—The numbers are aligned on their decimal points, which rest on the tab stop. You can change the alignment character to something other than a period (decimal point).

note

You can add dot leaders to each of the four tab types. Dot leaders are useful when the space between columns is wide because they help the reader's eye travel across the gap. They are especially useful when preparing a table of contents.

If you don't see the ruler at the top of the screen, turn it on by choosing **View**, **Ruler**. The default tab settings (every 1/2 inch) are shown with triangles in the tab area of the ruler (see Figure 7.3). The gray area identifies the margin area; the white area is the text area.

FIGURE 7.3

Using the ruler, you can set all types of tabs with just a few mouse clicks.

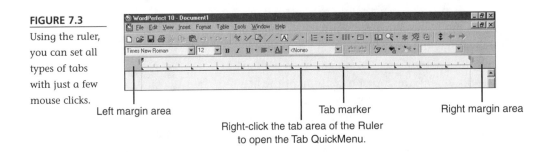

Left margin area   Tab marker   Right margin area

Right-click the tab area of the Ruler
to open the Tab QuickMenu.

In most cases, you want to clear the default tabs before you create tabs at specific settings. This way, you don't have to move past the default tabs—you can go straight to the specific tabs that you set.

To clear all tabs:

1. Right-click in the tab area of the ruler (refer to Figure 7.3) or right-click any tab marker to open the Tab QuickMenu (see Figure 7.4).

2. Click **Clear All Tabs** to delete the default tabs.

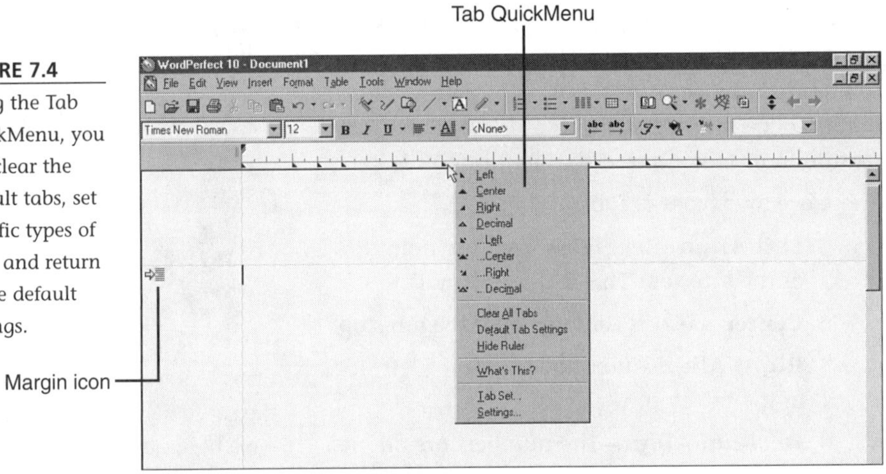

Tab QuickMenu

FIGURE 7.4

Using the Tab QuickMenu, you can clear the default tabs, set specific types of tabs, and return to the default settings.

Margin icon

Setting new tabs is fast and easy. All you have to do is click on the ruler where you want a tab to be, and voila!

To set a new tab:

1. Click in the tab area of the ruler, in the place where you want to create a tab (this inserts the default tab, which is a left-aligned tab).

2. To remove a tab, simply click and drag it off the ruler.

When you change the tab type, it stays selected until you select another tab type. So, if you change the tab type to Decimal, every time you click on the ruler, you'll set a decimal tab.

To change the tab type:

1. Right-click the tab marker to open the QuickMenu.

2. Choose a tab type from the QuickMenu.

3. Click on the ruler where you want to set the tab.

When you set a tab (or modify the default tab settings in any way), a margin icon appears in the left margin area (refer to Figure 7.4). Click the margin icon to display a tab bar, which shows the tab settings for the current paragraph. You can make changes to the tabs on the tab bar using the same methods that you use for the ruler. When you're finished, click anywhere in the document window to clear the tab bar.

After you've typed the text, you might decide to move things around a bit. Good news! You don't have to delete a tab and create a new one—you can just move it instead.

To move a tab:

1. Click and drag the tab marker (on the ruler or on the tab bar). When you do, a bubble appears, telling you where the tab will fall when you release the mouse button, and a guideline appears in the text so that you can see the effect on existing text (see Figure 7.5).

2. When you're satisfied with the tab position, release the mouse button to drop the tab.

When you're ready to return to default tab settings (so you can use regular tabs and indent later in the document), right-click in the document where you want to make the change and choose **Default _T_ab Settings**.

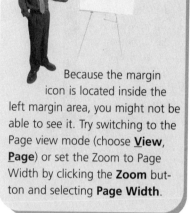

FIGURE 7.5

Even if you've already typed the text, you can freely move the tabs around. The guideline shows you where the text will be as you click and drag the tab.

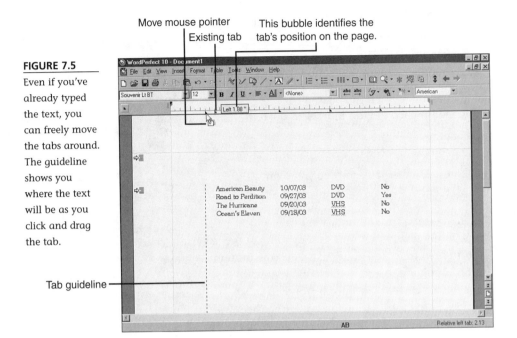

This is a good time to bring the Tab Set dialog box to your attention. Everything you can do from the ruler and more is available in this dialog box. Right-click the ruler and then choose **Tab Set** to open the Tab Set dialog box (see Figure 7.6). Alternatively, choose **Format**, **Line**, **Tab Set**.

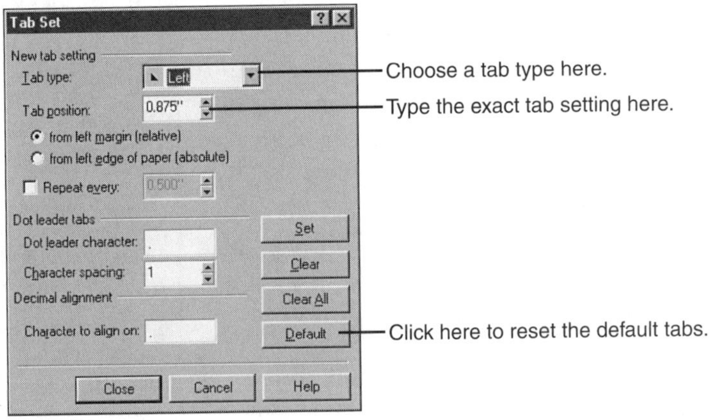

FIGURE 7.6

The Tab Set dialog box offers options that aren't available when you use the ruler.

Indenting Text

Indentation is often used to set quotations apart from the rest of the text. It also is used to emphasize text or to place a paragraph in a subordinate position beneath another paragraph. When you create a bulleted or numbered list, WordPerfect inserts an Indent command after the bullet or number so that the text you type isn't aligned under the bullet or number, but rather under the first word of the text. For more information on creating bulleted or numbered lists, see Chapter 11, "Lists and Outlines."

There are four ways to indent text:

- Indent moves every line within a paragraph to the next tab setting (to the right). By default, this moves the text over 1/2 inch every time you choose Indent.

- Double Indent moves every line in a paragraph in from the left and right sides, to the next tab setting. By default, this indents the text by 1/2 inch on the left and 1/2 inch on the right.

- Hanging Indent leaves the first line at the left margin—all the other lines are indented (on the left side) by 1/2 inch.

- A Back Tab temporarily releases the left margin so that the first line of a paragraph starts at the tab setting inside the left margin; all other lines are aligned at the left margin.

caution

The Indent feature uses the tab settings to indent your text. Changing the default tab settings affects how text is indented. If you plan on indenting text and setting specific tabs in the same document, don't change the tabs at the top of the document. Change them just before you want to type the tabbed text. Then, after you've typed the text, restore the default tab settings.

To indent a new paragraph, press **F7** and then type the text. Press **Shift+Ctrl+F7** for a double indent and **Ctrl+F7** for a hanging indent. As usual, if you've already typed the text, click in the paragraph before applying an indent style.

You can also choose Indent, Double Indent, and Hanging Indent, as well as Back Tab, from the Paragraph menu (see Figure 7.7). Choose **Format**, **Paragraph** to open the Paragraph menu.

If QuickIndent is enabled, you can quickly indent paragraphs with the Tab key. Press **Tab** at the beginning of the first *and* second lines. QuickIndent converts those tabs into an indent. You can also quickly create a hanging indent by pressing **Tab** at the beginning of any line *except* the first line in a paragraph.

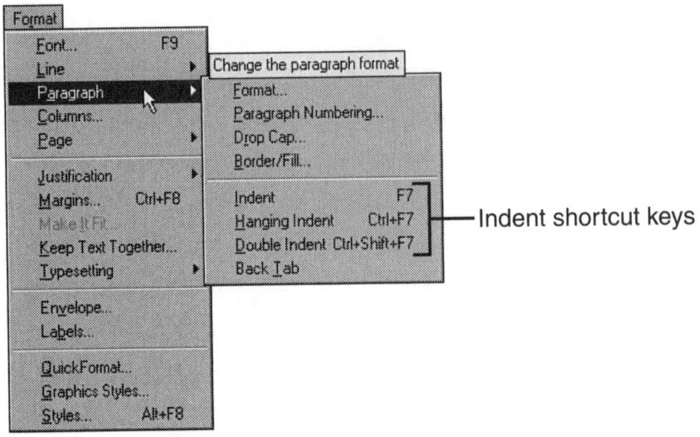

FIGURE 7.7

One of the
Indent com-
mands on the
Paragraph
menu, Back Tab,
doesn't have a
shortcut key
assigned to it.

Indent shortcut keys

To turn the QuickIndent feature on and off, choose **Tools**, **QuickCorrect**. Click the
Format-As-You-Go tab, and then enable or disable the check box next to
QuickIndent (in the list of Format-As-You-Go choices).

If you want the first line of every paragraph to be indented automatically (rather
than pressing Tab each time), use the First Line Indent option.

To set a first-line indent:

1. Choose **Format**, **Paragraph**, **Format** to open the Paragraph Format dialog
   box (see Figure 7.8).

2. Type the amount that you want the first line indented in the **First line
   indent** text box. (A tab indents the first line by 1/2 inch.)

3. Click **OK**. All new paragraphs from this point on will have the first line
   indented.

4. To remove a first-line indent, set the value back to **0** (zero) inches.

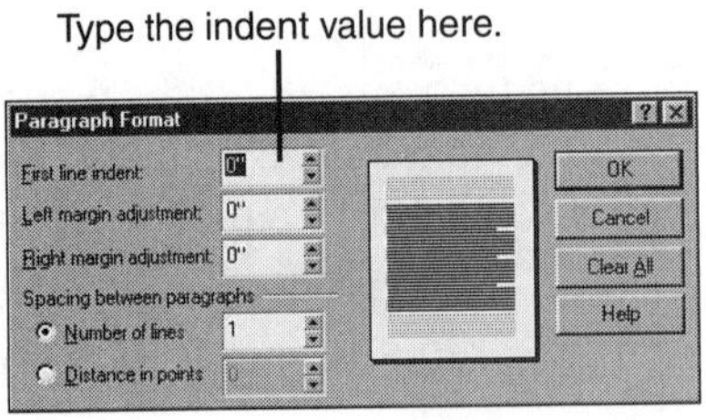

Type the indent value here.

FIGURE 7.8

Type the value
for the first-line
indent in incre-
ments of inches.
For example, 1/4
inch would be
.25".

Adjusting the Spacing Between Lines and Paragraphs

As you might remember from Chapter 1, "Getting Around and Getting Help in WordPerfect," the default line spacing setting is single-spacing. Some types of documents, such as manuscripts, grants, and formal reports, require a certain line-spacing setting for submission.

The accepted standard is to leave a blank line between paragraphs, so you just press Enter twice after you type a paragraph, right? That's not a problem—until you decide to change the line spacing to double. Now you've got the space of two lines between each paragraph. Furthermore, these extra lines leave space at the top of a page.

Making adjustments to the spacing between lines and paragraphs is another way to tailor your document to certain specifications and accepted standards.

Adjusting the Line Spacing

Let's say that you want to print out a document for someone else to review. You might consider changing to double- or triple-spacing, so that person has room for writing comments. After you incorporate that person's changes, you just switch back to single-spacing.

To change line spacing:

1. Click where you want the change to take effect (or select the text you want to change).

2. Choose **Fo_r_mat**, **_L_ine**, **_S_pacing** to open the Line Spacing dialog box (see Figure 7.9).

3. Either type a value or click the spinner arrows to increase or decrease the value in the **Spacing** text box. Use 1 for single-spacing, 1.5 for one-and-a-half spacing, 2 for double-spacing, and so on.

FIGURE 7.9

You can specify the number of blank lines you want between each line of text by typing the value or clicking the spinner arrows.

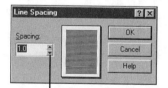

Spinner arrows

The new line-spacing setting takes effect at the beginning of the paragraph where the insertion point is resting, and it remains in effect throughout the rest of the document, or until you change the line spacing again. To give you an example of a document where you might change the line spacing, in a double-spaced document, it's common to switch to single-spacing for lists or quotations.

Adjusting the Spacing Between Paragraphs

Rather than insert extra blank lines, you can adjust the spacing between paragraphs. This way, you always get the same amount of space between each paragraph (no matter what you do to the line spacing), and you don't have extra blank lines floating around.

To change the paragraph spacing:

1. Click where you want the change to take effect.

2. Choose **Format**, **Paragraph**, **Format** to open the Paragraph Format dialog box (refer to Figure 7.8). In the **Spacing between paragraphs** section, you can enter the number of lines or the number of points that you want between each paragraph.

3. Either type the value or click the spinner arrows to increase or decrease the value.

Keeping Text Together

As you create or revise a document, you never have to worry about running out of room. WordPerfect creates a new page for you as soon as you reach the bottom of the current page. It's so transparent that you probably don't even stop to think about it. That is, until you preview the document and realize that you have headings and paragraphs separated by a page break.

You can prevent this situation by identifying the text that should stay together when a page break is encountered. You can use three features to do this: Widow/Orphan Protection, Block Protect, and Conditional End of Page. Choose **Format**, **Keep Text Together** to display the Keep Text Together dialog box (see Figure 7.10).

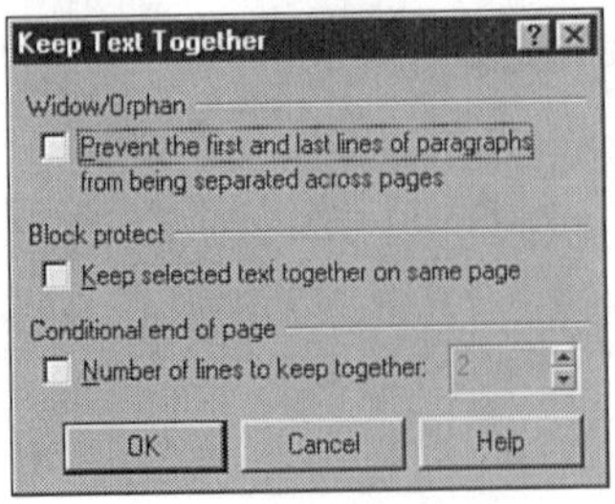

FIGURE 7.10

The options in the Keep Text Together dialog box prevent important information from being separated by a page break.

Enabling Widow/Orphan Protection

Widow/Orphan Protection prevents a single line of a paragraph being left behind at the bottom of a page or getting pushed to the top of the next page. The first line of a paragraph that gets left behind at the bottom of a page is called an *orphan*. A *widow* is the last line of a paragraph that gets pushed to the top of a page.

To turn on Widow/Orphan Protection:

1. Position the insertion point where you want Widow/Orphan Protection to start (usually at the top of the document).

2. Choose **Format**, **Keep Text Together** to open the Keep Text Together dialog box.

3. Enable the check box in the **Widow/Orphan** section.

Using Block Protect

Use the Block Protect feature when you want to keep a section of text together on the same page. As you edit the document, and the block moves near a page break, WordPerfect decides whether the block will fit on the current page. If it doesn't fit, the entire block gets moved to the top of the next page. Block Protect works well for keeping figures or tables and explanatory text together. You can also use it to protect numbered paragraphs, lists, and outlines.

To turn on Block Protect:

1. Select the text (and figures or tables) that you want to keep together.

2. Choose **Format**, **Keep Text Together** to open the Keep Text Together dialog box.

3. Enable the check box in the **Block protect** section.

caution

If you block protect large sections of text, you're likely to have big chunks of whitespace in the middle of your document.

Setting a Conditional End of Page

The Conditional End of Page feature keeps a certain number of lines together when a page break is encountered. You might use Conditional End of Page at the beginning of a heading so that you can specify how many lines of the following paragraph you want to keep with the heading.

To turn on Conditional End of Page:

1. Position the insertion point at the beginning of the heading.

2. Choose **For_mat**, **_Keep Text Together** to open the Keep Text Together dialog box.

3. Click **_Number of lines to keep together**.

4. In the text box, type the number of lines that you want to keep together. Count the heading line as one of the lines, and if there is a blank line between the heading and the paragraph, count that, too.

THE ABSOLUTE MINIMUM

This chapter started a three-chapter series on formatting. The topics covered in this chapter focused on formatting lines and paragraphs.

- You learned how to center a line of text using the Center feature. You also learned how to align text against the right margin with the Flush Right command.

- The Justification feature was introduced, and you saw how to justify text so that both margins are smooth.

- You learned how to use tabs to format information in columns.

- You learned how to properly indent text for quotations and numbered lists.

- Adjusting the spacing between lines and paragraphs makes it easier to read long passages of text.

- You learned that it isn't "good form" to have headings separated from the text, or a single line at the top or the bottom of a page, or to have key pieces of information split between two pages. You learned how to use the WordPerfect features that keep text together.

In the next chapter, you'll learn how to apply formatting to pages.

- Learn how to manually insert a page break to start on a new page.

- Switch to a different paper size or orientation.

- Learn how to subdivide a page into multiple sections.

- Discover how to include page numbers, headers, and footers in your documents.

- Use the Suppress and Delay Codes features to prevent certain page elements from printing.

- Add some punch with a plain or fancy border around a page.

- Use Make It Fit to shrink or expand a document into a certain number of pages.

8

WORKING WITH PAGES

In Chapter 7, "Working with Paragraphs," you learned how to format lines and paragraphs, which are pieces of a single page. This chapter deals with formatting that you apply to the entire page. Features such as headers and footers, page numbers, and borders are applied to a whole page, not just a section of a page.

In those situations where you don't want these elements included on a page, you can use the Suppress and Delay Codes features. For example, you might want the title page included in the page count, but you don't want to print a page number at the bottom of the title page.

Inserting a Page Break

You've probably already noticed that WordPerfect creates a new page for you whenever you fill up the current one. It happens automatically, so you don't even have to think about it. However, there are situations when you want to create a new page even though you haven't filled up the current page. Title pages come to mind, and so do headings that you want to place at the beginning of a new page.

To create a new page, you insert a page break on the current page. This type of page break is known as a *hard page*. The new page that WordPerfect creates for you is called a *soft page*.

To insert a hard page break, press **Ctrl+Enter**. In Page view mode, you'll see a gray space between the two pages (see Figure 8.1). In Draft view mode, a page break displays as a horizontal double line.

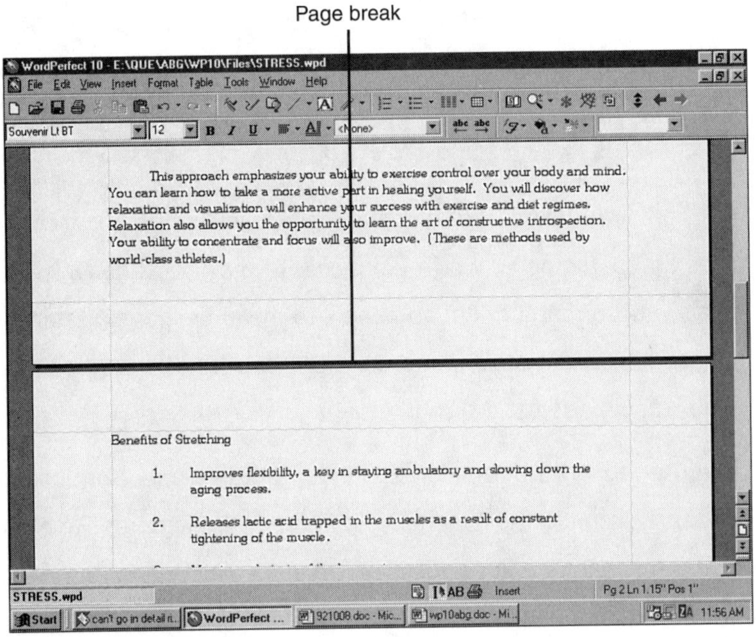

Page break

FIGURE 8.1

In Page view mode, a representation of the printed page is displayed, so you can see the space between pages.

When you insert a page break, a hard page code [HPg] is inserted in the document. To remove a page break, delete the [HPg] code using one of the following methods:

- Click at the end of the paragraph, just before a page break, and press **Delete**.

- In the Reveal Codes window, if the red cursor is to the left of a code, press **Delete**; if the red cursor is to the right of a code, press **Backspace**.

- You also can click and drag a code out of the Reveal Codes window to delete it.

Changing Paper Size and Orientation

By default, the paper size in the U.S. version of WordPerfect is 8 1/2 inches by 11 inches (other countries have different standards for paper size). Text is formatted in *portrait orientation*, which means the paper is taller than it is wide. Think of a portrait photograph.

tip

In a long document, you might decide to precede a major section with a hard page break so that each section begins on a new page. If, during heavy revisions, these hard pages get moved around to the wrong places, use Find and Replace to quickly strip out all the hard page codes (or only the ones that you don't need anymore).

If you create only standard business documents, you might never switch to a different paper size. However, when you need to create an envelope, print on legal-size paper, or rotate a document to landscape orientation, you switch to a different paper size.

To change to a different paper size:

1. Choose **Fo_r_mat**, **_P_age**, **Page Setup**, or choose **_F_ile**, **Page Setup**.

2. If necessary, click the **Page Setup** tab to display the paper sizes available for the current printer (see Figure 8.2).

Double-click a page size to select it.

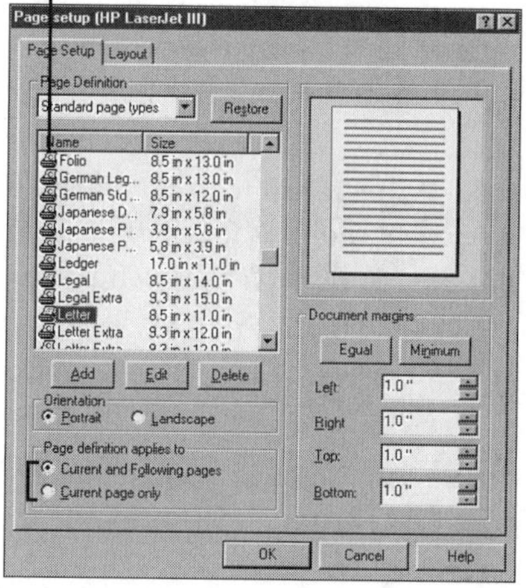

FIGURE 8.2

You can choose a different paper size or switch to a different orientation in the Page Setup dialog box.

3. Scroll down through the list of paper sizes and select a new paper size.

4. (Optional) If you want to rotate your text into a landscape orientation, click **Landscape**.

5. Select **Current page only** if you want to change the paper size only for the current page; or select **Current and Following pages** to apply the change to the current page and the rest of the document.

6. Click **OK** when finished.

Subdividing Pages

One physical page can be subdivided into multiple logical pages. Let's say that you need to design some invitations to a reception, and you want to print four of them on an 8 1/2×11-inch piece of card stock. You would subdivide the page into four logical pages each with a copy of the invitation. Another example might be a notice that you want to distribute to your child's classroom. I usually put two notices on a page so I can quickly tuck the notice into their folders. In this case, you would divide the page in half, so you can place one notice on the top and one on the bottom.

The physical page maintains the original dimensions of the paper. Logical pages are pieces of the physical page, but they are still considered individual pages for purposes of page numbering. For example, if you subdivide a page into six logical pages and then turn on page numbering, the logical pages are numbered 1 through 6. The Labels feature uses the same concept to separate a sheet of paper into individual labels.

To subdivide a page:

1. Choose **File**, **Page Setup** or choose **Format**, **Margins**.

2. Click the **Layout** tab, and then take a look at the Divide page section (see Figure 8.3).

3. Choose the number of columns and rows by either typing in the number or clicking the spinner arrows. The sample page illustrates how the paper will be subdivided.

4. Before you click **OK**, click the **Page Setup** tab and look at the margin settings. WordPerfect uses the current margins for each logical page, so if you keep the default 1-inch margins, you'll have a 1-inch border around each logical page that you won't be able to use. That's a lot of wasted space.

5. Click the **Minimum** button to quickly set the margins to the minimum allowed by your printer.

6. Click **OK**. Figure 8.4 shows the first logical page in a subdivided page. To move to the next page, press **Ctrl+Enter**.

FIGURE 8.3

By default, the number of columns and rows is set to 1.

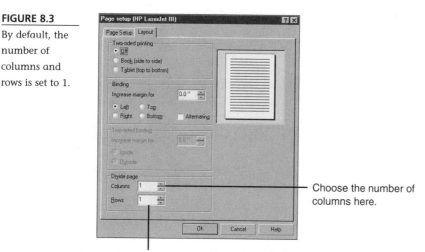

Choose the number of columns here.

Choose the number of rows here.

Logical page

Press Ctrl+Enter to move to the next logical page

FIGURE 8.4

Each logical page can be formatted as a separate page. In this example, a total of six logical pages are in one physical page.

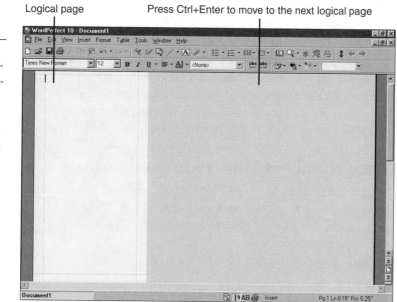

When you divide the current page, it affects all following pages in the document. To switch back to a single physical page, you'll have to go back into the Page Setup dialog box and set the rows and columns back to 1. Be sure the insertion point is at the top of the page that you want to switch back to, or you might accidentally revert a subdivided page back to a single physical page. If this happens, each subdivided page becomes a physical page, so you won't lose your text; it just gets spread out.

Choose **Undo** to get things back the way they were.

To go back to a single physical page:

1. Choose **File**, **Page Setup**.
2. Click the **Layout** tab.
3. Choose **1** in the Columns text box and **1** in the Rows text box.
4. Click **OK**.

Adding Page Numbers

Page numbers should be used on virtually every document longer than 4–5 pages. Page numbers help us to keep our place when we are reading, not to mention saving our reputations when we drop a stack of printouts on the office floor.

WordPerfect's page number feature has some depth to it. You can start by inserting page numbers at the bottom of every page and progress to creating customized page numbers using chapter and volume numbers. This book covers only the basics of page numbering, so if you want information on the more complex uses for page numbering, take a look at the WordPerfect Help topics.

tip

If you are creating invitations or announcements, it's common practice to center the text on the page. Because each section is a logical page, you format it just as if it were a full-size page. Click in the logical page that you want to center and then choose **Format**, **Page**, **Center**. Choose **Current page** if you want to center only the current page, or choose **Current and subsequent pages** to center all the pages from this point forward.

Inserting Page Numbers in a Predefined Position

The quickest way to add page numbers is to choose from the 10 different predefined locations where page numbers can be inserted. WordPerfect inserts the code for the page number and keeps the page numbers updated, no matter how many changes you make to the document.

To insert a page number:

1. Move to the page where you want the numbering to start.
2. Choose **Format**, **Page**, **Numbering** to display the Select Page Numbering Format dialog box.
3. Open the **Position** drop-down list to open the list of positions that you can choose from (see Figure 8.5).

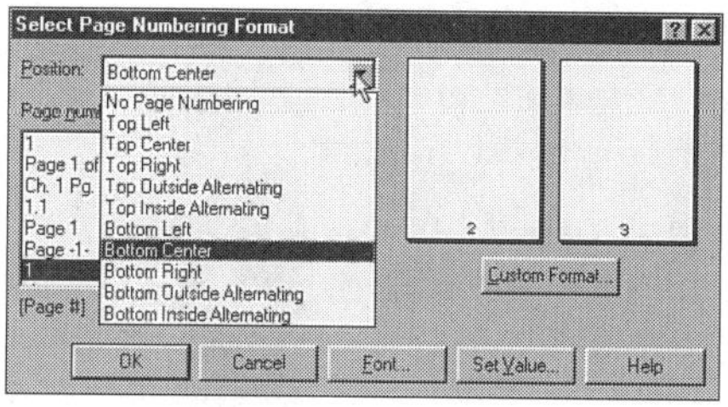

FIGURE 8.5

The quickest way to insert a page number is to choose one of the predefined page number positions.

4. Select a page number position from the list.

5. Click **OK** to insert a basic page number that starts on the current page and continues through the rest of the document. Figure 8.6 shows a document with simple page numbers at the bottom center of the page.

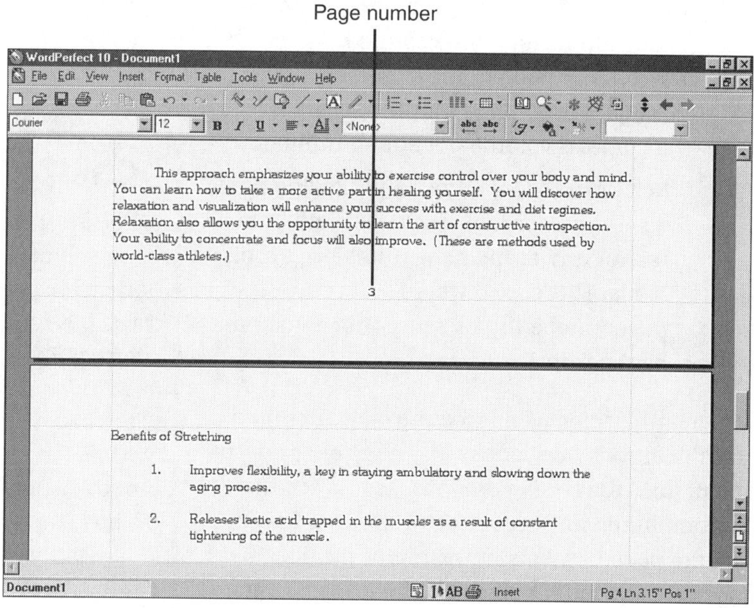

FIGURE 8.6

The most common page-numbering scheme is to position the number at the bottom center of every page.

Page number

Page numbers are printed on the top or bottom line in the text area of the page, *not* in the margin space. WordPerfect inserts a blank line to separate the page number from the rest of the document text. This reduces the amount of text that would normally fit on the page by two lines. If you decrease your top or bottom margin (depending on where you put the page numbers) to approximately 2/3 inch, you can regain the lost space, and the page numbers will appear to print in the margin space.

That's the quick way to insert a page number. If you want to get a little fancier, there are plenty of other page-numbering options to choose from:

- **Page numbering format list**—Choose from the list to select a different format for the page numbers, such as letter and Roman number styles.

- **Font**—Open the Page Numbering Font dialog box, where you can choose a font, font size, color, or attributes for the page number.

- **Custom Format**—Open the Custom Page Numbering dialog box. From here, you can create a combination page number style that can include the volume number, chapter number, or secondary page number. You can also create a customized "page x of y" page number style that includes a volume or chapter number.

- **Set Value**—Open the Values dialog box, where you can type the new number to use for any of the page numbering components. This is also where you can reset page numbering by setting the page number back to 1.

Frequently, different numbering styles are used for the introductory pages, the body of the document, and the closing sections. This is easily accomplished in WordPerfect. Select the format for the page numbers at the top of the document, again at the main body, and then again at the closing section. In addition to switching to a different number format, you can restart the page numbering.

Inserting Page Numbers Manually

Although there is plenty of flexibility in the 10 predefined page number positions, you're not limited to them. You can insert a page number anywhere in the document. You might, for example, want to refer to the current chapter number within the text. Or you might want to insert a chapter or volume number directly into a title.

To insert a page number elsewhere in a document:

1. Position the insertion point where you want the page number to appear.

2. Choose **Format**, **Page**, **Insert Page Number**. The Insert Page Number dialog box appears with options for inserting primary and secondary page numbers, chapter and volume numbers, and the total pages number (see Figure 8.7).

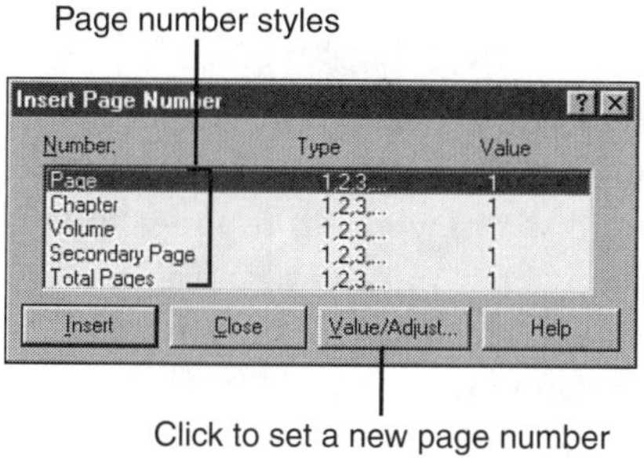

FIGURE 8.7

You can use the Insert Page Number dialog box to insert a page number in a location other than the predefined page number positions.

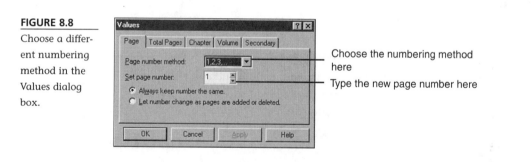

Page number styles

Click to set a new page number

3. Choose the type of number that you want to insert.

4. (optional) Click **Value/Adjust** to open the Values dialog box, where you can change to a different page number method (numbers, letters, or Roman numerals) or set the page number (see Figure 8.8). Click **Apply** and then click **OK** when you're finished.

FIGURE 8.8

Choose a different numbering method in the Values dialog box.

Choose the numbering method here

Type the new page number here

5. Click **Insert** (in the Insert Page Number dialog box). The number is inserted at the insertion point.

6. Continue inserting numbers as needed. Click in the document window and reposition the insertion point; then click in the dialog box to make it active again. Choose another number type and then click **Insert**.

7. Click **Close** when you're finished inserting page numbers.

Adding a Header or Footer

Headers are used for inserting information that you want printed at the top of every page; footers are for information that you want printed at the bottom of every page. Headers and footers can contain page numbers, titles, the filename, revision dates, the author's name or any other information about the document.

Creating a Header or Footer

Generally, you need to create the header or footer on the page where you want it to start. On pages where you don't want the headers and footers to print (such as the title page, first page of a letter, and so on), you can suppress the header and footer by selecting it in the Suppress dialog box. You can also use Delay Codes to postpone the effect of a formatting code. See the section "Suppressing and Delaying Codes" later in this chapter for more information.

To insert a header or footer:

1. Choose **Insert**, **Header/Footer** to open the Headers/Footers dialog box (see Figure 8.9).

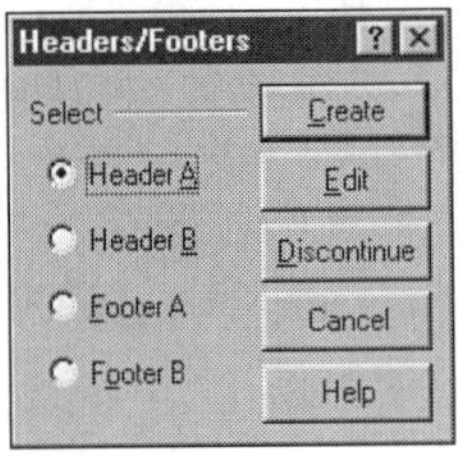

FIGURE 8.9

In the Headers/Footers dialog box, Header A is already selected.

2. Click the button for the header or footer you want to create.

3. Click **Create**. What happens next depends on which view mode you're using. Either way, the property bar now has some handy buttons you can use:

   - In Page view mode, the insertion point moves up to the top of the page, within the header guidelines (see Figure 8.10).

   - In Draft view mode, the insertion point moves to a separate header/footer-editing window. You won't be able to see the document text, only the text of the header as you type it.

caution

WordPerfect automatically inserts a blank line between the document text and the header or footer. Don't insert a blank line in the header or footer unless you want to increase the distance to two lines.

FIGURE 8.10

In Page view mode, you create and edit the header or footer onscreen, not in a separate window, as with Draft view mode.

Header area   Click to return to the document window

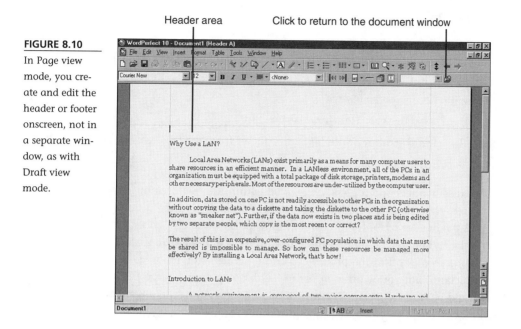

4. Type the text of the header or footer. Using the menus, add the necessary graphics, tables, and other formatting elements. (Features that can't be used in a header or footer are grayed out on the menus.)

CHOOSING A HEADER/FOOTER FONT

Header and footer text in the same font size as the document text is distracting at best, and downright ugly at worst. If you're using a 12-point font for the body text, step down at least 2 points, preferably 4 points, for the header or footer text.

Also, if you've selected a sans-serif font (such as Arial) for your headings and a serif font (such as Times New Roman) for your text, you might also consider using the sans-serif font for the header and footer text to further set it apart from the body text.

 5. Click the **Close** button, or press **Ctrl+F4**, to switch back to the document window.

If you are working in Page view mode, you'll see the header or footer text onscreen with the rest of the document text. In Draft view mode, you won't see header or footer text unless you edit the header or footer.

Working with Headers and Footers

For the most part, it's faster to create a new document by revising an existing document, especially if a lot of specific formatting is involved. If you're doing this, be sure you edit the header or footer to reflect the changes in the document.

To edit a header or footer:

1. Choose **Insert**, **Header/Footer**.
2. Select the appropriate header or footer from the Headers/Footers dialog box.
3. Click **Edit**.

Because headers and footers are printed within the text area of a page, you should decrease the margins to allow more space for the body text. It's more attractive to pull the header or footer into the margin space. Be sure to change the margins in the DocumentStyle (choose **File**, **Document**, **Current Document Style**), or your changes won't affect the placement of the headers and footers. In fact, any formatting codes that you want to apply to headers and footers, as well as the body text, should be inserted in the DocumentStyle rather than in the document itself.

As you continue to work with headers and footers, take note of the header/footer buttons on the property bar:

 ■ Click the **Header/Footer Prev** button to move to the previous header or footer.

 ■ Click the **Header/Footer Next** button to move to the next header or footer.

 ■ Click the **Page Numbering** button to insert page numbers. A drop-down list of options appears, so you can select the type of page number you want to insert.

■ Click the **Horizontal Line** button to insert a graphic line in the header or footer.

■ Click the **Header/Footer Placement** button to open the Header or Footer Placement dialog box (see Figure 8.11). The default is to print the header or footer on every page.

caution

Be sure the insertion point is on a blank line when you click the Horizontal Line button; otherwise, the graphics line will land right on top of your text.

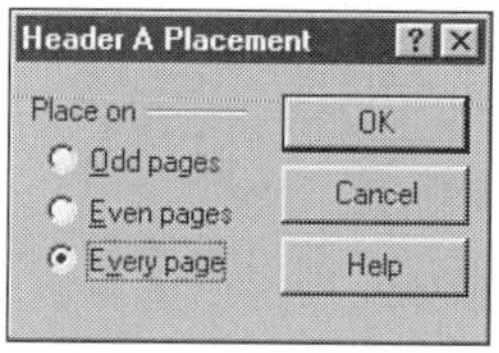

FIGURE 8.11

Specify on which
pages you want
the header or
footer to print in
the Placement
dialog box.

TWO HEADERS ON A PAGE

In WordPerfect, you can create up to two headers per page. It's nice to be able to create
one header for odd pages and another header for even pages. Another way you might
take advantage of this is to create two headers on the same page. One might contain
something standard, such as the title of the document and a page number. The other
would contain something that changes periodically in the document, such as a chapter
name. To keep the two headers from overlapping, place the first header's text at the left
margin and the second header's text flush against the right margin. Also, be sure you use
short titles and chapter names so they don't run into each other in the middle of the page!

■ Click the **Header/Footer Distance** button, and then type the distance that
you want between the header or footer and the body text in the Distance dialog box (see Figure 8.12).

FIGURE 8.12

You can adjust
the space
between the
header (or
footer) and the
text in the
Distance
dialog box.

Suppressing and Delaying Formatting

There are distinct advantages to placing all the formatting codes at the top of your
documents. For one, it's much harder to accidentally delete a code that is at the very
top of a document (versus at the top of any page). Another advantage is that everything is all in one place, and you don't have to go hunting around for a code.

So, you put all the codes at the top of the document, and they take effect on the first page. Fabulous! Except for one thing. You don't want the header and footer to print on the title page. So, how do you keep your codes at the top of the document, and keep the header and footer from printing? By using Suppress and Delay Codes.

Using the Suppress Feature

The Suppress feature is designed to prevent headers, footers, watermarks, and page numbers from printing on a particular page. Suppress is frequently used to keep these items from printing on a title page. Simply place a Suppress code at the top of every page on which you don't want a header, footer, page number, or watermark to print and let WordPerfect take care of the rest!

To suppress a header, footer, page number, or watermark:

1. Move to the page where you want to suppress the element.

2. Choose **Format**, **Page**, **Suppress**. The Suppress dialog box opens (see Figure 8.13).

3. Click the check box next to the elements that you want to suppress, or click the check box next to **All** to select all the elements at one time.

4. Click **OK**.

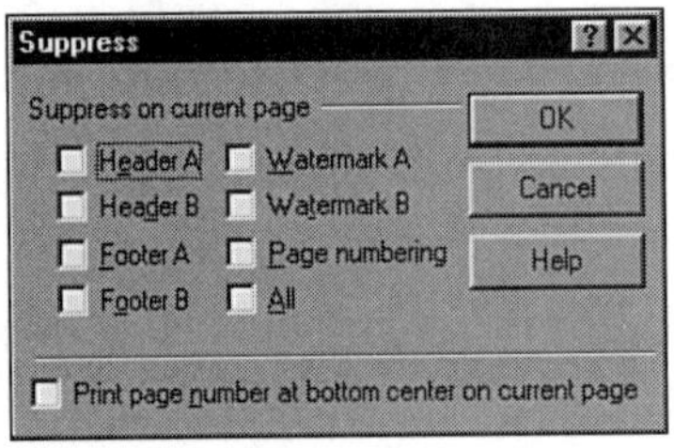

FIGURE 8.13

In the Suppress dialog box, choose the page elements you do not want to print on the current page.

Inserting a Delay Code

The Delay Codes feature is used to postpone the effect of formatting changes for a specified number of pages. Delay Codes are used when you want to skip more than one page (such as skipping past the table of contents, preface, or other introductory material before printing headers, footers, or page numbers).

To create a Delay Code:

1. Choose **Format**, **Page**, **Delay Codes**. The Delay Codes dialog box appears (see Figure 8.14).

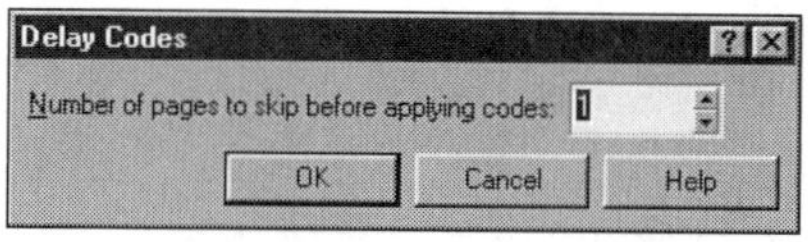

FIGURE 8.14

Type the number of pages that you want to skip in the Delay Codes dialog box.

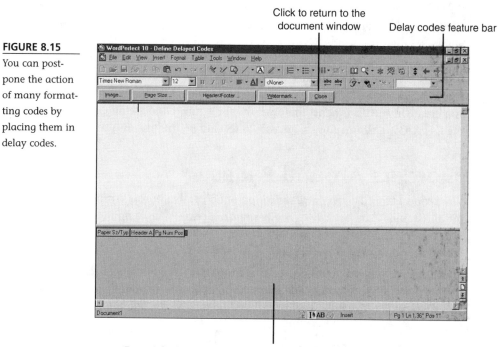

2. Type the number of pages in the **Number of pages to skip before apply-ing codes** text box (or click the spinner arrows to select the number).

3. Click **OK** to switch to the Define Delayed Codes editing window.

4. Use the menus or the buttons on the feature bar to insert the necessary formatting codes (see Figure 8.15).

FIGURE 8.15

You can post-pone the action of many format-ting codes by placing them in delay codes.

Click to return to the document window

Delay codes feature bar

Reveal Codes is on so you can see the codes as you insert them

5. Click the **Close** button to return to the document window.

Even if the insertion point is in the middle of a page, WordPerfect places this Delay Code at the top of the page: [Delay: #]. The # represents the number of pages you want to skip. (WordPerfect calculates the number of pages to skip based on physical pages, not page numbers.) If your insertion point is on page 5 and you set a Delay Code to skip 3 pages, the code [Delay: 3] is inserted at the top of page 5. On the page where the formatting takes effect, a [Delay Codes] code that contains the actual codes is inserted at the top of that page. Move the red Reveal Codes cursor to the left of this code to expand the code and reveal the codes within.

> **tip**
>
> You might consider putting Delay Codes in the DocumentStyle so they are safe from accidental deletion. To edit the DocumentStyle, turn on Reveal Codes and double-click the [Open Style: DocumentStyle] code at the top of the document.

The key to understanding the Delay Code feature is recognizing that you are actually inserting formatting codes into a code, not in the document. If you create Header B in a Delay Code, you can't edit that code from the document window; you can only create another Header B. The two headers are independent of each other. The header/footer that you create in a Delay Code overrides the header/footer that you create in the document. To adjust the formatting in a Delay Code, you must edit the Delay Code by turning on Reveal Codes and double-clicking the [Delay: #] code.

Adding Borders Around Pages

WordPerfect comes with a nice collection of decorative borders that you can place around a page. These ready-to-use designs are perfect for announcements, invitations, and a variety of presentation materials. Some of the designs can be used to create your own decorative paper.

There are two types of borders: line and fancy. The line borders are more formal, but they are also more versatile. There are 32 predefined line borders to choose from, and because you can edit these predefined borders to change the color and the line style, there are endless possibilities.

To add a border around the page:

1. Move to the page where you want to add a border.
2. Choose **Format**, **Page**, **Border/Fill**. The Page Border/Fill dialog box opens (see Figure 8.16).

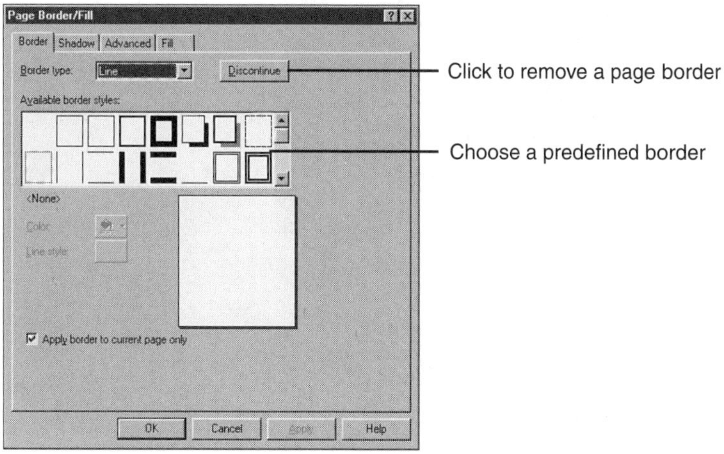

FIGURE 8.16

In the Page Border/Fill dialog box, you can choose the border that you want to place around the page.

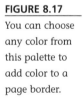

Click to remove a page border

Choose a predefined border

3. Scroll through the **A̲vailable border styles** list box to see all the predefined borders; then select a border. After you've chosen a border, you have the following options:

   ▪ You can change the color of the border. Click the **Color** button, and then click a color swatch on the palette (see Figure 8.17).

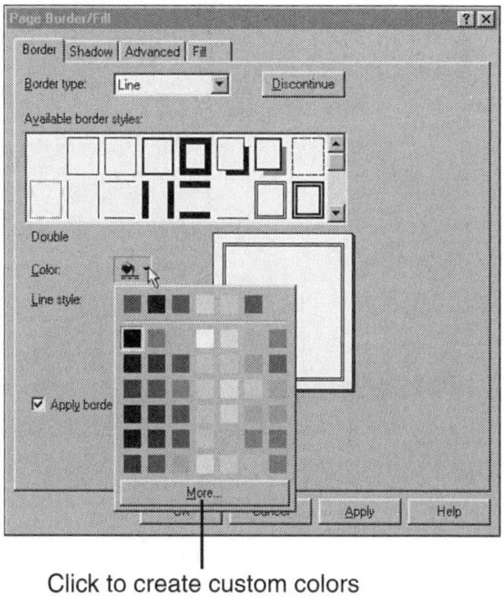

FIGURE 8.17

You can choose any color from this palette to add color to a page border.

Click to create custom colors

   ▪ You can change the line style used in the border. Click the **L̲ine style** button, and then click a line style from the palette (see Figure 8.18).

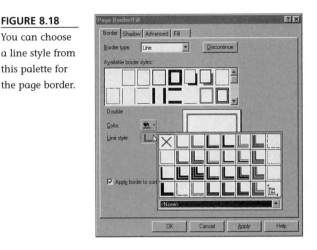

- Select **Apply border to current page only** if you want the border applied only to the current page. Otherwise, the border is applied to the current page and all other pages in the document.

- To remove a page border, click in the page; choose **Format**, **Page**, **Border/Fill** to open the Page Border/Fill dialog box; and click the **Discontinue** button.

Those are the "serious" borders. The fun borders are called "fancy" borders. There are 36 to choose from.

To select a fancy page border:

1. Choose **Format**, **Page**, **Border/Fill**.

2. Open the **Border type** drop-down list and choose **Fancy**. The list of fancy borders appears in the Available border styles window (see Figure 8.19). A preview of the selected border shows you how a page will look with the border.

caution

When you create a border using the line styles, WordPerfect automatically allows space between the text and the border, which is positioned on the margins. A fancy border can overwrite the text, so you might have to make some adjustments to the margins.

Click here to switch between Line and Fancy borders

Using the Make It Fit Feature

It happens to the best of us. You've just finished a carefully thought-out memo, and
you're ready to send it off. However, when you print it, you notice that the last two
lines of the memo have spilled over to the second page. Ack! You really need to get it
down to one page, so you sit down to play around with the margins and font size.

Stop! There is a feature that can do this for you, in just seconds. Make It Fit makes
text fit in the number of pages that you specify. Within reason, of course. You can't
make one page of text stretch out into three pages, and you can't take three pages
of text and expect to squeeze it into one page. The number of pages that you specify
must be at least 50% of the current size.

You can use Make It Fit on selected text or on the entire document; so if you want to
work on only a section of text, select it first.

To use Make it Fit on your document:

1. Choose **Format**, **Make It Fit** to open the Make It Fit dialog box (see Figure
   8.20). If you selected text, the Top margin and Bottom margin options won't
   be available.

2. Take a look at the current number of pages, and then type the number of
   pages that you want to fill in the **Desired number of pages** text box.

3. Select the options that you want Make It Fit to use to reformat the text.

4. Click **Make It Fit**.

If you have hard page codes in the document, you will get a message to warn you
that these codes might affect how well the document is formatted.

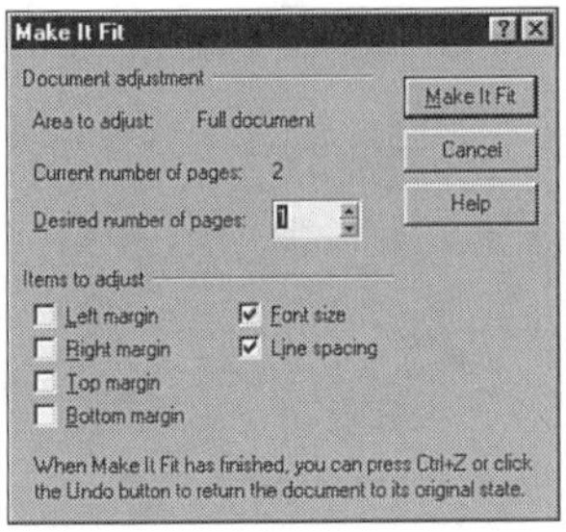

FIGURE 8.20

Make It Fit adjusts margins, font size, and line spacing to resize a document so that it fits within a certain number of pages.

THE ABSOLUTE MINIMUM

This is the second chapter in a three-chapter series on formatting. The topics in this chapter focus on formatting pages.

- You learned how to insert a page break so that you could start working on a new page.

- You saw that not every document is printed on an 8 1/2×11-inch piece of paper, and you learned how to switch to a different paper size and orientation.

- You saw how useful it is to subdivide a single page into multiple pages.

- Adding page numbers to a document can be done in just a few seconds with the Page Numbering feature.

- Adding headers and footers to a document allows you to display important information at the top and bottom of a page.

- You learned how to use the Suppress and Delay Codes features to prevent certain page elements from printing on a page.

- Borders are not essential formatting elements, but they are easy to work with, and they give simple documents a polished appearance.

- The Make It Fit feature is a great time-saver when you need to force a document into a certain number of pages.

In the next chapter, you'll learn how to create styles to automate repetitive formatting tasks and to ensure formatting consistency across documents.

- Learn about the different types of styles and create your own styles on-the-fly with QuickStyles.

- Apply the styles that come with WordPerfect to your own documents.

- Create and edit your own styles to speed up your formatting tasks and to ensure a consistent appearance.

- Use QuickFormat to copy the formatting from one section of text to other sections.

9

USING STYLES FOR CONSISTENCY

In Chapter 7, "Working with Paragraphs," and Chapter 8, "Working with Pages," you learned how to use most of the formatting commands that control lines, paragraphs, and pages. This chapter teaches you how to use those formatting commands to create *styles*. Styles speed up the formatting process and make it possible to make editing changes on-the-fly. They also ensure a consistent appearance among documents. For example, you could use styles for book manuscripts, presentation materials, financial reports, legal briefs, medical reports, and more.

Understanding Styles

A style is basically a collection of formatting commands, such as font type, size, underlining, and so on, that you put together and save with a name. The next time you want to apply those commands to some text, you use the style instead. Obviously, applying a style is much faster than repeating a series of steps to generate the proper format.

But that isn't the only reason you want to use styles. The real benefit is when you start fine-tuning the format. Let's say you decide not to italicize your headings. If you had italicized the headings by selecting the text and applying italic, you would have to go back to each heading and remove the italic code. Instead, you create a heading style so that all you have to do is remove the italics from the style and voilà! Every heading is automatically updated to reflect the new formatting in the style.

Think about this for a minute. You can format an entire project, such as a newsletter, and then go back and play around with the styles and have the changes reflected automatically, throughout the whole document. Furthermore, if you are trying to achieve some sort of consistency among the documents that you and your co-workers create, a set of standard styles is the way to go. There are two types of styles in WordPerfect: open and paired.

Open Styles

An *open style* is turned on and left on. The settings in the style stay in effect through the end of the document, or until another corresponding open style is found. The DocumentStyle, which contains the settings for the entire document, is an open style. Another example might be an open style that you insert in the document to start a different method of page numbering. That style remains in effect until another page numbering open style is found.

Paired Styles

A *paired style* is really two styles; an on style and an off style. A paired style is similar to the pair of bold codes that surround boldface text. The first code turns on bold; the second code turns it off. It's the same with paired styles. The first code turns on the style formatting; the second turns it off. Both paragraph (or heading) and character styles are paired styles.

A common example is a heading style that changes the font size, applies bold, and marks the text for a table of contents. The codes before the text increase the font size, turn on bold, and begin marking the text for the table of contents. The ending code switches back to the original font size, turns bold off, and ends the marking for the table of contents.

Using QuickStyle to Create Your Own Styles

What if I told you that all you need to create your own collection of styles is a formatted document or two? Seriously. You've already put in the time to set up everything—here's your chance to take advantage of it! All you have to do is click in the formatted text and then use QuickStyle to create a style out of it.

You could also type some "dummy" text in a blank document and format it the way you want. Position the insertion point in the formatted text, and then use the QuickStyle feature to save that formatting as a style.

To use QuickStyle:

1. Position the insertion point in the formatted text. For example, in Figure 9.1, the heading is 14-point Arial italic.

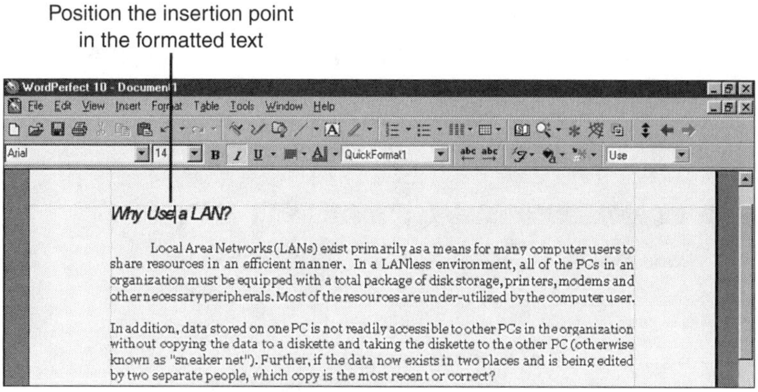

Position the insertion point
in the formatted text

FIGURE 9.1

You can format text first, and then use QuickStyle to create a style based on the format you used.

2. Position the insertion point anywhere in the selection or paragraph. You don't even have to select the text.

3. Choose **Format**, **Styles** (**Alt+F8**) to open the Styles dialog box.

4. Click **QuickStyle** to display the QuickStyle dialog box (see Figure 9.2).

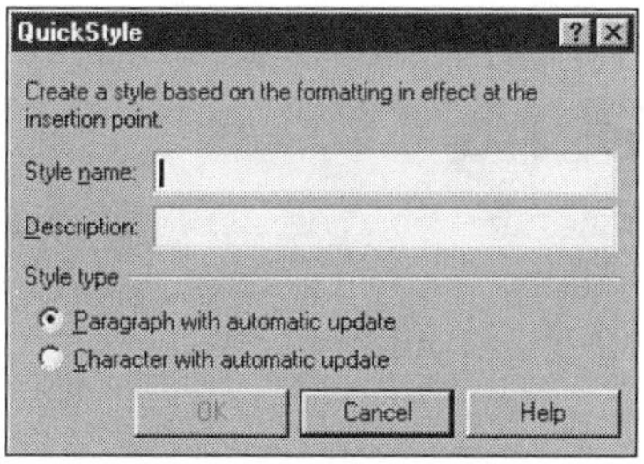

FIGURE 9.2

In the QuickStyle dialog box, you name the style and select the type of style you want to create.

5. Type a name for the style in the **Style name** text box. The name can be up to 20 characters long.

6. (Optional) Type a longer description in the **Description** text box. This can be useful later if you want to use the style but can't remember what it does by the name alone.

7. Choose **Paragraph** with automatic update if you want the style to apply to an entire paragraph, or **Character** with automatic update if you want to format only selected text.

8. Click **OK** to add the style to your current document and to return to the Styles dialog box. Your new style appears in the **Available styles** list (see Figure 9.3).

tip

You can also open the QuickStyle dialog box by opening the drop-down Styles list on the property bar and selecting **QuickStyle**.

New style

FIGURE 9.3
The newly created style appears in the list of Available styles.

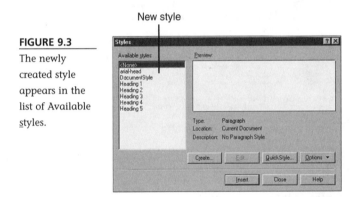

When you select a style, WordPerfect displays the effect of the style in the **Preview** box and also shows the description if you provided one.

Using WordPerfect's Heading Styles

WordPerfect has a few predefined styles that you can use in your documents. If you're in a hurry, or you don't care to learn how to create your own styles, you can use WordPerfect's heading styles to format your text.

To apply one of WordPerfect's heading styles:

1. Select the text that you want to format.

2. Click the **Styles** drop-down list on the property bar (see Figure 9.4).

FIGURE 9.4

The fastest way to select a style is to choose one from the Styles list on the property bar.

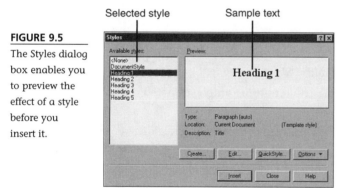

Style list

3. Click the style you want to use. WordPerfect applies the style to the text.

If you want to preview a style before you apply it, use the Styles dialog box instead. To select a style from the Styles dialog box:

1. Choose **Format**, **Styles** (**Alt+F8**). WordPerfect displays the Styles dialog box.

2. In the **Available styles** list, click the style you want to use. WordPerfect displays an approximation of the effect of the style in the **Preview** box (see Figure 9.5).

Selected style   Sample text

FIGURE 9.5

The Styles dialog box enables you to preview the effect of a style before you insert it.

3. Click **Insert** to apply the style to the selected text.

Building Your Own Styles

The heading styles are convenient, but they have limited use, so you'll probably want to start creating your own styles right away. You've already seen how the QuickStyle feature makes it easy to create styles from text that you have already formatted.

You can also create a style from scratch with the Styles Editor. The next time you start a new project, take a few minutes and create the styles that you will need. Then you can apply the styles as you generate the content.

To build your own style:

1. Choose **For̲mat**, **S̲tyles** (**Alt+F8**) to open the Styles dialog box.

2. Choose **C̲reate** to open the Styles Editor dialog box (see Figure 9.6).

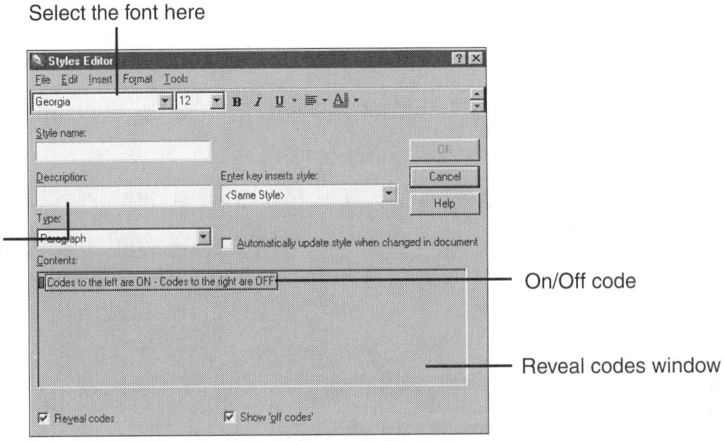

Select the font here

FIGURE 9.6

The Styles Editor allows you to create styles from scratch.

Type a description here

On/Off code

Reveal codes window

3. Type a style name in the **S̲tyle name** text box.

4. (Optional) Type a description (for example, centered, 14-point Arial text) in the **D̲escription** text box.

5. In the **Type** drop-down menu, choose **Paragraph** if you want the style to apply to an entire paragraph, or **Character** if you want to format only selected text.

6. Use the menus and the property bar in the Styles Editor to insert formatting codes just as you would in a document. The menus in the Style Editor do not contain all of WordPerfect's formatting commands and features; only the commands and features that can be used in a style are available.

7. When you're finished, click **OK** to save your style in the current document.

If necessary, place a check mark next to the **Show 'o̲ff codes'** option. In the Reveal Codes window, you should see a code that says Codes on the left are ON - Codes on the right are OFF. This is actually one of the more powerful aspects of the Style feature.

You can position a set of codes that should be in effect *before* the selected text, and another set of codes to be in effect *after* the selected text. You can also include text before or after this code if you want to include text in the style. For example, a heading style might have a font code to select a different font for the heading before the text, and another font code to switch back to the body text font after the heading text.

Editing Styles

Using the same techniques you learned in the previous section on creating your own styles, you can edit your styles and make adjustments to them. You can also edit the DocumentStyle, which contains the formatting codes for all new documents. This is how you can customize the default settings to suit your needs.

Revising Your Styles

After you create a style and apply it to some text, you can make changes to that style, and those changes will automatically be reflected in any text to which the style has been applied.

To edit a style:

1. Choose **Format**, **Styles** (**Alt+F8**) to open the Styles dialog box.

2. Select the style that you want to edit in the **Available styles** list.

3. Click **Edit** to open the Styles Editor dialog box (refer to Figure 9.6) and display the contents of the style.

4. Either use the menus to insert new codes, or double-click the existing codes to edit them.

5. Click **OK** when you're finished with your changes.

6. Click **Close** to close the Styles dialog box and update the document.

tip

If you want to create a new style that is similar to another style, you can save some time by editing the existing style rather than creating a new style from scratch. When you edit the style, give it a new name and then make your changes.

Customizing the Default Settings

As mentioned in Chapter 1, "Getting Around and Getting Help in WordPerfect," WordPerfect has a set of default format settings. The margins are 1 inch on all four sides, documents are single-spaced, there are tabs every 1/2 inch, and so on.

These settings are stored in the default template. Because of these defaults, you can start creating documents as soon as the software is installed.

After you've worked in WordPerfect for a while, you may develop a set of formatting standards that you use in your documents. Instead of making these selections every time you create a document, you can edit the default settings to meet your needs.

There are three ways to edit the default settings for the current document:

- Choose **File**, **Document**, **Current Document Style**.
- Choose **Format**, **Styles**. Select **DocumentStyle** in the **Available styles** list; then choose **Edit**.
- Turn on Reveal Codes (choose **View**, **Reveal Codes**; **Alt+F3**). In the Reveal Codes window, double-click the **Open Style: DocumentStyle** button at the beginning of the document.

WordPerfect displays the Styles Editor dialog box with the default language code in the Reveal Codes window (see Figure 9.7). Make the necessary changes. The selections that you make here will be reflected in the document as soon as you switch back to it.

FIGURE 9.7

Edit the Document Style to customize the default settings.

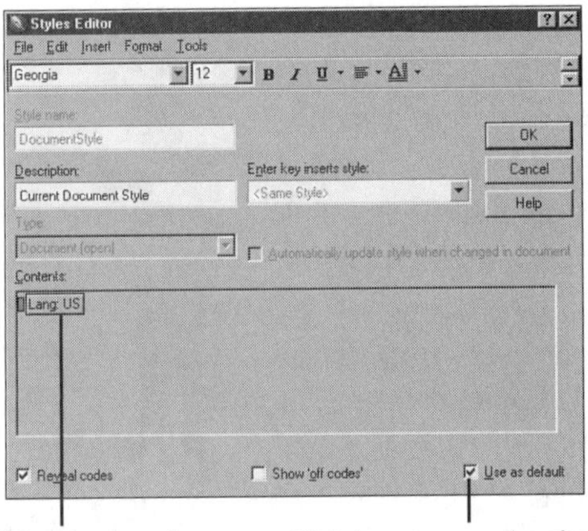

Default language code

Click here to save the changes to the default template

If you want your new settings to affect all new documents, you'll have to save the changes to the default template. Place a check mark in the **Use as default** check box. You'll be prompted to apply this new style to all new documents. Click **Yes** to save your changes, or **No** to abandon the changes.

Changes to the default template do *not* change the styles in documents that you have already created. Such changes apply only to new documents that you create after updating the default template.

Using QuickFormat

WordPerfect's QuickFormat feature enables you to create a temporary style that you can then apply to other parts of the document. It's perfect for those situations where you need to do some repetitive formatting, but you don't really need to create a style.

1. Begin by applying the formatting you want to a section of text. This is the formatting that will be copied to other sections of the document.

2. Position the insertion point anywhere in the formatted text.

3.  Choose **Fo**r**mat**, **QuickFormat**, or click the **QuickFormat** button on the toolbar. WordPerfect displays the QuickFormat dialog box (see Figure 9.8).

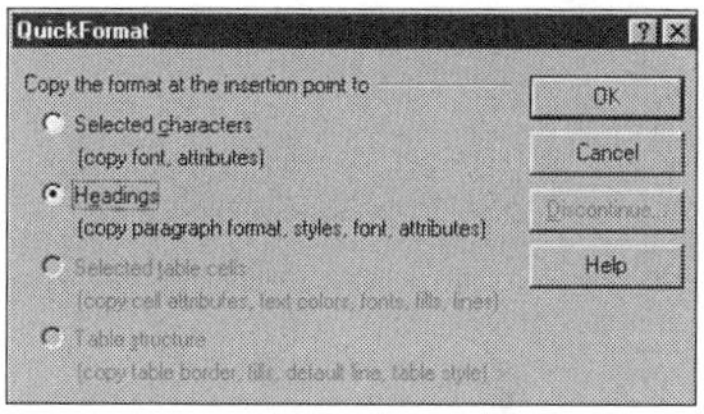

FIGURE 9.8

The QuickFormat dialog box enables you to apply a captured format to text.

4. Click **H**e**adings** or **Selected** c**haracters**, depending on how you want to use the style.

5. Click **OK**. A new mouse pointer appears; this one is shaped like a paint roller (see Figure 9.9).

6. If you selected **Headings**, click the paragraph that you want to format; otherwise, click and drag the mouse pointer across the text that you want to format.

7. Continue through the document, clicking each heading or selecting sections of text to apply the QuickFormat style.

8. To turn off QuickFormat, choose **Fo**r**mat**, **QuickFormat**; or click the **QuickFormat** button on the toolbar.

FIGURE 9.9

The mouse
pointer changes
to indicate that
you will apply a
heading style
when you click
the mouse.

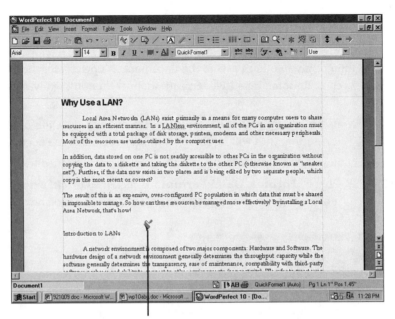

The QuickFormat paint roller pointer

THE ABSOLUTE MINIMUM

This is the last chapter in a three-chapter series on formatting. This chapter covered the use of styles.

- Right off the bat, you used the QuickStyle feature to create styles based on text you had already formatted.

- WordPerfect includes heading styles that you can use right away to apply to headings and titles in your documents.

- You learned how to build your own styles in the Styles Editor.

- The DocumentStyle code can be revised to customize the default settings for all new documents.

- The QuickFormat feature creates a temporary style that you can use to repeat formatting in a document.

In the next chapter, you'll learn how to use one of the most versatile features in WordPerfect—the Table feature. From a simple list with several columns to forms to a mini spreadsheet, you'll use the Table feature often.

PART III

Organizing Information

IN THIS CHAPTER

- Learn how to create and edit tables to help you organize information.

- Discover how to add fancy table lines, borders, or shading.

- Learn to use tables for basic spreadsheet-like calculations.

- Learn how to convert existing text into a table, or table text to regular text.

10

CREATING AND FORMATTING TABLES

So, you're not even sure what a table is, let alone why you might want to use one? That's a fairly typical response, but after you learn how easy and useful WordPerfect tables can be, you'll wonder how you ever got along without them.

Any time you need to organize information in rows and columns, such as a team roster or an inventory list, you'll want to use a table. In fact, with very little effort you can use tables to create simple lists, invoices, schedules, calendars, programs, dialogue scripts, and more. And even if you're not quite ready to venture off into the world of spreadsheets, you can still use WordPerfect to perform spreadsheet-like calculations.

Creating Tables

The basics steps for creating a table are simple. Begin by trying to determine how your information needs to be organized. How many columns of information will you need (for example, name, address, phone number, and email)? Then if you can, estimate the number of rows you need (for example, the number of people on your team roster—see Figure 10.1).

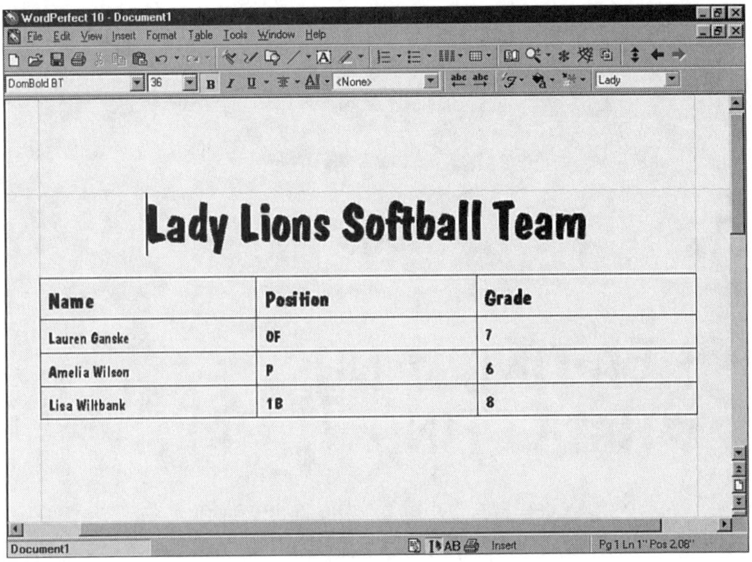

FIGURE 10.1

WordPerfect tables can be used for all sorts of tasks, such as team rosters, calendars, invoices, and much more.

For now, let's just create a simple table, and then I'll explain what you've done:

1. On the menu, choose **Table**, **Create**.

2. In the Create Table dialog box, leave the number of columns at 3, and change the number of rows to **4** (see Figure 10.2).

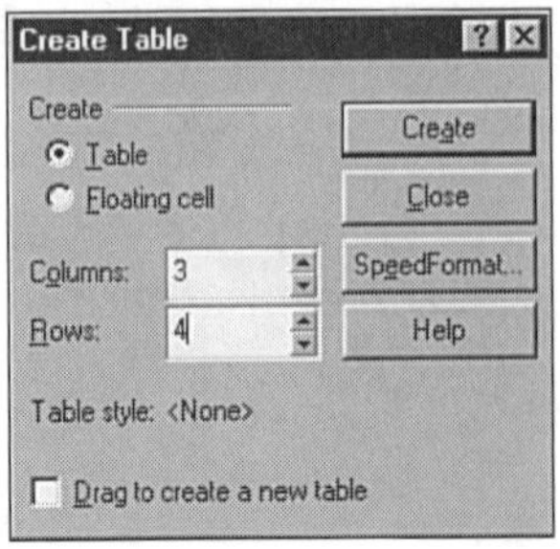

FIGURE 10.2

Use the Table Create dialog box to choose the number or rows and columns you want in your table.

3. Click **Create** to create the table shown in Figure 10.3.

FIGURE 10.3

Tables help organize information into rows and columns, quickly and easily.

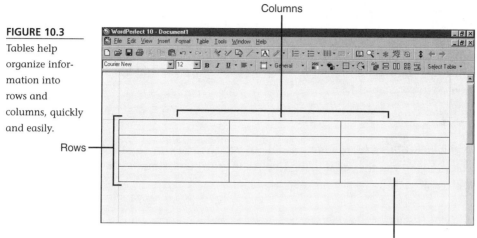

Tables look and function a lot like spreadsheets. In fact, the terminology is the same: information is placed in *cells*, which are the intersection of *rows* and *columns*. For example, in the table shown in Figure 10.3, the last cell (row 4, column C) is named cell C4.

That was pretty easy, wasn't it? Well, believe it or not, there is an even easier way to create a table: Simply click the **Table QuickCreate** button on the toolbar and, holding down the mouse button, drag the mouse down and to the right until you obtain a grid that matches the number of rows and columns you want (see Figure 10.4). Release the mouse button, and there you have it!

tip

Don't forget to use Undo button if you make a mistake either creating or modifying a table. Just click the **Undo** button, or press **Ctrl+Z**.

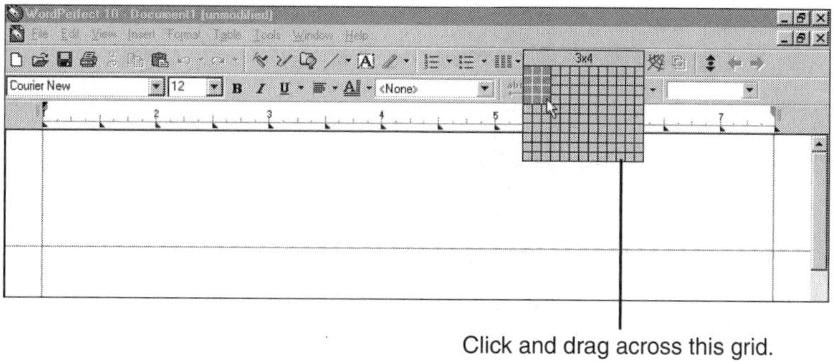

FIGURE 10.4

Dragging the mouse on the Table QuickCreate button is a quick and easy way to create the exact size table you want.

Click and drag across this grid.

Working with Tables

One of the biggest advantages of using a table is the ease in which you can work with information in a table. Think about each table cell as a miniature document with its own margins and formatting. You can enter and edit text in a cell just as you do in a document.

Typing in Tables

A cell can contain more than one line of text. As you enter text, WordPerfect wraps the words within the cell, adding lines to the row to accommodate what you type (see Figure 10.5).

This row has two lines.

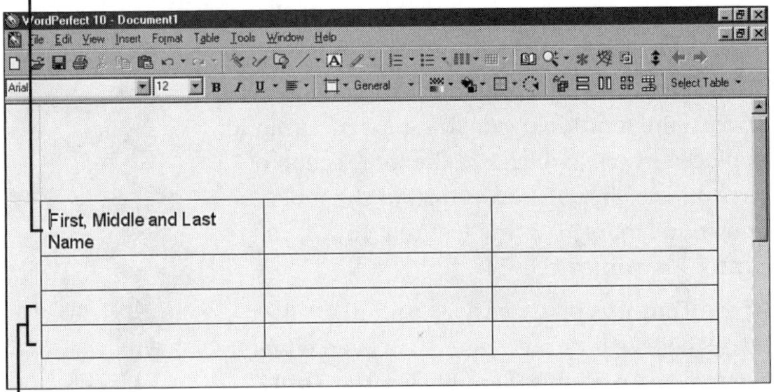

FIGURE 10.5

Notice that lines are automatically added to the row to accommodate the text.

These rows are not affected.

To move around in a table:

- Click anywhere in a table to move the insertion point.
- Press the **Tab** key to move to the next cell to the right, or, when you reach the end of a row, Tab moves you to the first cell of the next row.
- Press **Shift+Tab** to move back to the previous cell.

Adjusting the Column Widths

When you create a WordPerfect table, certain default settings apply:

- The rows and columns are evenly spaced.
- There's no special formatting of the contents of the cells.

- Single lines separate the cells of the table.
- There's no special border around the table.
- The tables are full-justified (the tables themselves extend from margin to margin).

tip

Sometimes you just want to be sure that the column is wide enough to display the information on one line. To adjust a column width to match the cell contents, choose **Size Column to Fit** from the **Table** menu. You can also right-click anywhere in a table and choose **Size Column to Fit** from the Table QuickMenu.

The real beauty of WordPerfect tables is that you can easily make all kinds of adjustments to these default settings. When you make changes to the shape, size, and number of table cells, columns, and rows, you are editing the layout of the table, or the table structure.

Okay, so you don't necessarily want evenly spaced columns or rows. After all, you don't need the same amount of space for a phone number as you do for a name, right?

Let me show you how to adjust the column widths. (We'll talk about how to change some of the other features later in this chapter.)

To change column widths:

1. Position the mouse pointer over a line separating the two columns you want to change. The mouse pointer changes to a thick vertical bar with left and right arrows (see Figure 10.6).

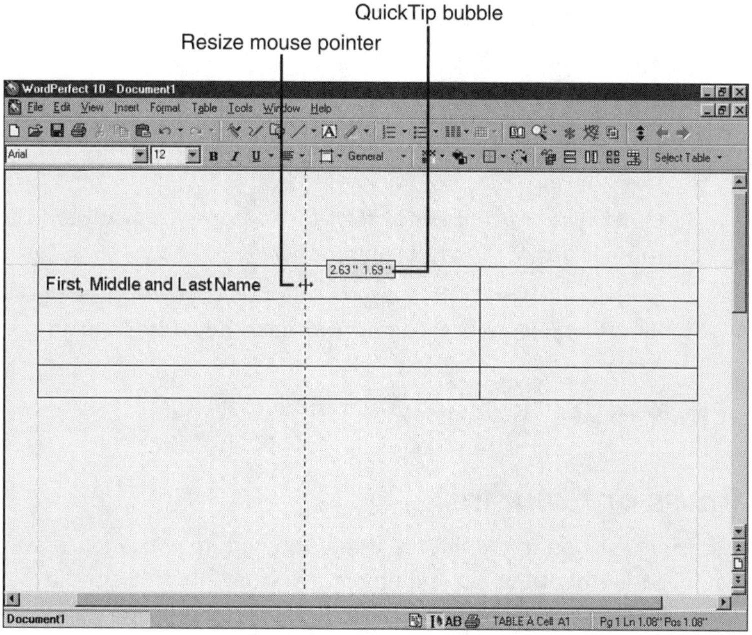

FIGURE 10.6
Use the mouse to drag table column lines and change the width of table columns.

2. Click and drag the **column separator line** to the right or to the left, thus widening one column and narrowing the other. A QuickTip bubble tells you how wide the column(s) will be when you release the mouse button.

3. When you get the column widths that you want, release the mouse button.

You can repeat this process with other columns until your table looks just the way you want it.

Adding Rows and Columns

A common problem in using tables is that you're never sure just how many rows or columns you're going to need. One easy way to add rows at the bottom of the table is to press the Tab key in the last column of the last row. Rows and columns also can be added anywhere in a table.

To add rows or columns to a table:

1. Position the insertion point where you want to add a new column or row.

2. Choose **Table**, **Insert**. WordPerfect displays the Insert Columns/Rows dialog box (see Figure 10.7).

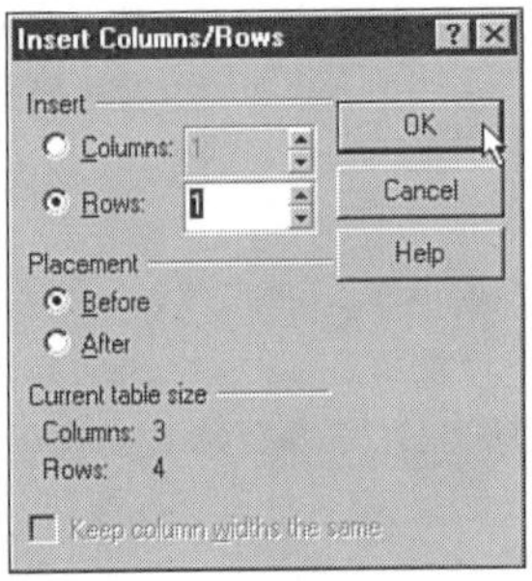

FIGURE 10.7

The Insert Columns/Rows dialog box enables you to change the number of rows or columns in your table.

3. Either type the number of rows or columns you want to insert, or click the spinner arrows to select the number.

4. By default, WordPerfect inserts columns or rows *before* the current cursor position. If you want them to appear *after* the current cursor position, choose the **After**.

5. Click **OK** to insert the rows or columns.

Deleting Rows or Columns

Occasionally, you overshoot the mark and end up with more rows or columns than you need. Rather than leave them empty, delete them from the table.

To delete rows or columns:

1. Position the insertion point in the first row or column you want to delete.

2. Choose **Table**, **Delete** to open the Delete Structure/Contents dialog box (see Figure 10.8).

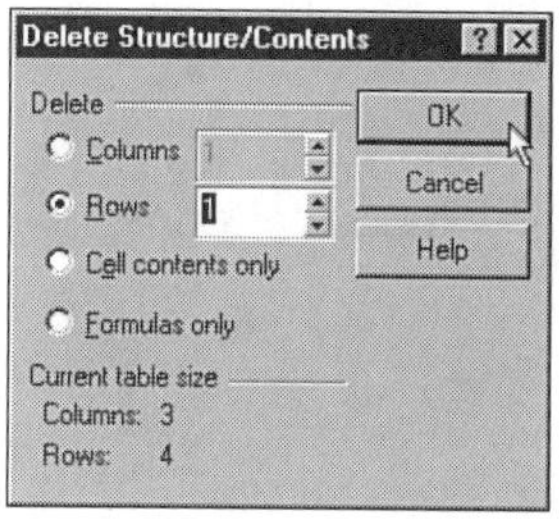

FIGURE 10.8

Use the Delete Structure/Contents dialog box to remove unneeded table rows or columns.

3. Specify the number of rows or columns you want to delete and click **OK**.

Remember, when you delete rows or columns, the contents are also erased. Click the **Undo** button, or choose **Edit**, **Undo** (**Ctrl+Z**) if you accidentally delete important data.

Joining and Splitting Cells

Another useful way to modify the layout of your table is to join cells or to split them. For example, you might want to make the entire top row of your team list a single cell to use as a title row. To do this, you need to join the cells in the top row.

Or you might decide that you need two separate pieces of information in place of one single cell. In this case, you need to split a single cell into two cells.

To join cells:

1. Click in the **first cell** you want to join (for example, cell A1).

2. Click and drag the mouse to the **last cell** in the group you want to join (for example, D1).

3. Choose **Table**, **Join**, **Cell**. WordPerfect automatically joins the selected cells, combining any information that was in those cells into the new cell.

tip

The absolute easiest way to insert or delete rows is to use the keyboard. Position the insertion point where you want to add or delete a row, and press **Alt+Insert** to add a row, or **Alt+Delete** to delete a row. If you don't like taking your hands off the keyboard, these two shortcuts are real timesavers!

From now on, WordPerfect will treat the joined cells as a single cell. If you want to revert to the original cell division, you can split the cells.

Also, there are times when you need to create additional cells in a row or column. This is particularly useful if you're trying to create a special form.

To split a cell:

1. Position the insertion point in the cell you want to split.

2. Choose **T**a**ble**, **Split**, **Cell**.

3. In the Split Cell dialog box, specify how many columns (horizontal cells) or rows (vertical cells) you want.

4. Click **OK**.

Figure 10.9 shows an example of a form where several cells have been joined, whereas others have been split.

FIGURE 10.9

You can join or split cells in a table to create useful table layouts, such as in a form.

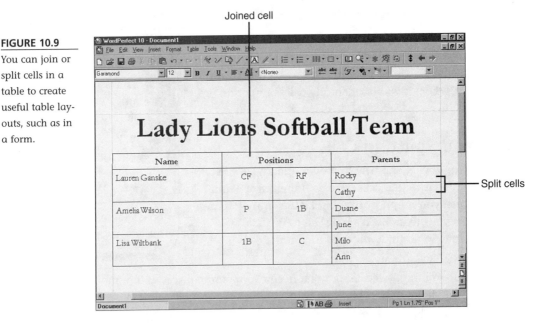

Joined cell

Split cells

Formatting Tables, Columns, and Cells

We've just talked about features that help you create the layout, or structure, of a table. But you also want your text to look good, and that's why it's important to understand how text attributes and text alignment are applied to table cells.

Formatting the Entire Table

When you want to apply a broad brush and format elements of the entire table, you use the Table tab of the Table Format dialog box.

To format a table:

1. Position the insertion point in the table. If you don't, you won't be able to open the Table Format dialog box.

2. Choose **Table**, **Format**, or press **Ctrl+F12**. Or, my personal favorite, right-click in the table and choose **Format**. WordPerfect displays the Properties for Table Format dialog box (we'll just call it the Table Format dialog box).

3. Click the **Table** tab to make changes to the entire table (see Figure 10.10).

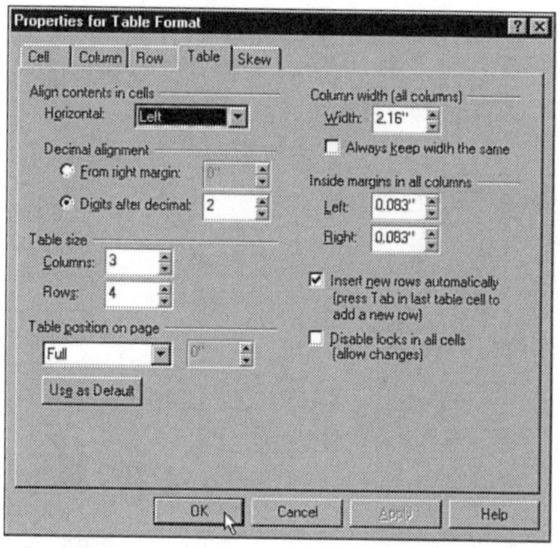

FIGURE 10.10

Use the Table tab of the Table Format dialog box to make changes to the entire WordPerfect table.

Each time you choose a text formatting option, you have to consider whether that attribute should apply to the entire table, to a column, or to a cell or group of cells. Changes you make to a specific cell or group of cells have precedence, or priority, over changes you make to columns. Changes made to cells or to columns have precedence over changes made to the entire table.

Keep this in mind, especially as you format columns. Any changes to a cell that you may have made (and forgotten about) will not change when you specify something different with column or table formatting.

tip

As you format your table, it's often useful to move from the general to the specific. For example, format your entire table first, then your columns, and then your cells. This helps avoid precedence conflicts.

In the Table tab of the Table Format dialog box you can see what the current format settings are and make changes to the table format, position, or size. For example:

- **Align contents**—Normally, all cell contents are left aligned. Click the drop-down menu to make text center, right, or decimal aligned.

- **Table size**—Although you can easily add or delete rows or columns, you can also change here the number of rows or columns in your table.

- **Table position**—WordPerfect tables stretch from margin to margin. You can also center or right- or left-align a table instead.

Formatting Text in Columns

To modify the text formatting of all the cells in a column, position the insertion point in the column you want to format, choose **Table**, **Format**, and in the Table Format dialog box, click the **Column** tab. WordPerfect displays the dialog box controls for formatting columns (see Figure 10.11).

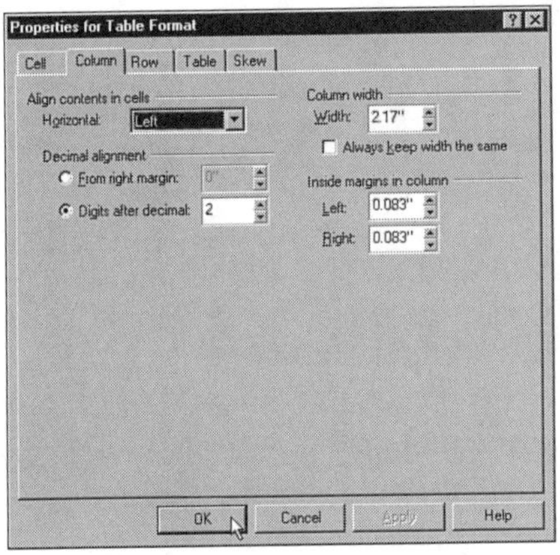

FIGURE 10.11

To format columns, use the Column tab in the Table Format dialog box.

> **caution**
>
> Don't forget that if you have already formatted an individual cell, column formatting will not change that cell's format. To correct this, position the insertion point in the individual cell, access the Table Format dialog box, and on the **Cell** tab, click **Use same alignment as column**.

One of the most commonly needed column formats is the horizontal alignment of text. In the Align contents in cells area of the Table Format dialog box, you can click the **Horizontal** drop-down menu to choose Left, Right, Center, Full, or All alignment.

Formatting Rows

Working with rows is different from working with cells or columns because you're not really applying formatting to cell contents within a row. Instead, you're only changing row structure and function.

It might seem logical to click the Row tab to format all the cells in a row. Not so! You must first select all the cells in the row, then access the Table Format dialog box, and choose cell format options.

As you've probably noted, WordPerfect automatically determines the amount of vertical space in a row based on the amount of text in its cells. The cell requiring the most vertical space sets the height for the entire row.

You can easily and quickly change a row's height by dragging the bottom line of the row up or down. WordPerfect displays a QuickTip showing the size the row will become when you release the mouse button (see Figure 10.12).

tip

If the cell row seems too high, check to see whether you have an extra hard return in any of the cells in that row. Delete the hard return, and the row will return to its normal height.

QuickTip

FIGURE 10.12

You can easily change the height of a WordPerfect table row by dragging the horizontal line below the row.

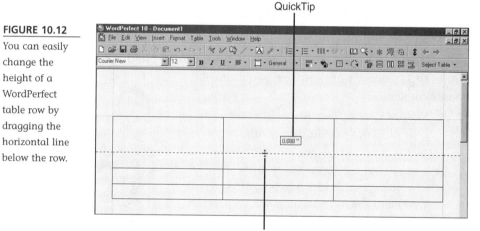

Resize mouse pointer

Sometimes you need to set a specific row height—for example, if you want to create a calendar in which all rows are the same height, regardless of the number of events on any given day.

To set a fixed row height:

1. Select the **row** or **rows** you want to format.

2. Open the Table Format dialog box (by choosing **Format** from the **QuickMenu** or from the **Table** menu).

3. Click the **Row** tab. WordPerfect displays options for formatting a row (see Figure 10.13).

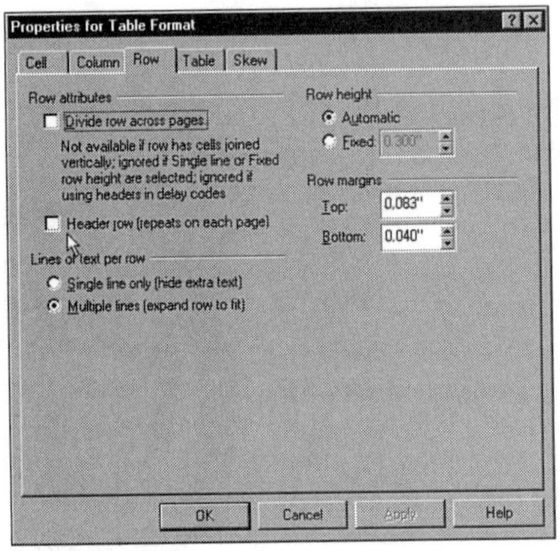

FIGURE 10.13

To alter the
structure of a
row, click the
Row tab in the
Table Format
dialog box.

4. Click **Fixed** and in the text box type the height of the row (for example, 1.0"
   for a calendar row).

5. Click **OK** to apply the change and return to the table.

Once in a while, you'll have table cells with a lot of text in them, or you'll have
extremely long tables, with many rows. In the Table Format dialog box (refer to
Figure 10.12), two options can help you deal with
those situations:

- **Divide row across pages**—If you have
  cells with an unusually large amount of
  text, WordPerfect forces the entire cell to
  wrap to the next page. That can leave a lot
  of blank space. If instead you want to break
  the cell at the page break, just click **Divide
  row across pages**.

- **Header row**—If you create a table several
  pages long, you may want certain information (such as column headings) to repeat at
  the top of each page. Such rows are called
  header rows. To create a header row, first
  position the insertion point in the row you
  want to designate as a header row; then in
  the Table Format dialog box, click the **Row**
  tab and click the **Header row** check box.

> **note**
>
> When the insertion
> point is positioned in a
> header row, WordPerfect displays
> an asterisk (*) next to the cell ref-
> erence in the general status area
> of the application bar (for exam-
> ple, Cell A1*) to indicate that the
> row is a header row.

Formatting Cells

Within cells, you format text as you normally do in a document. Simply select the text and add whatever attributes you want. However, you can also format a cell so that any text you add to the cell automatically looks like everything else in the cell.

Formatting Text Attributes

B   For example, if you want all the text in a cell to be bold, first select the cell (move the mouse pointer to the edge of the cell, and click when the pointer turns to an arrow, as shown in Figure 10.14); then click the **Bold** button on the toolbar or press **Ctrl+B**.

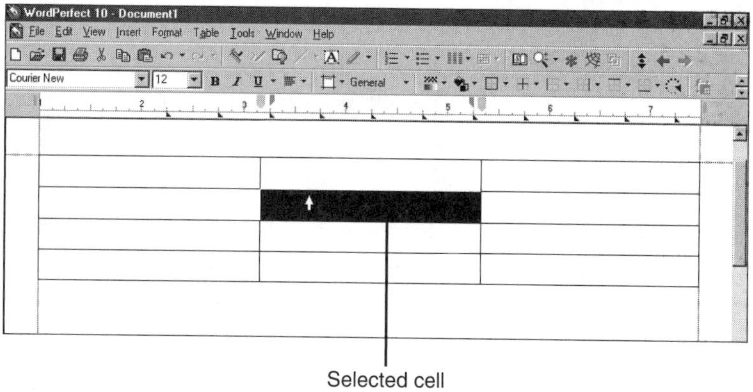

FIGURE 10.14

You can apply text attributes to cells using the same methods that you use for text outside a table.

Selected cell

Formatting Cell Attributes

In the preceding section, you learned how to change table cell text attributes, such as bold, font size, and so on. To change other format options for a single cell, position the insertion point in the cell you want to change; then choose **Table**, **Format**. WordPerfect displays the controls for formatting cells (see Figure 10.15).

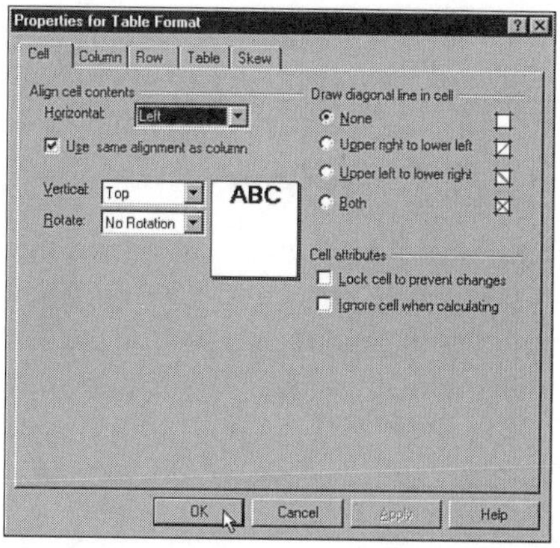

FIGURE 10.15

To format specific cells in a table, use the Cell tab in the Table Format dialog box.

To change the format of a group of cells, simply select the cells you want to change and open the Table Format dialog box. The changes you choose from the Cell tab then apply to each of the selected cells.

WordPerfect offers several useful options for formatting cells, such as those found in the Align cell contents area:

- **Horizontal**—Click the drop-down menu to choose Left, Right, Center, Full, or All alignment for all text in the selected cells.

- **Use same alignment as column**—If you previously formatted a cell, and now want to make it the same as all other cells in the column, click this option.

- **Vertical**—Normally, WordPerfect aligns all text in a cell at the top of the cell. Instead, you can choose Bottom or Center to align text vertically at the bottom or center of the cell.

- **Rotate**—The default selection for text is No Rotation. You can rotate the text within a cell by choosing 90 Degrees, 180 Degrees, or 270 Degrees from the **Rotate** menu.

If you create tables or forms for someone else's use, you may find it useful to lock certain cells. Locking a cell prevents any changes to the cell, either to the structure or the contents. To lock a cell, click the **Lock cell to prevent changes** check box.

You can do some complex calculations in tables. In fact, users have told me of their relief when they discovered that they could build spreadsheets in WordPerfect and didn't have to learn another program. In most cases, a table with calculations will have column headings and other cells that contain text, mixed in with the cells that contain values. To avoid throwing off your calculations, tell WordPerfect to ignore that cell when calculating the values. To ignore a cell, click the **Ignore cell when calculating** check box.

Finally, you can include two-part information in a cell. Choose one of the options in the Draw diagonal line in cell section to add diagonal lines to cells. This would be useful if you need to track the number of potential attendees and the actual number of people who attended in a single cell.

Changing Lines, Fills, and Borders

Although the layout and content of your table are most important, with WordPerfect you can also make your tables stunningly attractive. It's easy to change the lines around table cells so you can highlight important cells. You can quickly switch to a different border to make the table more attractive. A fill can be added to emphasize important information.

Using SpeedFormat

By default, single lines separate WordPerfect table cells and create a border around the table, but no other special formatting is assigned. To help you quickly add special line formatting, WordPerfect provides several preset styles.

To use SpeedFormat to apply a table formatting style:

1. Position the insertion point anywhere within the table.

2. Choose **Table**, **SpeedFormat**. WordPerfect displays the Table SpeedFormat dialog box (see Figure 10.16).

3. Select a style in the **Available styles** list box. WordPerfect shows you what it looks like in the preview box. For example, if you select the **Fancy Fills** style, WordPerfect formats your table with a centered title bar and with shading and line changes to set off the data (refer to Figure 10.16).

tip

Although you can change the design and format of a table at any time, SpeedFormat usually works best if applied before making other format changes. Therefore, if you know what kind of look you want, use SpeedFormat immediately after creating your table.

FIGURE 10.16

When you select a SpeedFormat style such as Fancy Fills, you apply a predefined set of formats, lines, and fills to your table.

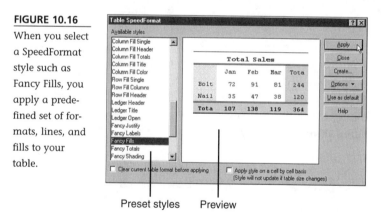

Preset styles   Preview

Not all designs match the function of the table you are creating. For example, the Single Bold Title style actually changes the structure of your table. If you don't like the format you select, you can simply select other styles until you find the one that works best for your table.

Changing the Lines

SpeedFormat might just be overkill, especially if all you want to do is change the line style for a few lines. To change individual cell lines, follow these steps:

1. Select the **cells** you want to change. For example, if you want to change the line beneath the cells in the first row, select all the cells in the first row.

2. Choose **Table**, **Borders/Fill**. WordPerfect displays the Table Borders/Fill dialog box (see Figure 10.17).

3. Determine which side of the cell(s) you want to change and then click the corresponding palette button to select a line style (see Figure 10.18). For example, you might click the **Bottom** button, and choose **Double Heavy** from the palette.

4. WordPerfect displays a sample of what you have selected (see Figure 10.19). If you like what you see, click **OK** (or click **Apply** if you want to stay in the dialog box and make other changes).

You might not want any lines at all. For example, you might want to organize your information but not have it look like a table. With all the lines removed, your text looks like you formatted into columns. The bonus is that tables are much easier to work in than columns.

caution

If you make changes to your table lines first and then apply a SpeedFormat or change the default table line, you might not get the result you want because the original changes take precedence. In some cases, it is easier to start over than to sort it all out. Choose **Table**, **SpeedFormat**; click **Clear Current Table Format Before Applying**; and then select the **<None>** style.

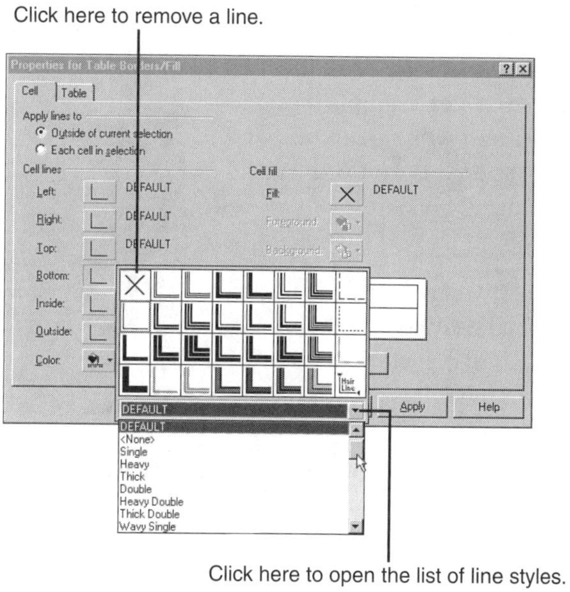

Click here to remove a line.

FIGURE 10.18

You can select a line style from the line style palette, or click the palette's drop-down menu for a more complete list of line styles.

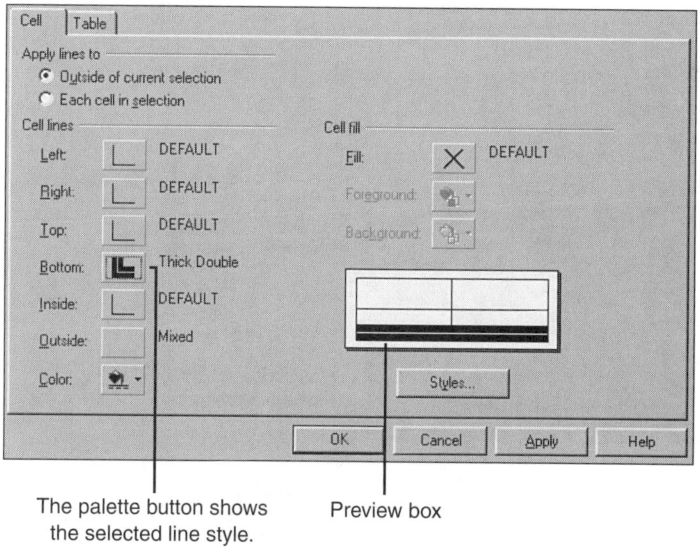

Click here to open the list of line styles.

FIGURE 10.19

The preview box in the Table Borders/Fill dialog box lets you see the effect of your choice before applying it to your table.

The palette button shows the selected line style.

Preview box

To remove all the table lines:

1. Click the **Table** tab while in the Table Borders/Fill dialog box.

2. Choose **None** as the default **L**ine style. Alternatively, you can choose **Ta**ble, **Sp**e**edFormat** and select the **No Lines No Border** style.

Changing the Fill Pattern

Fills are nothing more than color or shaded cell backgrounds. A fill color can be applied as a solid color, or in a pattern with foreground and background colors. The idea is that you can have some fun with this if you want.

tip

If you plan to include text in a filled cell, it's best to use a light shade of gray, 10% or less, or a light color such as yellow. Otherwise, text won't show up very well.

To add fill patterns to a cell:

1. Click in the **cell** where you want a fill. If you want to add a fill to more than one cell—for example, the entire first row of cells—select all the cells you want to change.

2. Choose **Table**, **Borders/Fill**. WordPerfect displays the Table Borders/Fill dialog box (refer to Figure 10.17).

3. Click the **Fill** palette button (see Figure 10.20) and select a fill pattern.

Click to open the Fill palette.

No Fill

FIGURE 10.20

You can select a fill style from the fill style palette, or click the palette's drop-down menu for a more complete list of fill styles.

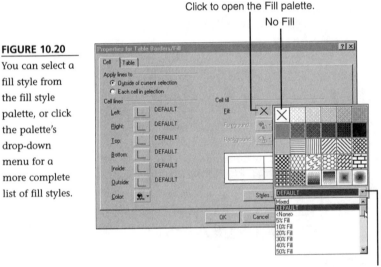

Click to open the list of fill patterns.

4. Click **OK** to apply the fill pattern.

Choosing a Table Border

By default, a WordPerfect table has no border, so you can quickly improve the appearance of a table by applying one of the border styles.

To add a border style:

1. From the **Table** menu or from the **QuickMenu**, choose **Borders/Fill**.

2. In the Table Borders/Fill dialog box, click the **Table** tab to display table-related lines and fill options (see Figure 10.21).

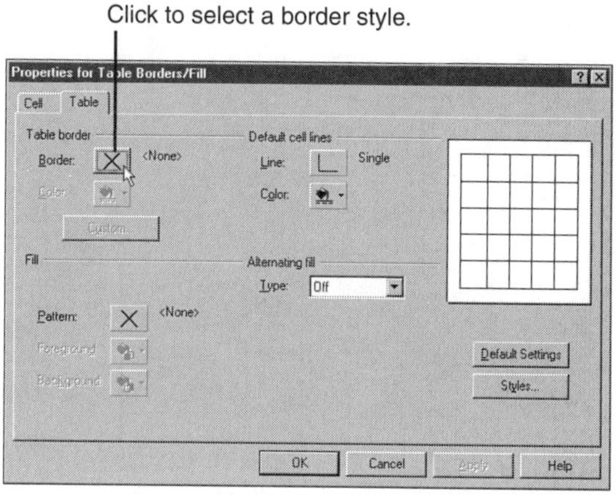

Click to select a border style.

FIGURE 10.21

You can use the Table tab of the Table Borders/ Fill dialog box to apply a table border.

3. In the **Table border** area, choose a border style by clicking the **Border** button. Note the resulting effect in the preview box.

4. Click **Apply** to apply the change and remain in the dialog box, or click **OK** to apply the change and return to your table.

Using WordPerfect Tables for Calculations

WordPerfect isn't a full-blown spreadsheet program, but for many different types of calculations, WordPerfect is definitely up to the task. For example, you might want to calculate a total of reservations for your team's final banquet. WordPerfect can do that and much more. In fact, users can construct small spreadsheets in WordPerfect and turn to Quattro Pro only for larger, more complex spreadsheets. See the Appendix section for three bonus chapters on creating spreadsheets in Quattro Pro.

Using QuickSum

Suppose that you have a team list, with a column indicating the number of persons attending the team banquet (see Figure 10.22).

FIGURE 10.22

The QuickSum feature lets you add up a column of numbers, such as in this list of team dinner reservations.

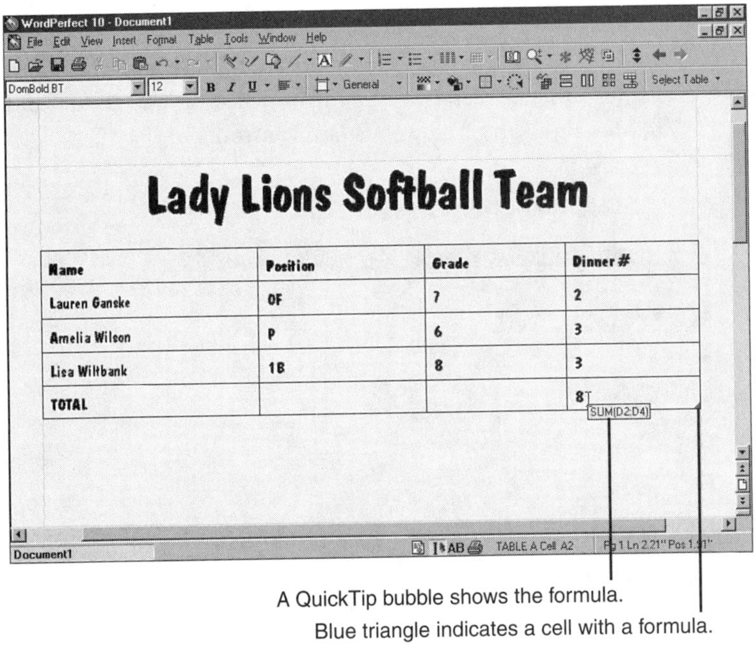

Lady Lions Softball Team

Name	Position	Grade	Dinner #
Lauren Ganske	OF	7	2
Amelia Wilson	P	6	3
Lisa Wiltbank	1B	8	3
TOTAL			8

SUM(D2:D4)

A QuickTip bubble shows the formula.

Blue triangle indicates a cell with a formula.

To create a formula that calculates the total:

1. Position the insertion point in the cell where you want the total to appear.

2. Choose **Table**, **QuickSum**. WordPerfect inserts a formula that adds up all the cells above the formula in a column, or all the cells to the left of the formula in a row. Notice the blue triangle in the lower-right corner—this indicates a cell with a formula.

If you edit numbers in cells that are included in a QuickSum, the total is automatically recalculated as you work. In a large table, the recalculating process can slow down the operation of your system. In some cases, you might prefer to turn off the automatic recalculate and calculate manually when you are finished editing.

To turn off the automatic recalculate:

1. Choose **Table**, **Calculate**. WordPerfect displays the Calculate dialog box (see Figure 10.23).

2. Choose **Off** in the Automatic calculation section.

note

A QuickSum formula in a column adds all the numbers in cells directly above it; a QuickSum at the end of a row adds all the numbers to the left of it. If a cell is empty, QuickSum doesn't calculate any cell above the empty one, so make sure that you have numbers in all the cells, even if some of the numbers are zero.

To manually recalculate a table:

1. Choose **Table, Calculate** to open the Calculate dialog box.

2. Choose **Calc Table.** Alternatively, you can right-click the table and choose **Calculate** from the table QuickMenu.

Inserting Formulas

QuickSum is a great feature, especially when you are frequently totaling up numbers in a column. You can create spreadsheet-like formulas in a WordPerfect table that perform a variety of calculations on the figures.

The same math addition and subtraction operators (+, –) that you learned in elementary school are used to build formulas in WordPerfect tables. An asterisk (*) is used as a multiplication symbol instead of an ×, and the slash (/) is used as a division symbol. So, if you want to multiply two cells and divide by a third, your formula might look like this: C5*F14/A2.

Let's say that you have a simple invoice where you want to multiply the number of items sold by the cost of each unit. To insert a formula:

1. Choose **Table, Formula Toolbar**. WordPerfect displays the Formula toolbar (see Figure 10.24).

2. Position the insertion point in the cell where you want the formula (for example, in column D of the second row).

3. Click in the **Formula Edit** box (to the right of the blue check mark button) to begin the formula edit process.

4. You can type the cell references and math symbols by hand, but you can also just click on the cells you want to include and add the math operators. For example, you could type A2*C2. Or you could click in cell **A2**, type the **asterisk**, and then click in **C2**. The result is the same.

5. Press **Enter**, or click the blue **check mark** button to place the formula in the target cell (for example, D2).

FIGURE 10.24

The Formula toolbar helps you create and edit spreadsheet formulas.

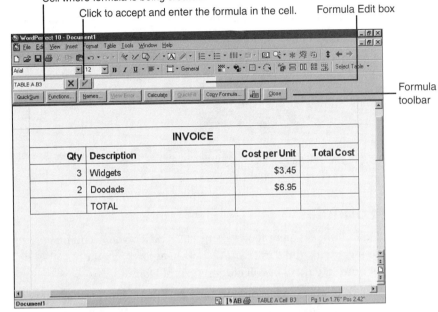

Cell where formula is being created.

Click to accept and enter the formula in the cell.

Formula Edit box

Formula toolbar

It's easy to get mixed up, so if it doesn't work right the first time, just click **Undo** and try again. You'll get the hang of it in no time.

You could repeat the preceding steps for each row of the invoice, but an easier way is to copy the formula. WordPerfect automatically adjusts the formula for each row:

1. Position the insertion point in the cell with the formula.

2. On the Formula toolbar, click **Copy Formula**. WordPerfect displays the Copy Formula dialog box (see Figure 10.25).

3. Click the **Down** radio button and then indicate how many times to copy the formula (for example, 3).

4. Click **OK**, and WordPerfect copies the formula down (in our example, to the next three cells).

tip

You probably noticed the $ signs in Figure 10.24. What you probably don't realize is that you don't have to type them. Instead you can save yourself time and trouble by letting WordPerfect automatically format your numbers for you.

Choose **Table**, **Numeric Format**. WordPerfect shows you a dialog box that lets you change the numbering style for cells, columns, or the entire table. You can format numbers for currency, percentage, fixed decimal places, and more.

Formula being copied

FIGURE 10.25

Use the Copy
Formula dialog
box to copy for-
mulas instead of
re-creating
them.

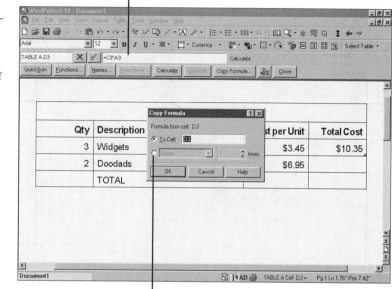

Click to copy the formula down.

Notice that you can also copy a formula directly to a specific cell. Simply type the
cell address in the **To** cell text box in the Copy Formula dialog box.

Inserting Functions

Okay, now things are getting technical. What's a function? It's nothing more than a
word that describes a mathematical process. For example, SUM is a function that
adds, or sums, all the values in a given group of cells.

Suppose, for example, that you now want to add all the extended prices on your
invoice. You could use the QuickSum feature, but you can also use the SUM function. The SUM function is more flexible because you are actually building the formula and indicating which cells to sum instead of letting QuickSum figure it out.

To insert a function in a formula:

1. Position the insertion point at the bottom of the list of numbers.

2. Click in the **Formula Edit** box on the Formula toolbar.

3. Type **SUM(D3:D6)**. This simply means, "sum all the numbers in cells D3
   through D6."

4. Click the blue **check mark** button, or press **Enter**. WordPerfect puts the
   function formula in the proper cell and makes the calculation (see Figure
   10.26).

FIGURE 10.26

Functions, such
as SUM, are sim-
ply shortcuts
that enable
you to make
spreadsheet-type
calculations.

Type the formula.

Result

QuickTip shows the formula.

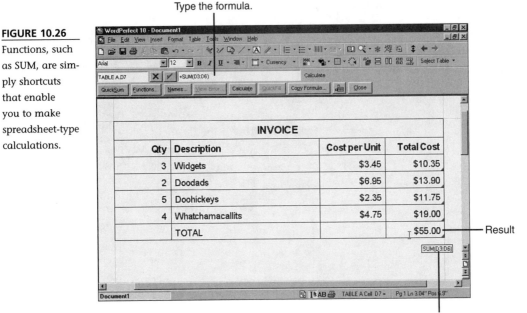

WordPerfect's table formulas are based on spreadsheet technology. Although
WordPerfect tables are not suited for heavy-duty spreadsheet applications like
Quattro Pro, they're just fine for the day-to-day calculations we have to make. Many
of us can avoid spreadsheet programs altogether just by using WordPerfect tables.

WordPerfect has more than 500 built-in functions. For more information on the
functions and how to insert them into a formula, search for "table functions" in the
Help Index.

Converting Text to a Table, or a Table to Text

"Now you tell me about tables," you say. You already painstakingly created some
rows and columns of data, but would rather see this information in a table. Or, per-
haps you want to convert a table list to a simple text list.

Fortunately, WordPerfect provides a simple method for creating a table from text formatted in tabular columns (columns with tabs between them). In fact, this capability may be one of the easiest yet most practical uses for tables.

Converting Tabular Columns to Tables

Suppose that you have a list of company employees that includes names, offices, and telephone numbers. Single tabs separate the three columns of data, as follows:

Lin, Ting-Yi	VH299	7-6543
Rohde, Kathy	VH287	7-1408
Samuels, Jodi	VH246	7-4965

To convert data in tabular columns to a table:

1. Select all the text to the end of the last line of data.

2. Choose **Table**, **Convert**. WordPerfect displays the Convert: Text to Table dialog box (see Figure 10.27).

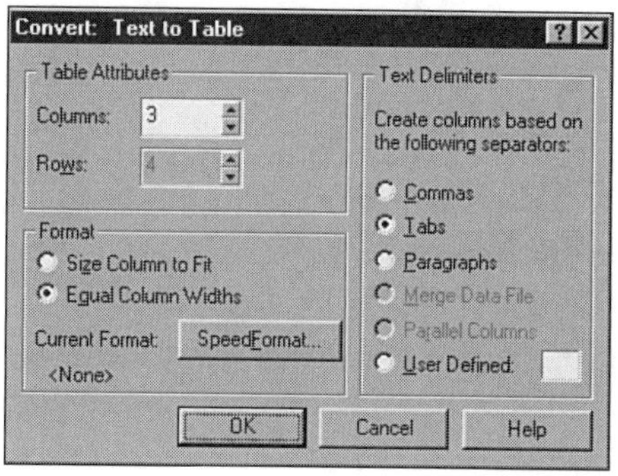

FIGURE 10.27

When you convert text to a table, the Tabs option is selected by default.

3. Take a look at the options and make any necessary selections; then click **OK**. WordPerfect converts your tabular columns of data into a table (see Figure 10.28).

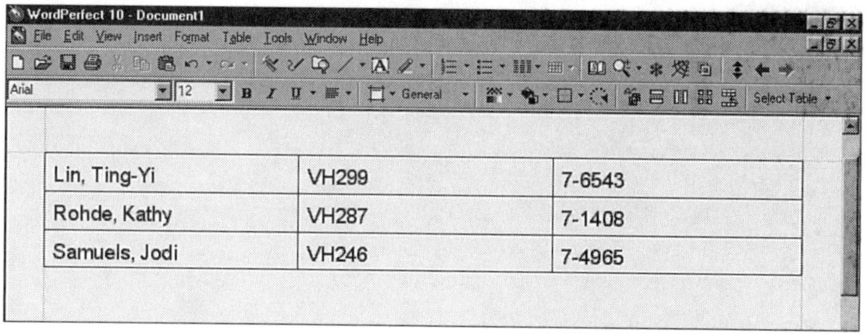

FIGURE 10.28

After converting data from tabular columns into a table, you might need to adjust the column width and other formatting to improve the layout of the data.

Converting Tables to Other Formats

At some point, you may want to use your table data in another format. For example, you need to export the information to a format that can be used in a non-WordPerfect database.

To convert table data to another format:

1. Position the insertion point in the table and choose **Table**, **Convert**. WordPerfect displays the Convert: Table to Text dialog box, shown in Figure 10.29.

2. Select one of the following options to separate the cells:

   ▥ You can separate the data from each cell in a row with commas, hard returns, tabs, or with any other character you specify. Note that rows of data themselves are separated by hard returns.

   ▥ You can change the data into a WordPerfect merge file format, where each cell is separated by an ENDFIELD code, and each row is separated by an ENDRECORD code.

> **caution**
>
> Although converting text to tables is easy, the key to a successful conversion is making sure that a single tab separates the text columns. If, for example, you use more than one tab to separate some of the entries, WordPerfect adds extra cells in the table for the extra tabs. The result can be messy. If this is the case, use **Undo** to restore the text columns. Remove the extra tabs and try again.

FIGURE 10.29

The Convert: Table to Text dialog box enables you to convert table data into other formats.

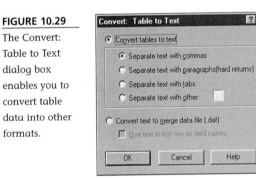

THE ABSOLUTE MINIMUM

In this chapter, you learned how to work with one of the most versatile features in WordPerfect—tables. From start to finish, you learned how to create a table, how to edit cell contents, how to format the table, and how to include calculations on values.

- You saw how easy it is to create tables, using the dialog box, or by clicking and dragging across the Table palette.

- You learned how quick it is to move around in a table by clicking the mouse, or by pressing **Tab** and **Shift+Tab**.

- It's a simple process to adjust column widths, to add/delete rows and columns, and to join or split rows/columns, as you fine-tune the table structure.

- You now understand how to format table elements, taking the order of precedence into account.

- Borders, lines, and fill can all be altered to fit the situation and to emphasize important parts of the table.

- Formulas can be inserted to calculate values just like you would in a spreadsheet program. Quite a few spreadsheet calculations can be performed in WordPerfect tables using the built-in functions.

- It's easy to convert an existing table into text, or to convert tabbed columns into a table, so if you already have content that you want in a table, you won't have to retype anything.

In the next chapter, you learn how to organize information into lists and outlines.

IN THIS CHAPTER

- Learn how to create lists with bullets or numbers.
- Explore how to change bullet and number styles.
- Discover how useful outlines can be and how easy they are to create and edit.
- Learn how to collapse or expand outlines, and how to change outline styles.

11

USING LISTS AND OUTLINES

WordPerfect is great for creating and editing paragraphs of text, but it's also well-suited to creating structured lists and outlines that make it easy for the reader to quickly grasp the important items or ideas in your document. To illustrate, I could go on and on about various types of lists, including descriptions about each type. On the other hand, I could simply create a bulleted list, which I suspect you'll find quicker and easier to understand. Lists or outlines are perfect for

- To-Do lists

- Agendas for an upcoming meeting

- Notes for a speech you have to give

- Summary notes for a class you've attended

- Executive summaries for more extensive reports

- Summary items for overhead transparencies

Working with Lists

You could just use the "brute force" method to create lists or outlines like those shown in Figure 11.1 (type a number, type the text, type the next number, and so on). Or, you could take a few minutes to learn how this powerful WordPerfect feature can automate your list making and, over the course of the next several months, save yourself literally hours of time and trouble. Figure 11.1 shows the three different types of lists that can be created in WordPerfect.

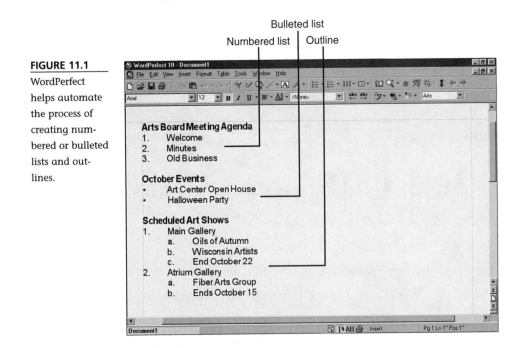

FIGURE 11.1

WordPerfect helps automate the process of creating numbered or bulleted lists and outlines.

Creating Bulleted Lists

A *bulleted list* uses bullets, or symbols, to delineate the different levels in a list. The default bullet is a medium-sized solid black bullet, but you can switch to a different type of bullet, or you can use one of the symbols from the WP character sets.

To create a bulleted list:

1. Choose **Insert**, **Outline/Bullets & Numbering**. WordPerfect opens the Bullets & Numbering dialog box.

2. Click the **Bullets** tab to display a list of predefined bullet list styles (see Figure 11.2).

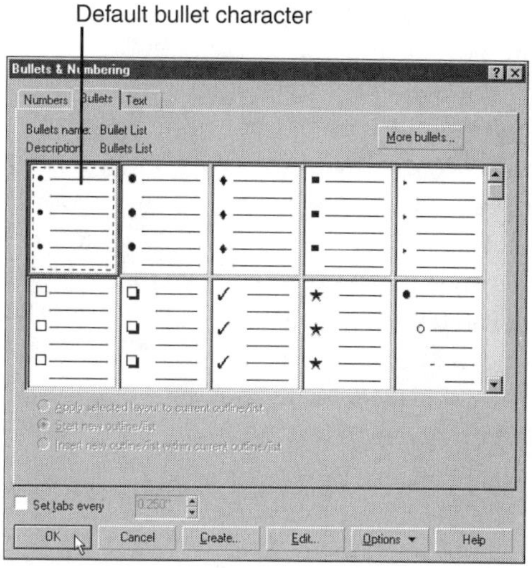

Default bullet character

FIGURE 11.2

The Bullets tab of the Bullets & Numbering dialog box offers several bullet styles for your list.

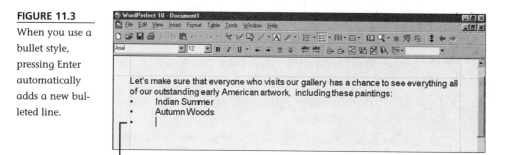

3. Click the bullet style you want to use and click **OK**. WordPerfect inserts the chosen bullet style, which includes the bullet character and an indented paragraph.

4. Type the text of the first bullet.

5. Press **Enter**. WordPerfect inserts a new bullet (see Figure 11.3).

FIGURE 11.3

When you use a bullet style, pressing Enter automatically adds a new bulleted line.

Let's make sure that everyone who visits our gallery has a chance to see everything all of our outstanding early American artwork, including these paintings:
- Indian Summer
- Autumn Woods

New bulleted line

6. Repeat steps 4 and 5 until you finish the list, and then press **Enter** one last time.

7. Press **Backspace** to erase the last bullet and to turn off the bullets. You can also press **Ctrl+H**, or click the **Bullet** button on the toolbar if you prefer.

You can also start a bulleted list by clicking the **Bullet** button on the toolbar, which places the currently selected bullet style in your document. If you don't like the current bullet style, select the list; then click the **drop-down arrow** on the **Bullet** button to see a palette of available bullet styles. Hover the mouse pointer over a bullet style to see the effect in WordPerfect's RealTime Preview, or click **More** to go to the Bullets & Numbering dialog box (refer to Figure 11.2). To turn off the bullet style, simply click the **Bullet** button again.

tip

Another quick and simple way to start a bulleted list is to type an asterisk (*) and then press **Tab**. WordPerfect's QuickBullets feature automatically starts a bulleted list, which you then continue by adding bullets, or turn off the bullet feature as you do with any bulleted list.

Creating Numbered Lists

For some reason, when using a word processing program, most of us forget how good computers are with numbers. Everything you do on a computer is broken down into zeros and ones, so calculating numbers is what computers do best. This comes in handy when WordPerfect automatically updates your numbered lists as you revise the document.

To create a numbered list, follow these steps:

1. Choose **Insert, Outline/Bullets & Numbering**.
2. Click the **Numbers** tab to choose a number style (see Figure 11.4). Use the scrollbar to see all the styles.
3. If you simply click **OK** without choosing a different style, WordPerfect uses the default style that includes a number, followed by a period and an indent code.
4. Type some text, and when you press **Enter**, WordPerfect automatically increments the number for you.
5. Press **Backspace** to turn off the numbered list.

You can start a numbered list quickly by clicking the **Numbering** button on the toolbar. Choose different styles by clicking the drop-down arrow on the Numbering button.

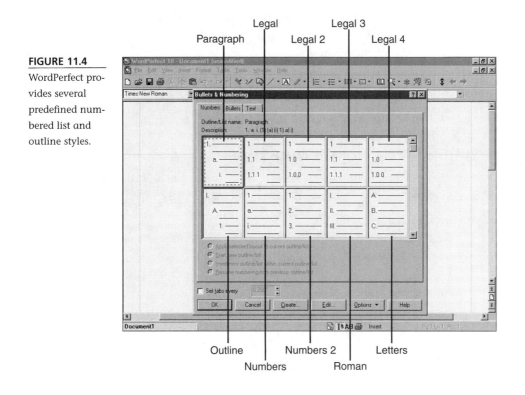

Legal

Legal 3

Paragraph   Legal 2   Legal 4

FIGURE 11.4

WordPerfect provides several predefined numbered list and outline styles.

Outline   Numbers 2   Letters

Numbers   Roman

Editing Lists

It stands to reason that as soon as you complete a list of items, something will come up, and you'll need to edit those items. You'll need to know how to add or delete list items and how to add blank lines.

Here are a few of the more useful and important ways of modifying a bulleted or numbered list:

- Add an extra blank line between list items. As you create the list, press **Enter** a second time before typing the list item. If you've already typed an item, place the insertion point on the line, press **Home** to move to the beginning of the line (after the number), and then press **Enter** to add a new blank line.

- Add a new list item. Position the insertion point at the end of an existing list item; then press **Enter**. WordPerfect automatically inserts a new bullet or number. If you are working in a numbered list, notice how WordPerfect automatically inserts the correct number. Also, notice that if you add or delete a numbered item, WordPerfect adjusts all the numbers following the inserted item.

- Remove a line. Simply delete all the text on the line, and press **Backspace** to delete the bullet or number. Press **Backspace** again to remove the blank space between the list items.

- Turn off bullets or numbers. When you're finished with the list, click the **Number** or **Bullet** button on the toolbar to turn off the automatic bulleted or numbered list.

Changing the Bullet or Numbering Style

WordPerfect makes it easy to change your mind, or to exercise artistic freedom. You can change the bullet or number style even after you have created the list.

To change the bullet or numbering style for a list:

1. Position the insertion point anywhere in the list area. For some options, you might want to position the insertion point on the first item in the list.

2. Open the Bullets & Numbering dialog box by choosing **Insert, Outline/Bullets & Numbering**.

3. Click the **Numbers** or **Bullets** tab, depending on the style you want to change to (refer to Figures 11.4 or 11.2, respectively). You can change any list from one style type to another. For example, you can change a numbered list to a bulleted list, and vice versa.

4. Click the style you want. The three options at the bottom of the tab now become available (see Figure 11.5).

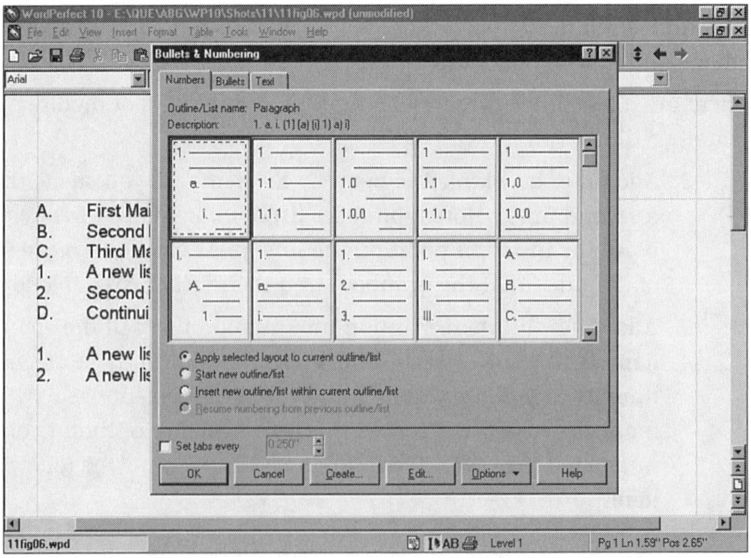

FIGURE 11.5

When you select a different bullet or numbering style, you have additional options as to how to apply that style.

Only two of the options are likely to be generally useful to you. These are

- **Apply selected layout to current outline/list**—This option simply changes the style for the entire list.

- **Start new outline/list**—This option starts a new style at the insertion point. If you are in the middle of a list, the new style applies to all items from that point forward. If you are at the end of a list, it simply starts a new list, beginning at number 1 if you are using numbers (see Figure 11.6).

FIGURE 11.6

You can use numbering/outline options to create new lists, or to change the style of all or part of an existing list.

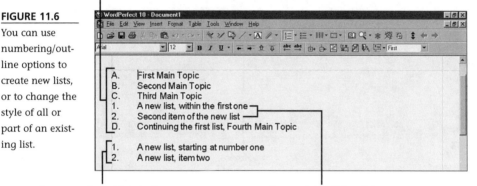

A list style that uses letters

A new numbered list starting again at number 1

A new style within a list

Working with Outlines

Outlines are a lot like lists, but they add another dimension of detail. For example, in a list, every item has the same relative importance (1, 2, 3, and so on). Outline items, on the other hand, are arranged in different levels of importance (1, 1a, 1b, 2, and so on). Consider the two lists shown in Figure 11.7.

In Figure 11.7, the second list's sublevels provide additional details about the major topics in the list.

WordPerfect's outlines are easy to work with, and the little bit of time required to learn about them is more than justified by the time and effort they can save you. For example, outline items are automatically renumbered as you add, delete, or rearrange them.

Main topics

FIGURE 11.7

Outlines look a
lot like lists, but
outline sublevels
provide more
flexibility in
organizing infor-
mation.

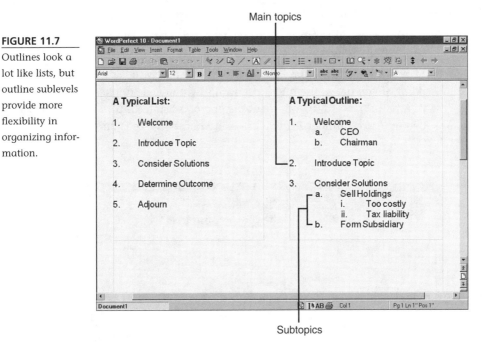

Subtopics

Creating Outlines

WordPerfect offers several outline styles, but the default is called Paragraph numbering. Let's first step through the basics to show you just how easy it is to create a
multilevel outline. We can return to the details after that.

To create an outline:

1. Choose **Insert**, **Outline/Bullets & Numbering**. WordPerfect displays the
   Bullets & Numbering dialog box.

2. Click the **Numbers** tab. The Paragraph style is selected by default (refer to
   Figure 11.4).

3. Click **OK**. WordPerfect places a number, followed by a period and an indent.

4. Type the content of the first outline item (refer to the outline in Figure 11.7
   for sample text you can type).

5. To insert the next number, press **Enter**. If you want to move the number
   down another line before you type, press **Enter** again.

6. To create the next level, press **Tab**. WordPerfect moves to the next tab stop
   and, in this case, changes the number to a letter.

7. Type the content of the first subtopic.

8. Press **Enter**. WordPerfect inserts the next number or letter at the same level as the preceding paragraph.

9. Type the second subtopic and press **Enter**.

10. Before typing, press **Shift+Tab** to move back to the left and switch to the previous outline level.

11. Continue typing and inserting numbers until you finish the outline. Here is a quick reference of keystrokes:

    ▪ Press **Enter** to add a new numbered line.

    ▪ Press **Tab** to move to the next level.

    ▪ Press **Shift+Tab** to return to a previous level.

12. Press **Enter** one last time and then press **Backspace** to delete the extra outline number and to turn off outlining.

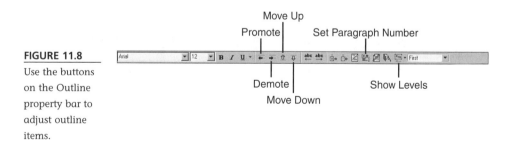

tip

A quick way to begin or end a numbered paragraph outline is to click the **Numbering** button on the toolbar, or to just press **Ctrl+H**.

Using the Outline Property Bar

Whenever the insertion point is located within a list or outline, the Outline property bar appears (see Figure 11.8). Several of these buttons add functionality that most of us will rarely use. Some, however, might just be useful shortcuts. Buttons that are covered in this chapter include the following:

Move Up
Promote | Set Paragraph Number

FIGURE 11.8

Use the buttons on the Outline property bar to adjust outline items.

Demote | Show Levels
Move Down

 ▪ **Promote**—Changes an outline item to a higher level (for example, a main topic rather than a subtopic).

 ▪ **Demote**—Changes an outline item to a lower level (for example, a subtopic rather than a main topic).

■ **Move up**—Moves an outline item up in the outline.

 ■ **Move down**—Moves an outline item down in the outline.

■ **Set Paragraph Number**—This is useful for starting a new outline (at number one) when another outline already exists in the document.

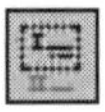

■ **Show Levels**—Expands or collapses an outline.

Editing an Outline

The nifty thing about outlines is how easy it is to add, move, or delete outline items. WordPerfect automatically numbers and renumbers everything so you don't have to worry about it. You can insert items in the middle of an outline, rearrange outline items, and promote/demote outline items, all in just a few quick steps.

Inserting Items in an Existing Outline

Let's say that you've decided to follow the advice of your high school English teacher and create all the main topics of your outline, and then go back and add subtopics, and even sub-subtopics. When you go back to add the subtopics, you'll be adding items to an existing outline.

To add an outline item to an existing outline:

1. Position the insertion point at the end of the line preceding where you want to add a new line.

2. Press **Enter**. WordPerfect adds a new number at the same level of the preceding line (see Figure 11.9).

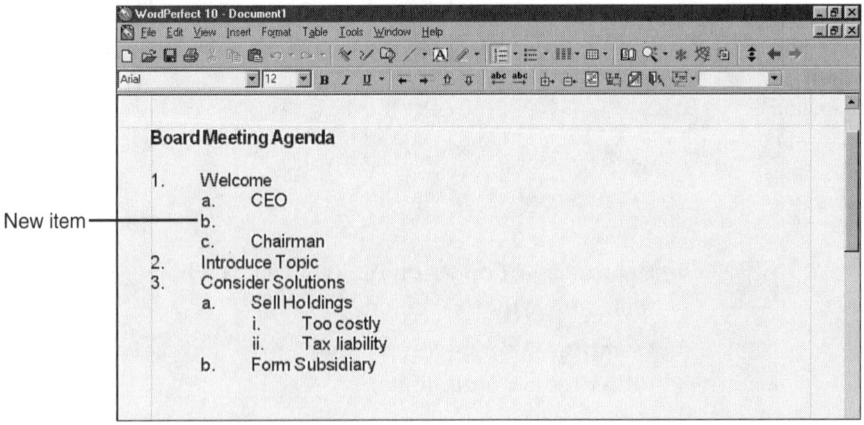

FIGURE 11.9

When you insert a line in the middle of an outline, WordPerfect automatically numbers the new line and renumbers all the following lines.

New item

3. If you want to change the outline level of the new item, press **Tab** to move to the right, and **Shift+Tab** to move to the left.

4. Type the text of the outline item.

Rearranging Outline Items

It's also easy to rearrange the items in an outline. For example, you decide that item five really belongs after item two, so you need to cut item five (and everything that falls beneath it) and move it under item two. One easy method is to move an item using the Outline property bar. The other is to move an item by cutting and pasting.

To move an item using the Outline property bar:

1. Position the insertion point on the item to be moved.

2. Click the **Move Up** button or the **Move Down** button on the Outline property bar.

To move an item along with its related subtopics, or to move several outline items at once, you simply select and then cut or copy the outline items. However, positioning the insertion point can be tricky. Instead, follow these easy steps:

1. Position the mouse pointer in the left margin area next to the item to be moved. The pointer turns into an arrow that points up and to the right (see Figure 11.10).

FIGURE 11.10

Click in the left margin next to the outline items you want to select.

New mouse pointer shape

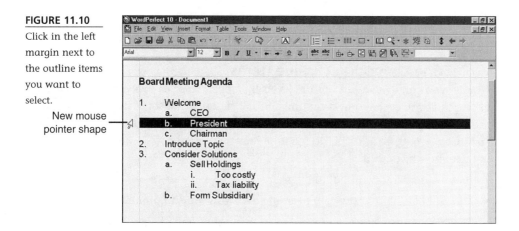

2. To select just one outline item, double-click in the margin area. WordPerfect selects the entire outline item (refer to Figure 11.10).

3. To select several outline items, click and drag the mouse downward. You might have to drag the mouse to the far right of the last line to select everything in that last line (see Figure 11.11).

4. With the items selected, use your favorite method to cut or copy.

5. Next, move the insertion point to the line *after* the item where you want to paste the outline items.

6. Press the **Home** key *twice*. Pressing Home only once moves the insertion point to the beginning of the text in the line, but after the number. Pressing Home twice moves it to the absolute beginning of the line, before the number.

7. Use your favorite method to paste the outline items.

Note that when you cut outline items, WordPerfect renumbers everything following it, and when you paste them back, WordPerfect once again automatically adjusts the outline numbers.

Promoting/Demoting Outline Items

Finally, you can also adjust outline levels by *promoting* or *demoting* outline items. For example, if you decide that a certain subtopic deserves the same importance as a main topic, you can *promote* it. In other words, you can change the numbering from "a" to "1". Conversely, if you decide to reduce the importance of an item, you can demote it in the outline.

To promote or demote an outline item:

1. Position the insertion point on the item you want to promote or demote.

2. Press **Home** *once* to move the insertion point to the beginning of the line, but following the outline number.

3. Press **Shift+Tab** to promote the item (move it to the left). You can also click the **Promote** button on the Outline property bar.

4. Press **Tab** to demote the item (move it to the right), or click the **Demote** button on the Outline property bar.

Collapsing and Expanding Outlines

WordPerfect makes it easy to develop two or more different outlines from the same original outline. Let me give you an example. You might need to prepare an agenda for those attending a meeting that shows only the main outline items. However, you need a second, more detailed agenda so you can make sure that everything goes according to schedule. All you have to do is create the full agenda or outline and then hide the sublevels you don't want others to see. This is called *collapsing* an outline. You could then print the collapsed copy of your agenda for the participants and an expanded copy of the agenda for your use.

caution

If you select <None>, WordPerfect hides the entire outline and turns off the Outline property bar. To get your outline back, you have to choose **View**, **Toolbars**; select the **Outline Tools** toolbar; and then click the **Show Levels** button and choose the number of levels you want to display.

To collapse an outline, showing only the main topics:

1. Position the insertion point somewhere in the outline so that the Outline property bar appears (refer to Figure 11.8).

2. Click the **Show Levels** button. WordPerfect displays a list of levels, One through Nine, and <None> (see Figure 11.12).

FIGURE 11.12

The Show Levels button enables you to collapse or expand your outline.

![Screenshot of WordPerfect 10 showing the Board Meeting Agenda outline with the Show Levels dropdown displaying One through Nine and None]

Board Meeting Agenda

1. Welcome
   a. CEO
   b. President
   c. Chairman
2. Introduce Topic
3. Consider Solutions
   a. Sell Holdings
      i. Too costly
      ii. Tax liability
   b. Form Subsidiary

3. Click the number of levels you want to display, for example, **One**. WordPerfect collapses the outline to display only the first level outline items (see Figure 11.13).

FIGURE 11.13

A collapsed outline shows only the major topics. The subtopics are still there. You just expand the outline to see them again.

Board Meeting Agenda

1. Welcome
2. Introduce Topic
3. Consider Solutions

4. To display all levels again, repeat steps 1–3, choosing **Nine**.

Changing the Outline Style

The default outline style in WordPerfect is Paragraph (1., a., i., and so on). You probably remember this as the traditional outline style you learned in high school. There are other outline styles as well. Fortunately, WordPerfect makes it easy to change outline styles.

To change to a different outline style:

1. Position the insertion point anywhere in the outline.

2. Choose **Insert**, **Outline/Bullets & Numbering**. WordPerfect displays the Bullets & Numbering dialog box (refer to Figure 11.4).

3. Choose the outline style you want, and click **OK**. WordPerfect automatically changes the outline style (see Figure 11.14).

note

If you have more than one outline in your document, changing the style for one outline changes the style for all outlines. To apply a style change to just one outline, select the outline before changing the style.

FIGURE 11.14

The structure of
an outline does
not change
when you apply
a different out-
line style.

New outline style

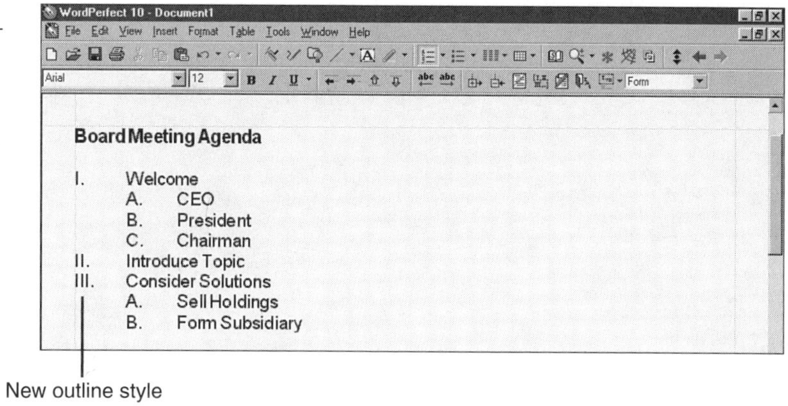

THE ABSOLUTE MINIMUM

In this chapter, you discovered some easy and practical ways to organize information other than in plain paragraphs. Whether you're creating a simple To-Do list or a complex outline for a speech you have to give, WordPerfect lists and outlines are just the ticket.

- You discovered how easy it is to create and edit bulleted lists.
- Numbered lists are also useful because you can add, remove, or move items, and WordPerfect automatically renumbers your list.
- You saw how you could switch to a different bullet or number style after you create a list.
- Outlines give you the added dimension of subtopics, and again, WordPerfect automatically keeps track of the proper outline numbering.
- You learned how to edit outline items and how to collapse and expand your outlines.
- Changing to a different outline style won't affect the structure of the outline.

In the next chapter—Chapter 12, "Working with Graphics"—you get to play with graphic images, lines, and other visual elements that spice up and enhance the content of your documents.

PART IV

ADDING VISUALS

- Learn how to insert horizontal and vertical graphic lines.

- Find out how to import graphics into WordPerfect.

- Learn how to create and use text boxes.

- Add borders and fills to graphics and text boxes, and learn how to wrap text around them.

- Learn how to add a watermark to your pages.

- Explore creating and layering your own drawings (shapes).

12

WORKING WITH GRAPHICS

Words are great. They're the stuff of *Hamlet*, *War and Peace*, and *The Catcher in the Rye*. Just think what the authors of those famous works could have done with a word processing program like WordPerfect! Although you and I are pretty good with words, we could use a little help in making our words communicate more effectively. That's where graphics come in.

Graphic elements range from simple lines or shapes that we create ourselves, to clip art created by artists who are much better at art than we are. WordPerfect makes it easy to insert and manipulate graphics in a document.

Working with Graphic Lines

Although they might not seem like it, lines in WordPerfect are a simple form of graphics. In fact, some of the things you learn about graphic lines will help you as you work with more complex things such as shapes or clip art.

Inserting Standard Lines

There are two basic types of lines in WordPerfect: horizontal and vertical. The most commonly used type is the horizontal line, which helps the reader visually separate sections of your document. For example, when you create a memo, you often separate the heading information (To:, From:, Re:) from the body of the text with a line that extends from one margin to the other. The default horizontal graphic line is a thin line that stretches from the left to the right margin (see Figure 12.1).

To create the default horizontal line:

1. Position the insertion point on the line where you want to create the graphic line.

2. Choose **Insert**, **Line**, **Horizontal line** (**Ctrl+F11**).

FIGURE 12.1

The default horizontal line extends from the left margin to the right margin.

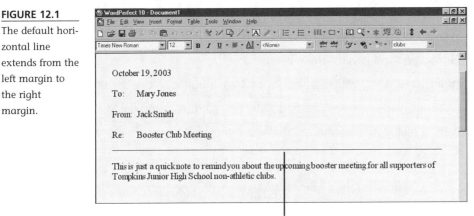

Default horizontal line

WordPerfect places a perfectly measured horizontal line in your document (refer to Figure 12.1). No muss, no fuss! "But," you ask, "why can't I just type a bunch of underlines?" Graphic lines have distinct advantages over lines created with characters.

First, if you change your margins, the line might end up being too long and will wrap to the next line, or it might be too short, not reaching all the way to the right margin. Second, if you change your font, the width of the underline characters changes and again your line might be too long or too short. Graphic lines, on the other hand, fit neatly from margin to margin, regardless of the margin settings or the text font. Figure 12.2 shows both graphic and character-based lines, before and after changing the font size and the margins.

FIGURE 12.2

Character-based lines don't always fit after changing the font or margins.

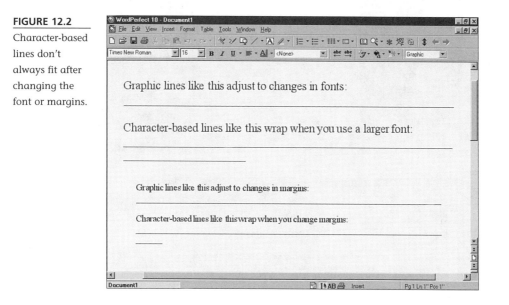

The other graphic line type, vertical lines, has a different purpose. Often they are used with newspaper style columns and help the reader follow the flow of the text (see Figure 12.3).

To insert a vertical line, position the insertion point at the left margin and simply choose **Insert**, **Line**, **Vertical Line**. WordPerfect inserts a vertical line at the left margin that extends from the top to bottom margins (see Figure 12.4). Note, however, that because the default vertical line is nearly on top of the text, you'll probably want to move the line over a little.

FIGURE 12.3

Vertical lines are
often used to
separate
columns of text.

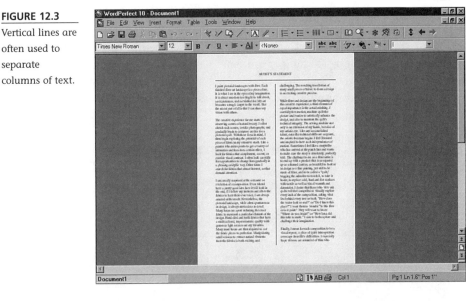

FIGURE 12.4

The default ver-
tical line practi-
cally stands on
top of the text,
so you may
need to adjust
its location.

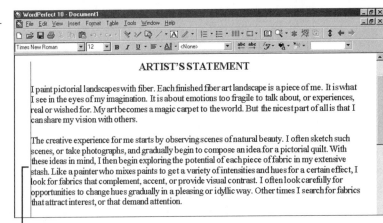

Default vertical line

Customizing Graphic Lines

Fortunately, you can customize your lines to meet your needs. One way is simply to
drag the lines to another location. The other is to create a line that is as long and as
thick as you want, located exactly where you want it. Suppose you want to move the
vertical line you just created a bit to the left, into the left margin.

To move a graphic line:

1. Position the mouse pointer over the graphic line until the pointer leans to the right.

2. Click the mouse, and small black boxes appear at each end of the line and also in the middle (see Figure 12.5). These boxes are called *sizing handles* and can be used to manipulate a graphic image.

FIGURE 12.5

Sizing handles are used to change the shape of a graphic element.

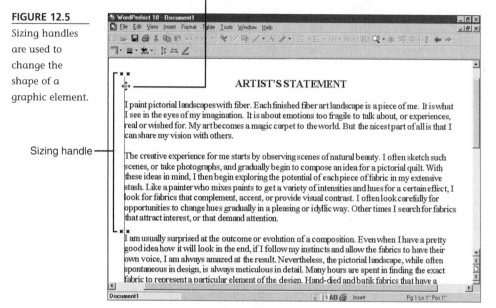

Four-way arrow pointer

Sizing handle

3. Position the mouse pointer over the selected graphic until it turns into a four-way arrow, which is the move pointer (refer to Figure 12.5).

4. Click and hold down the mouse button while you drag the line to its new location.

5. When the line is where you want it, release the mouse button. If you don't get it quite right, repeat steps 3 and 4 until you do (see Figure 12.6).

It doesn't make any difference whether you're moving a horizontal or vertical line; the steps to move it are the same. You select the line by clicking on it; then move it by dragging it to a new location.

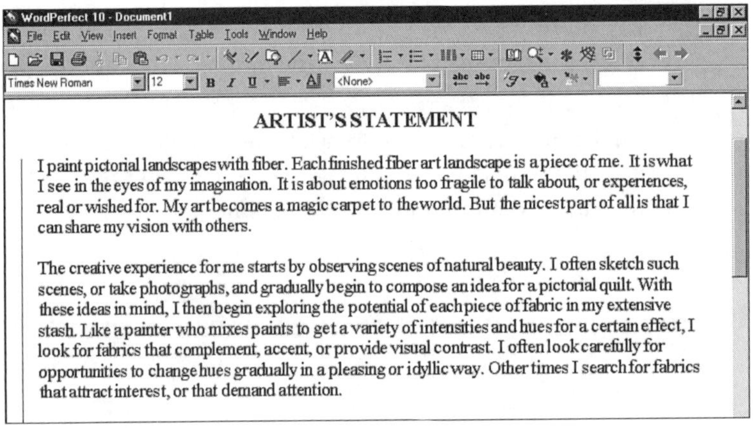

FIGURE 12.6

The vertical line
has been moved
away from the
text into the left
margin.

Most of us prefer simply to drag graphic elements to position them and use sizing handles to resize them. However, sometimes you need more precise control of a line: the length, the width or thickness, the color, or the position on the page. Suppose that you want to create a three-inch signature line at the end of a legal agreement.

To create a custom line:

1. Position the insertion point where you want to insert the line.

2. Choose **Insert**, **Line**, **Custom Line**. WordPerfect displays the Create Graphics Line dialog box (see Figure 12.7).

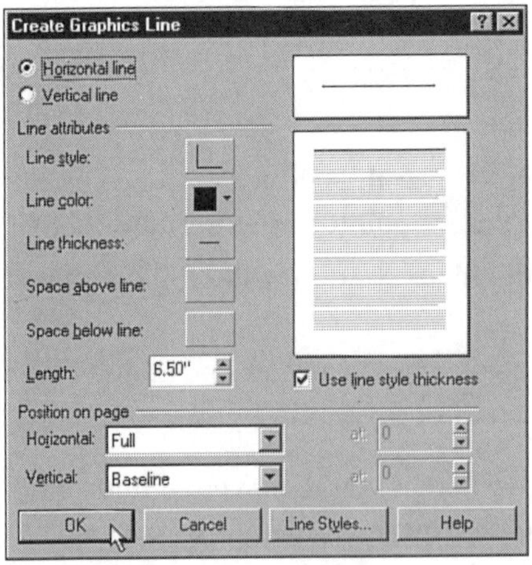

FIGURE 12.7

Using the Create
Graphics Line
dialog box, you
can create a cus-
tom line of any
length, thick-
ness, color, or
location.

3. Change the line options as desired. For example:

   ■ **Vertical line/Horizontal line**—Choose the type of line you want to create. This selection determines some of the other options available to you.

- **Line attributes**—Choose the style (single, double, dashed, and so on), color, thickness, spacing, and length.

- **Position on page**—If you set a horizontal line's horizontal position to Left, whatever size line you create will begin at the left margin. To place a vertical line between columns, choose the horizontal position **Align with Columns**. If you choose **Set** in either the **Vertical** or **Horizontal** drop-down lists, the length of the line will be from the current insertion point position to the right or bottom margin.

4. The preview box shows you what your line will look like. When you're satisfied, click **OK**. WordPerfect inserts the line in your document (see Figure 12.8).

FIGURE 12.8

You can use horizontal, vertical, or custom lines all in the same document.

Horizontal line

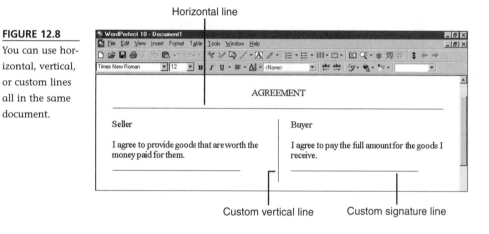

Custom vertical line   Custom signature line

Inserting Graphic Images

Graphic lines are simple and are rather practical graphic elements. However, I'll bet you really want to know about putting pictures in your document. You've probably heard about clip art, but that is just one of the many graphic elements you can add to a WordPerfect document. Some of the things you can add include

- WordPerfect's own clip art images
- Images you scan yourself
- Graphic images from the Internet
- Background graphics called watermarks
- Graphic shapes such as stars, boxes, or arrows

Working with graphics is fun! But try not to get too carried away. At the very least, you might find yourself spending a lot of time trying to get things just right. At the worst, you'll focus so much on the graphical "eye candy" that you neglect to write good text.

Inserting Clip Art

The easiest place to start is with WordPerfect's own clip art images—predesigned artwork that comes with the WordPerfect program. The steps to insert and manipulate these graphic images also apply to most other graphic elements, including graphic lines, which you just learned about.

To insert a clip art image in your document:

1. Position the insertion point at the location where you want to insert the graphic image.

 2. Choose **Insert**, **Graphics**, **Clipart**, or click the **Clipart** button on the toolbar. WordPerfect displays the Scrapbook dialog box (see Figure 12.9), which contains clip art, along with photos, video, and audio clips.

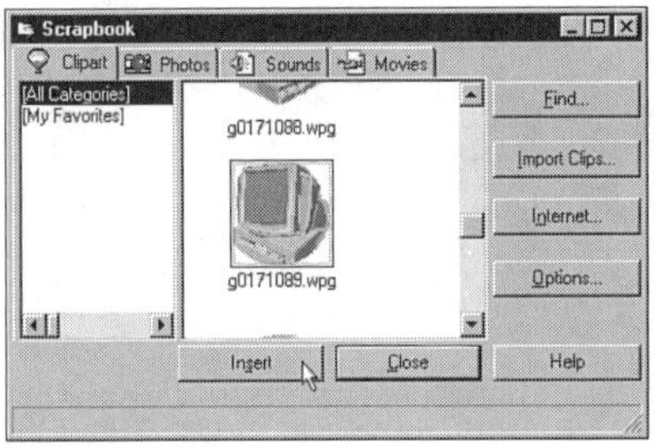

FIGURE 12.9

The WordPerfect Scrapbook provides access to more than 10,000 clip art images (on CD-ROM), as well as photos, audio, and video clips.

3. Scroll through the list of images and select the one you want.

4. Click **Insert** to place the image in your document. Or, if you prefer, you can double-click an image to insert it in the document.

5. Click **Close** to clear the Scrapbook dialog box.

Notice how the image pushes aside the text that surrounds it, in the shape of a rectangle (see Figure 12.10). You'll also note that a special Graphics property bar appears to help you manipulate and modify the image.

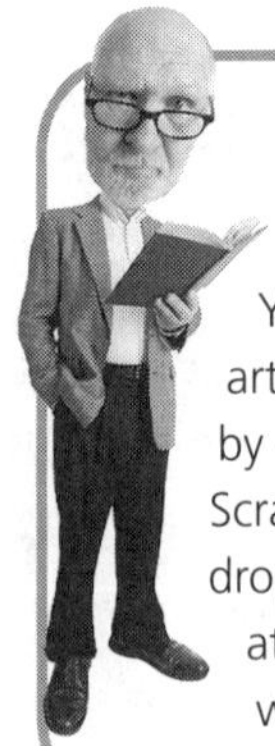

tip

You can also place a clip art image in your document by dragging it from the Scrapbook dialog box and dropping it in your document at the precise location where you want it.

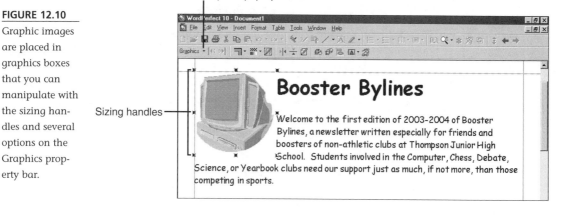

Graphics pop-up menu

FIGURE 12.10

Graphic images are placed in graphics boxes that you can manipulate with the sizing handles and several options on the Graphics property bar.

Sizing handles

The rectangle that surrounds the image is called a *graphics box*, and when selected it is surrounded by eight black boxes called sizing handles (refer to Figure 12.10). If you click elsewhere in the document, you deselect the graphic box and the handles disappear. When you click an image, you select the object and the sizing handles reappear.

Note that if you accidentally insert the wrong image, you can delete it. Just select the image and press **Delete**.

Moving and Sizing an Image

Before we talk about other types of images, you probably want to know how to make the clip art behave the way you want it to. It may be too large or too small, and almost certainly it won't be positioned exactly where you want it.

To move an image:

1. Click *once* on the image to select it; the sizing handles appear. Remember that double-clicking takes you to the graphics editor.
2. Position the mouse pointer over the image until it turns to the four-sided move pointer.
3. Click and drag the image to the new location.
4. Release the mouse button.

caution

Be careful not to double-click a clip art image after you've inserted it into your document. Doing so actually transfers you to the Corel Presentations graphics program where you can edit the clip art image itself. Menus and toolbars change drastically. If this does happen, simply click outside the image area to return to WordPerfect and your document.

Part of the problem in placing the graphic might be that the image is too large or too small. You can change the size of a graphic image this way:

1. Select the image and then move the mouse pointer to one of the corner sizing handles until the pointer turns to a two-way arrow. This is called a *resizing pointer* (see Figure 12.11).

FIGURE 12.11

To resize a graphic image, drag the corner sizing handles.

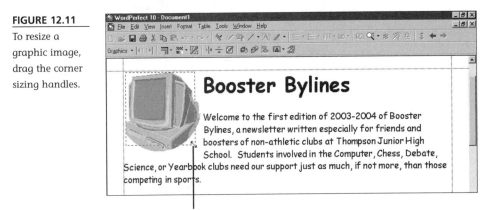

Resizing pointer

2. Click and drag the sizing handle toward the center of the image to make it smaller, or away from the center to make it larger.

3. Release the mouse button. You might need to further adjust the location of the image as described previously.

Dragging the corner sizing handles keeps the image proportional. If you want to distort an image, drag the top, bottom, or side sizing handles. You can produce some interesting images using this method.

Importing Graphics

WordPerfect's clip art is extensive and useful. But often the precise image you need just can't be found in WordPerfect's clip art library. Fortunately, you can import almost any type of graphic, from almost any source. The Internet has a vast collection of free clip art that you can download and use freely in your documents. You can also convert graphics created in other applications to WordPerfect format. Finally, if you have a printed copy of an image, you can scan it and insert it into a document.

Inserting Other Graphic Types

Whether you use a graphic image created in another graphics program, a scanned graphic, or an image from the Internet, the procedure for inserting it is the same.

WordPerfect capably converts to the WordPerfect format a variety of graphics, such as the GIF, JPG, TIFF, or PCX graphics format. For a complete list of the formats that you can convert in WordPerfect, search for "graphic file import formats" in the Index tab of the Help Topics dialog box.

To convert a graphic from another format, all you have to do is insert the image, and WordPerfect takes care of the rest. If, for some reason, WordPerfect doesn't recognize a graphic format, it tells you, and you'll have to find another format for the image you want.

To insert a graphic image from a non-WordPerfect file:

1. Position the insertion point approximately where you want to place the graphic image.

2. Choose **Insert**, **Graphics**, **From File**. WordPerfect displays the Insert Image dialog box. It looks a lot like the File Open dialog box, and you use it the same way to locate and insert a graphic image that you've saved to your disk. You may have to browse to locate the file you want.

3. Select the file you want to use, and click **Insert**. WordPerfect converts the file to a WordPerfect format and inserts it into your document (see Figure 12.12).

4. At this point, you can move and size the image just like you did the clip art image.

note

Graphics come in two basic flavors: vector and bitmap. WordPerfect's own clip art images are *vector* graphics, which are created by using mathematical calculations. When you stretch such an image, the lines remain smooth because WordPerfect knows how to recalculate to fill in the lines. *Bitmap* graphics, on the other hand, such as those you find on the Internet or that come from scanned images, are made up of individual blocks of color called *pixels*, which aren't quite so easy to manipulate. In particular, bitmap images do not enlarge as cleanly as vector art does. Very small bitmap images tend to have "jaggies" (jagged edges) when you stretch them to make them larger.

FIGURE 12.12

You can insert nearly any kind of graphic image, including scanned images or graphics from the Internet.

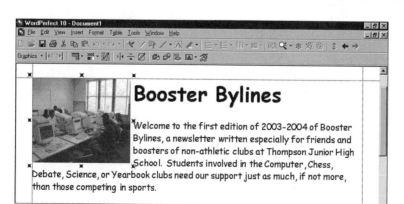

Using Images from a Scanner

Any image, black-and-white or color, can be scanned and inserted into a document. The quality of the scanned image is directly related to the quality of the scanner. If you aren't satisfied with the scanned image, you might consider paying a print shop to scan the image for you.

To scan an image directly into your WordPerfect document:

note

If you have a scanner and you want more information on how to use it effectively, take a look at Que's *The Scanning Workshop* by Richard Romano, ISBN 0-7897-2558-4.

1. Position the insertion point where you want the image.

2. Choose **Insert**, **Graphics**, **Acquire Image**. Depending on the scanner you have, a scanning software program appears. Each scanning program is different, but you should consider these options, if available:

   - Choose the type of scan that matches the image: color, grayscale, or black and white.

   - Crop (trim) the scan to just that part of the overall image you want.

   - If you can, specify the size of the resulting image. For example, the original may be only 1/2" by 1/2", but if you scan it at 2" by 2" the result will be much cleaner and you won't have to stretch the image. Likewise, you can make a much larger image smaller so that it doesn't take up so much space on your hard drive.

   - Apply settings such as color balance or brightness and contrast.

3. When you're ready, scan the image. The scanning program sends the result directly to WordPerfect (see Figure 12.13).

4. Size and move the image just as you would any graphic.

FIGURE 12.13

You can scan directly into WordPerfect from your scanning program.

Scanned image

Using Images from the Internet

You can even use images you obtain from the Internet. But first, a word of caution—just because you *can* use Internet images, doesn't necessarily make it *legal*. Copyright laws apply to Internet graphics just as they apply to print graphics. Depending on how and where your document will be used, you might need to seek permission to use Internet images in your documents.

To download an Internet image and use it in a WordPerfect document:

1. Locate an image using your Internet browser; then right-click the image you want to download.

2. In Netscape choose **Save <u>I</u>mage As**, or in Internet Explorer choose **Save Picture As**.

3. Provide a name and local destination (for example, `c:\My Pictures\ happyface.jpg`). Don't change the filename extension for the image—for example, `.gif` or `.jpg`.

4. Click **<u>S</u>ave** to save the image.

5. Switch to WordPerfect and choose **<u>I</u>nsert**, **<u>G</u>raphics**, **<u>F</u>rom File**.

6. Browse to the location where you saved the image, select the image, and click **Insert**.

WordPerfect converts the image from the Internet format (`.gif` or `.jpg`) and places it in the document. See Figure 12.14 for an example of an Internet image, at both normal and enlarged sizes. You then can move or size the image.

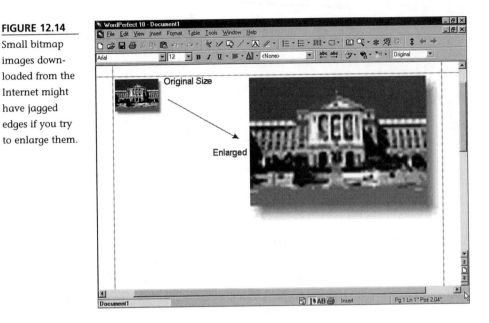

Creating Text Boxes

Text boxes in a graphics chapter? You might be wondering how text boxes fit in a chapter on graphics. Well, the box that contains the text is a graphics box, so you treat text boxes just like graphic images.

What's nifty about text boxes is that you can create some text, such as a sign or a label, and then move it on top of other text or graphic images.

To create a text box:

1. Position the insertion point approximately where you want the text box to begin.

2. Choose **Insert**, **Text Box**. WordPerfect places an empty text box at the right of the screen (see Figure 12.15).

3. Type the text you want. You can change the font style, size, color, or other attributes, and you can include hard returns, just like you would with regular text.

4. When you're finished editing the text content of the box, you might want to size the text box to match the contents. Note that when you size a text box, unlike a graphics box, the size and shape of the contents do not change.

5. To move the box, move the mouse pointer to the edge of the text box. When it changes to a move pointer (refer to Figure 12.15), click and drag the box. Drop the box into a new position.

Move pointer

FIGURE 12.15

Text boxes let
you put text in a
box that you
can place any-
where on the
document, even
in the margins.

The creative experience for me starts by observing scenes of natural beauty. I often sketch such scenes, or take photographs, and gradually begin to compose an idea for a pictorial quilt. With these ideas in mind, I then begin exploring the potential of each piece of fabric in my extensive stash. Like a painter who mixes paints to get a variety of intensities and hues for a certain effect, I look for fabrics that complement, accent, or provide visual contrast. I often look carefully for opportunities to change hues gradually in a pleasing or idyllic way. Other times I search for fabrics that attract interest, or that demand attention.

If, after the text box is deselected, you want to make some changes to the text, you need to select the box first. When a text box is selected, a border appears around the box. When you see the blinking insertion point inside the box, you can edit the text.

Setting Border, Wrap, and Fill Options

Graphics boxes—whether they contain clip art, scanned images, or text—are like containers you place into your text. The way your document's text flows around these graphics boxes is called *wrap*. A box can also have a visible border, and it can be filled with a pattern or color.

Wrapping Text Around Graphics Boxes

You can make your text wrap around graphics boxes in several ways. By default, WordPerfect text moves aside to make room for graphics boxes, but you can change the settings to have the text appear in front of, or behind, the box (see Figure 12.16).

To change how text wraps around a box, right-click the graphics box and choose **Wrap** from the context menu. WordPerfect displays the Wrap Text dialog box (see Figure 12.17). You can also click the **Wrap** button on the Graphics property bar, but to see the Graphics property bar, you must have first selected the graphics image or text box (click on the edge of a text box to select it). Some of the more useful options from the Wrap Text dialog box are illustrated in Figure 12.16.

note

With the Contour option selected, text wraps around the image in the box, not the box itself (refer to Figure 12.16). This eliminates the extra whitespace between the graphic and the text. Note that if you add a border of any kind to a contoured graphics box, the wrap option reverts back to Square.

FIGURE 12.16

Wrapping text means making room around a graphics box for the text that surrounds it. You can also place graphic images in front of or behind the text.

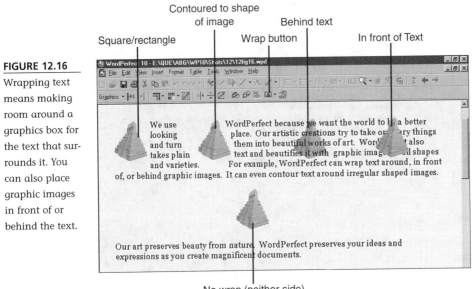

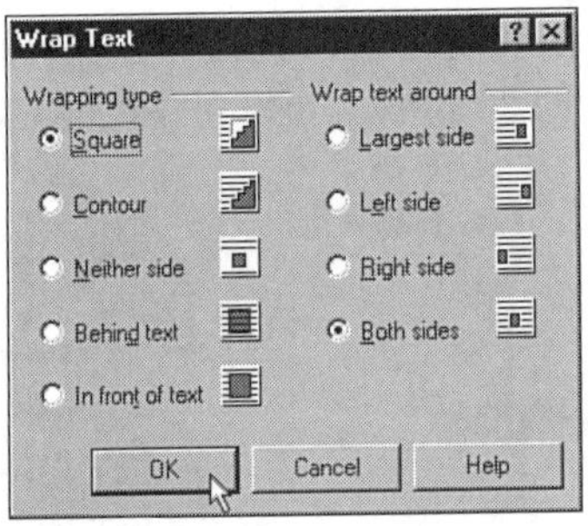

FIGURE 12.17

The Wrap Text dialog box shows you various ways to wrap text around graphics boxes.

Adding Borders to Graphics Boxes

If you really want to set off your graphics, you can put a border around them. By default, text boxes already come with a single line border. You can switch to a more decorative border in just a few steps.

To change the border around a graphics box:

1. Click the graphics box that needs a border. Remember, you have to click the edge of a text box to select it.

2. Click the **Border Style** button on the Graphics property bar. WordPerfect displays a palette of border styles (see Figure 12.18).

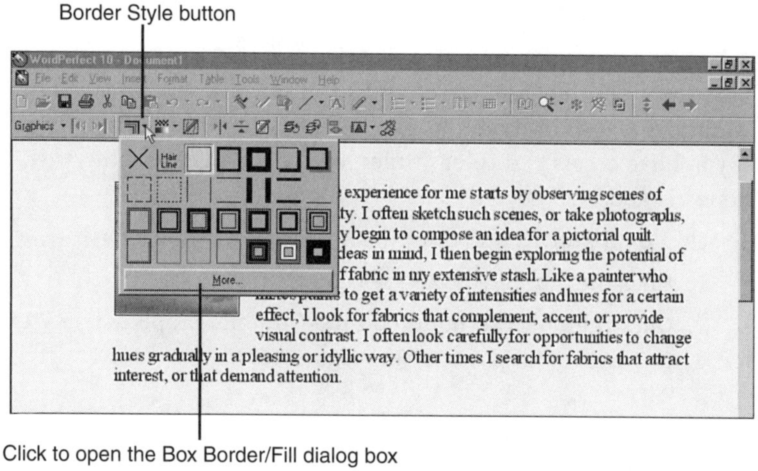

Border Style button

FIGURE 12.18

Select graphics box border styles from the Graphics property bar. Click the box with the X in it to remove a border.

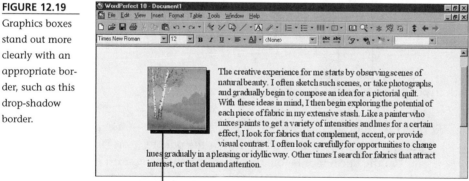

Click to open the Box Border/Fill dialog box

3. Hover the mouse pointer over the border you want to activate in RealTime Preview, which shows you how the border will look if you apply it to the graphic.

4. Select a border style from the palette. WordPerfect adds it to your graphics box (see Figure 12.19).

FIGURE 12.19

Graphics boxes stand out more clearly with an appropriate border, such as this drop-shadow border.

Drop-shadow border

If you're feeling particularly adventurous, you can click the **More** button on the Border Style palette to display the Box Border/Fill dialog box where you can change line or shadow colors and styles, and more.

Adding Fills to Graphics Boxes

For effect, you can also provide a background pattern or shading to your graphics box, whether or not you use a border. Let me give you some examples. You might want to add a shaded background behind a clip art image, or to text in a text box. If you have access to a color printer, you can use colors; otherwise, the shading is done in shades of gray.

To select a fill pattern and color:

1. Click the graphics box to select it.

2. Click the **Box Fill** button on the Graphics property bar. WordPerfect displays a palette of fill patterns (see Figure 12.20).

Box Fill button   New fill pattern

FIGURE 12.20

Gradient shading is just one of many fill patterns you can apply to graphics boxes.

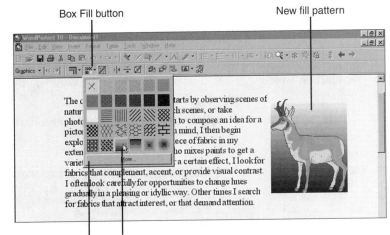

Gradient Fill

Click to open the Box Border/Fill dialog box

3. Hover the mouse pointer over the pattern you want—for example, one of the gradient shadings on the bottom row of the palette. WordPerfect previews the effect in the document before you select it (refer to Figure 12.20).

4. Click the fill pattern you want to use. WordPerfect applies it to the graphics box.

Unfortunately, all the patterns on the palette are shades of gray. If you want to add color, click **More** on the Box Fill button. WordPerfect displays the Box Border/Fill dialog box, with the Fill tab selected (see Figure 12.21). Click the color buttons (in this case, Start Color and End Color) and select the colors that you want to use. Click **OK** when you're finished.

FIGURE 12.21

The Box Border/Fill dialog box helps you add color to fill patterns.

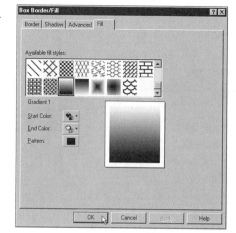

Adding Watermarks

If you hold a quality piece of bond paper up to the light, you'll see a pattern, usually the name of the company that manufactured it. This is called a *watermark*. In WordPerfect, watermarks are much more versatile and can serve a useful purpose. They're nothing more than lightly shaded versions of graphics or text images that seem to lie behind the body of text. Figure 12.22 shows you what a typical watermark might look like.

FIGURE 12.22

A watermark image is text or a graphic image, displayed at 25% brightness.

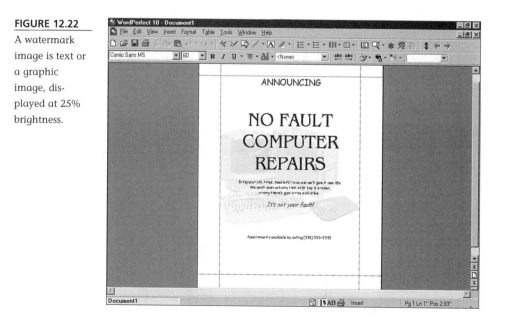

To create a watermark:

1. Position the cursor at the beginning of the document.

2. Choose **Insert**, **Watermark**. WordPerfect displays the Watermark dialog box (see Figure 12.23).

3. If this is a new watermark, and the first one you've created in this document, choose **Watermark A** and click **Create**. Otherwise, choose another option, such as editing an existing watermark, or creating a second watermark (Watermark B). WordPerfect displays a blank, full page where you create or edit the watermark graphic (see Figure 12.24).

note

Watermarks function like headers in that they appear on every page, beginning at the page where you insert the watermark code and continuing until you turn off the watermark.

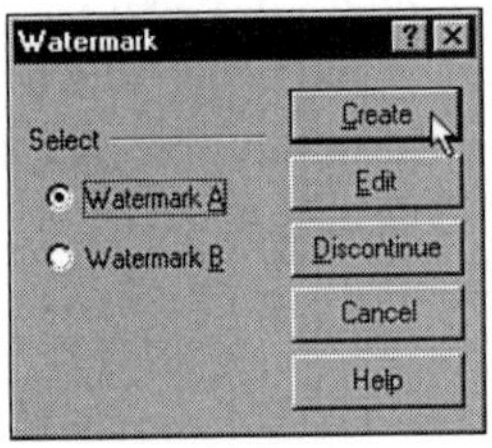

FIGURE 12.23

You can use the Watermark dialog box to create or edit background watermark graphics.

Watermark

Select
- Watermark A
- Watermark B

Create
Edit
Discontinue
Cancel
Help

4. You can use graphics from any source that you would use in the document itself. For example, you can choose **Insert**, **Graphics**, **Clipart** (or **From File**).

5. Insert the image to place it on the Watermark screen (see Figure 12.25).

Note that the graphics box, complete with sizing handles, fills the entire page. You can size and position the graphic image just as you do any other graphic image, using the mouse and the sizing handles.

FIGURE 12.24

Watermarks are created in a separate watermark editing screen.

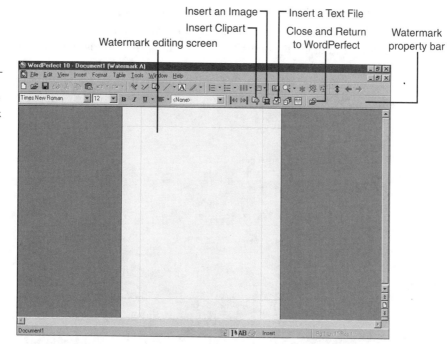

Insert an Image

Insert a Text File

Insert Clipart

Close and Return to WordPerfect

Watermark editing screen

Watermark property bar

FIGURE 12.25

You manipulate a watermark graphics box just like any other graphics box.

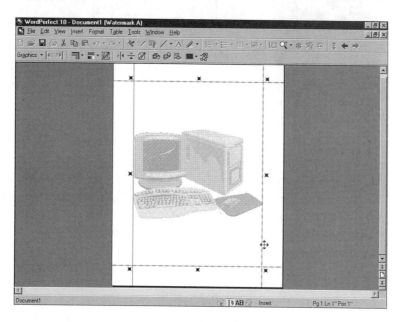

The image itself is shaded lightly so as not to interfere with the text that will appear on top of it. Normally you won't want to make this any darker, and in fact, you might want to make it even lighter. To change the brightness or contrast of the watermark image, either click the **Image Tools** button on the Graphics property bar, or right-click the image and then choose **Image Tools**. WordPerfect displays an Image Tools dialog box where you can choose from palettes of brightness and contrast (see Figure 12.26).

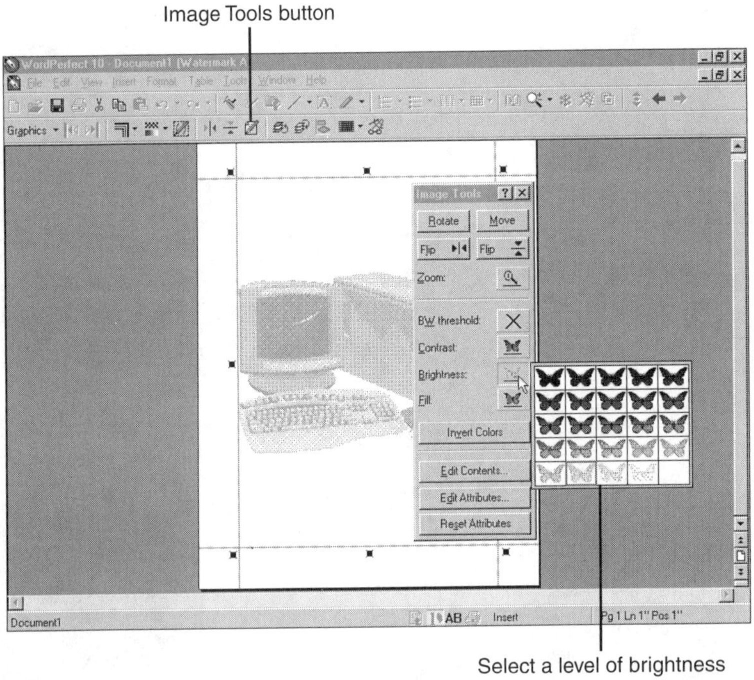

Image Tools button

FIGURE 12.26

You can use the Image Tools dialog box to change the brightness or contrast of a graphic image.

Select a level of brightness

When you're satisfied with the look of the watermark, either choose **File**, **Close** if the watermark graphic is selected, or click the **Close** button on the Watermark property bar. WordPerfect switches back to the document window, where you can see how the watermark looks behind the text (refer to Figure 12.22).

Inserting Shapes

Are you ready to become your own artist? Okay, maybe not, but at least you can create your own graphic shapes—such as boxes, circles, stars, arrows, or even smiley faces—and insert them into your documents.

 There are several ways to access the graphic shape tools, but perhaps the easiest is to click the drop-down menu on the **Draw Combined Shapes** button on the toolbar. WordPerfect then displays a palette of choices (see Figure 12.27), which include several line styles, closed objects, and callout styles. By default, this button shows a diagonal line, but after you insert a shape, the picture on the button changes to the shape you inserted in your document.

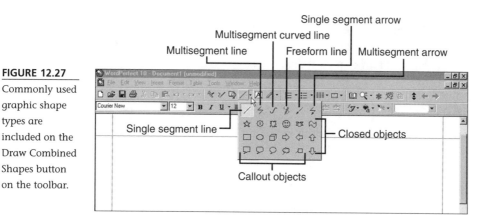

FIGURE 12.27

Commonly used graphic shape types are included on the Draw Combined Shapes button on the toolbar.

You can also get to shapes by choosing **Insert**, **Shapes** and selecting from the Draw Object Shapes dialog box, which gives you a more extensive selection of predefined shapes (see Figure 12.28). For now, let's focus on the Draw Combined Shapes button. What you learn here will work with all the other shapes as well.

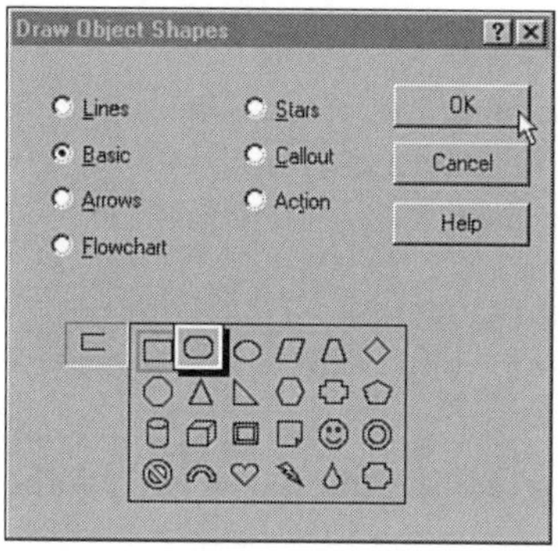

FIGURE 12.28

A more extensive arrangement of predefined shapes is available from the Draw Object Shapes dialog box.

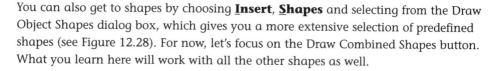

WordPerfect's graphic shape types fall into three basic categories (refer to Figure 12.27 for examples). Although each has similar characteristics, you create, edit, and manipulate each slightly differently:

- **Lines**—Each of the line types has a beginning and end, and you can add arrow heads or tails to them.
- **Closed shapes**—These include boxes, circles, action buttons, and specialty shapes.
- **Callout shapes**—These are similar to closed shapes, but you can type text in them to make it easier to create callouts, which are like speech or thought bubbles found in cartoons.

Adding Line Shapes

Suppose that you want to draw a line that connects a graphic image to some text in your document. You can use the line shape to quickly draw a horizontal or vertical line in your documents.

To draw a line shape:

1. Click the drop-down menu on the **Draw Combined Shapes** button and click the line style you want to use from the palette (refer to Figure 12.27). WordPerfect displays the icon for that style on the button, and the button appears to be selected.

2. Move the mouse pointer to the text area and note that it becomes a crosshair pointer.

3. Position the pointer where you want the line to begin.

4. Click and drag to the opposite end of the line.

5. If you're creating a single-segment line, release the mouse button to add the line on top of your text. For other types of lines, either double-click the line to finish, or release the mouse button to complete the line.

    - If you're creating a multisegment line, click once to start the line, click again to change directions, and double-click to complete the line.
    - Freeform drawing works just like drawing with a pencil. Click and drag to draw, and release the mouse button to complete the line.

After you complete your line shape, note that WordPerfect places the shape in a graphics box, complete with sizing handles (see Figure 12.29). The shape also covers any text or other objects that lie beneath it. You can adjust the size of the box or move the box as needed.

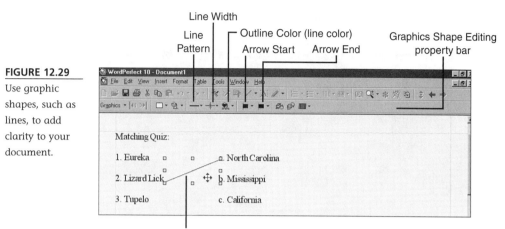

FIGURE 12.29

Use graphic shapes, such as lines, to add clarity to your document.

With the shape selected, WordPerfect adds the graphics line editing tools to the Graphics property bar (refer to Figure 12.29). These tools enable you to add arrow heads or tails; add shadows; or change line width, pattern, or colors.

Adding Closed Object Shapes

The line ends of closed object shapes come together, as in a circle, so the inside area is closed. These objects have thin single lines and are filled with an aquamarine-like green color (doesn't *everyone* like ocean colors?).

Let's use a five-point star as an example for creating a closed object shape:

1. Click the drop-down palette on the Draw Combined Shapes button to display the list of available shapes (refer to Figure 12.27).

2. Click a closed object, such as the five-point star. WordPerfect displays the star on the button, and the pointer turns into crosshairs.

3. Position the mouse pointer at one corner of the area you intend to fill with the shape (for example, the upper-left corner).

4. Click and drag the crosshair pointer to the opposite corner (for example, the lower-right corner). Continue holding down the mouse button while you move the pointer, until you have exactly the right size and proportions. If you accidentally release the mouse button, click **Undo** and try again.

5. Release the mouse button to place the object on the document (see Figure 12.30).

FIGURE 12.30

Closed objects and callout shapes are filled with color. Note the glyph, which is used to change the style of a graphic shape.

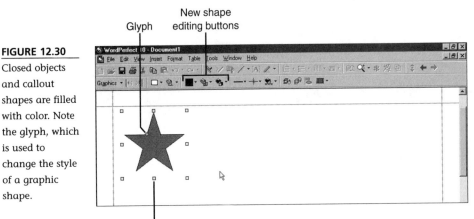

If the object has one or more *glyphs*—small pink-colored diamond handles—you can manipulate the shape or the perspective of the shape. For example, on the five-point star, you can drag the glyph toward the center of the object to create a skinny starfish look, or drag it away from the center to create a sheriff's fat star look. Whenever you see such a glyph, experiment with it to see what happens when you drag it.

With the closed object shape selected, WordPerfect modifies the graphics shape editing tools on the property bar (refer to Figure 12.30). The buttons on this toolbar are the same as those used for lines, except that the Fill Style, Foreground Color, and Background Color buttons replace the Arrow Start and End buttons.

Adding Callout Shapes

You might not even know that the "speech bubble" you often see in cartoons is also called a *callout*. Callouts are similar to closed object shapes and are created in the same way. However, WordPerfect also creates a text box inside the closed shape, where you can type text to go along with the callout. Figure 12.31 shows a callout with text and a white fill background.

To fill in the callout text, simply type text in the box just like you would in any text box. By default, such text is centered both horizontally and vertically, but you can change the text just as you would any other text in your document.

You might want to resize the box, or change its fill color. You can also drag the glyph at the end of the callout pointer to make it point where you want.

FIGURE 12.31

A callout is a closed object shape with a text box.

Glyph to move callout pointer

Text box sizing handle

Layering Graphics

You may have already noticed that after you draw several images and move them around, a graphic image ends up covering another. This can be an advantage. For example, you could layer a text box and an arrow on top of a scanned photo. Other images or filled shapes, however, are opaque and may cover up something you want the reader to see.

Think of your document as a flat table, and each time you create a graphic image, you lay it down on the table. Sometimes, however, you want to change the order of the objects you have laid down.

For example, you created an arrow and then later decided to add a box that you want to appear behind it. Because it was created first, the arrow is at the bottom of the pile. Fortunately, it's simple to change the order of a graphic element.

To change the order of an object:

1. Select the item by clicking it.

2. Click the **Graphics** button on the Graphics property bar to display a menu of options.

3. Choose the option you need that will send the object all the way to the back, send it back just one level, bring it all the way to the front, or bring it forward just one level.

You can also click the **Object(s) forward one** and **Object(s) back one** buttons on the Graphics property bar.

By changing the order of objects and layering them on top of each other, you can creatively present ideas and concepts that would never be possible with words alone (see Figure 12.32).

FIGURE 12.32

You can layer graphics objects and change their order to more clearly illustrate your document.

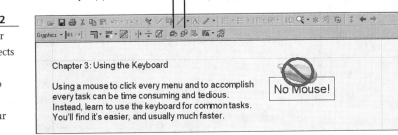

THE ABSOLUTE MINIMUM

In this chapter, you learned that a well-chosen picture could be worth a thousand words. Graphic elements come in various forms and are easy to add to a WordPerfect document.

- Right away you discovered how easy it is to add graphic lines that don't get messed up when you change fonts or margins.

- You used clip art and other images to spice up your document, and you learned how easy it is to resize graphic images and move them exactly where you want them.

- Graphic images can come from many sources: WordPerfect's own clip art scrapbook, your scanner, or even the Internet.

- Text boxes are just another type of graphics box that you can position anywhere on the page, even on top of other text or graphic images.

- You found that watermarks are cool-looking background graphics that add class to your documents.

- Now you know how to create your own graphic shapes, such as lines, arrows, boxes, and even callouts, to better illustrate what you're trying to say.

In the next chapter, you'll learn how to incorporate data from other sources into your WordPerfect documents.

IN THIS CHAPTER

- Learn how to use copy and paste to copy data from another program into WordPerfect.

- Use Corel's Clipbook to maintain a library of clips that can be pasted into a document.

- Set up links between a WordPerfect document and data in other programs.

- Learn how to work with files in other formats, as well as some tricks for using data in unsupported formats.

13

USING DATA FROM OTHER SOURCES

You can bring information from other applications into WordPerfect using simple copy and paste techniques. The Windows Clipboard acts as a go-between, transferring the information between applications. Thanks to the capability to attach files to email messages, it's also common to communicate with people all over the world. You must be able to open and edit a file even if it wasn't created in WordPerfect. Then, you'll need to save that file back to the native format so the recipient can continue working with it. That's where the capability to convert files from other formats and save files to other formats comes in.

Copying Data from Other Programs

WordPerfect can do many things, but it can't do everything. You will occasionally have to switch to another application for a project. You can have the best of both worlds here, because you can pull that information into a WordPerfect document. You can do a simple copy and paste, or you can set up a link so that if the information is updated, the changes are automatically reflected in the document. Either way, it's simple to set up in WordPerfect.

Using the same techniques you learned in the "Moving and Copying Text" section in Chapter 4, "Revising Documents," you can copy information from another program and paste it into WordPerfect. The Windows Clipboard acts as a "go-between," temporarily holding the cut or copied information until you can paste it in a WordPerfect document.

To move or copy information between programs:

1. Open the source program (for example, Microsoft Word).

2. Select the information you want to move or copy.

 3. Click the **Cut** or **Copy** button to cut or copy the selection.

4. Switch to the target program (for example, WordPerfect).

5. Click the **Paste** button to paste the selection.

The Clipboard can hold more than one selection, so if you need to copy several passages of text, you can copy all of them at one time and paste them when you're ready instead of switching back and forth between the applications for each copy and paste operation. When you are ready to paste, the selections are inserted in the order that you copied them to the Clipboard.

To cut or copy multiple selections to the Clipboard:

1. Select the first section of text.

2. Either cut or copy the text.

3. Select the second section of text.

4. Choose **Edit**, **Append**.

5. Repeat steps 3 and 4 to store additional selections.

When you paste information from another program into WordPerfect, the pasted information can include styles and other formatting from the source program. Text from Microsoft Word, for example, comes in with all the codes necessary to retain the original formatting of the text.

To paste text without the formatting:

1. Choose **Edit**, **Paste Special**.
2. Click **Unformatted Text** in the list box.

Using Corel's Clipbook

The Clipbook is a new tool that Corel included in Service Pack 2 for WordPerfect Office 2002. Clipbook is a Clipboard program that improves on the Windows Clipboard. You can now copy multiple sections of text and graphics objects to the Clipbook, which you can then insert into any Windows application. Furthermore, you can create customized collections of clips and store them in clipboards for special projects. You can create an unlimited number of clipboards.

For example, you can create clipboards of boilerplate sections of text that can be used to generate "form" documents in just a few keystrokes. I have been using Clipbook to save replies to frequently asked questions on the Corel newsgroups. You might want to use it to store items unique to certain projects that you work on. On a network, Clipbook gives system administrators centralized control over standard paragraphs, letterhead logos, and more instead of using QuickWord or QuickCorrect entries, which must be updated individually.

Loading the Clipbook Program

The first time you start Clipbook, you'll have to use the Start menu. Click **Start**, **Programs**, **WordPerfect Office 2002**, **Utilities**, **Corel Clipbook**. I promptly created a shortcut on my desktop so that I don't have to scroll through the Programs menu each time. If you want to do the same, open the **Utilities** menu, right-click **Corel Clipbook**, and then choose **Send To**, **Desktop** (create shortcut).

When you select Corel Clipbook from the Programs menu, you won't see a program window on the screen, so you might think you've done something wrong. Take a look at the taskbar—you should see a nice little Clipbook icon in the system tray (next to the time). You can double-click the icon to open Clipbook.

The Clipbook window displays the cut or copied item, along with information about the clip, such as the source, the size, and when the clip was created (see Figure 13.1).

The name of the clipboard is displayed underneath the menu bar. When you first start using Clipbook, the default clipboard is called Clipboard 1. As you continue to build your clipboards, you can designate another clipboard as the default. Whatever clipboard is currently the default is the one where all the clips that you cut or copy will be placed.

FIGURE 13.1

Each clipboard can hold up to 36 different clips, labeled 0–9 and A–Z.

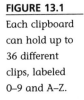

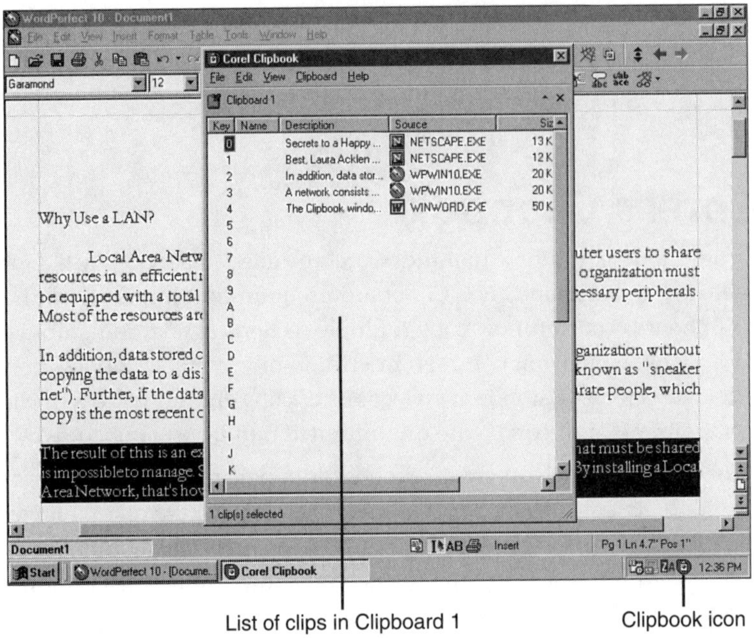

List of clips in Clipboard 1

Clipbook icon

Using the Clipbook

When the Clipbook program is loaded, pressing the shortcut keys for cutting (**Ctrl+X**) or copying (**Ctrl+C**) opens the Clipbook window, where you can select a key under which the cut or copied item is stored. While the Clipbook is loaded, it overrides the Windows Clipboard, so the text is being saved to the Clipbook only.

To paste items from the Clipbook into any Windows application, simply press **Ctrl+V**, and then double-click the letter or number of the item to be pasted. You can also right-click any letter or number in the Key column of the Clipbook, and then choose cut, copy, or paste to move the information.

If you prefer, you can use the mouse to move information to and from the Clipbook. To paste the information in the document and remove it from the Clipbook (cut and drop), click the **Key** letter or number and drag the item to your document. If you

> **note**
>
> The Clipbook is actually a file, so you can set up the Clipbook on a network drive so that the contents can be shared with other users. In the Clipbook dialog box, choose **Clipboard**, **Network** to display the menu items. The help topics have more information on networking clipboards.

want to leave a copy in the Clipbook (copy and drop), hold down the **Ctrl** key, click the **Key** letter or number, and drag the item to your document. When the mouse pointer moves into the WordPerfect document, the insertion point appears so that you can see where the text will be inserted when you release the mouse.

To see more information about a clip—for example, to see what kind of clip it is—right-click the Clipbook **Key** and choose **Properties**. You can assign a title and description in the Clip Properties dialog box (see Figure 13.2).

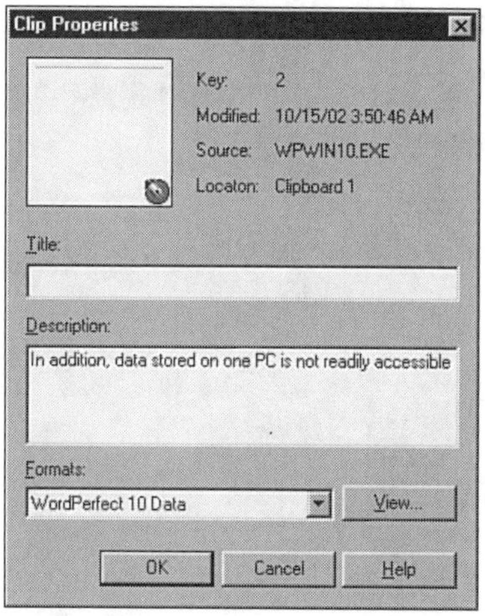

FIGURE 13.2

A title and description can be created for each clip in a clipboard.

Using OLE to Link and Embed Data from Other Programs

Copying and pasting is one way to share data from one Windows application to another, but with Object Linking and Embedding (OLE), you can do more. You can *link* data between two programs so that if the data changes in the originating program, it is automatically updated in WordPerfect. Linking is very important if you use data that requires constant updating, such as spreadsheets or databases. If you create a link to data, any changes to the data in the original application are automatically reflected in WordPerfect.

When you paste information from another program, WordPerfect *embeds* the information and remembers where the data came from. Embedded information can be edited from within WordPerfect—all you have to do is double-click it. WordPerfect creates an editing window with all the menus and toolbars from the original program.

The main difference between linking and embedding is that linked information maintains an active connection between the data in the WordPerfect document and the data in the original application. When you embed something in a WordPerfect document, you forego a link to the original data, but you do maintain a connection to the application. In either case, all you have to do to edit the data is double-click it. WordPerfect opens the original application and integrates it into the document window so you can revise the data without ever leaving WordPerfect.

Using OLE to Create a Link to Existing Data

You can insert OLE objects in WordPerfect documents and take advantage of existing information created in other applications.

To create an OLE link:

1. Choose **Insert**, **Object** to open the Insert Object dialog box (see Figure 13.3).

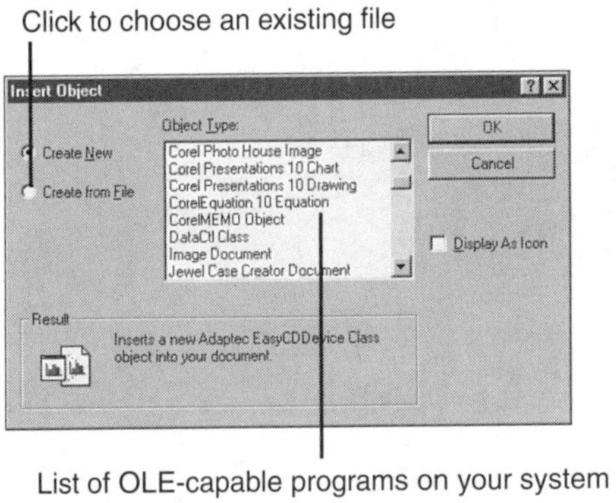

Click to choose an existing file

FIGURE 13.3

Use the Insert Object dialog box to select which type of OLE object you want to insert.

List of OLE-capable programs on your system

2. Click **Create from File**. The dialog box changes, and you now have a File text box and a Link check box (see Figure 13.4).

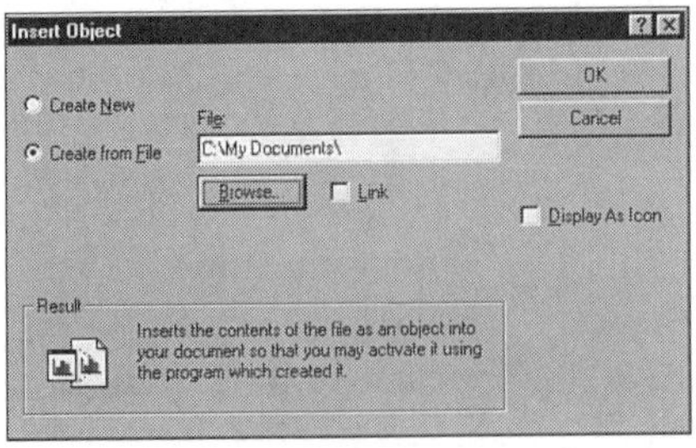

FIGURE 13.4

Use the Browse button if you don't remember the exact name and location of the object file.

3. Click the Browse button to locate the file you want to insert.

4. By default, WordPerfect inserts the file as an embedded object. However, if you put a check mark in the **Link** check box, WordPerfect inserts the object as a linked object.

5. Click **OK** to insert the object in your document.

If you drag and drop the information from another program to WordPerfect, WordPerfect automatically establishes an OLE link. The procedure is similar to dragging and dropping text between WordPerfect documents.

Locate the area in the WordPerfect document where you want to paste the data. Switch to the source program and select the information. If you want to leave a copy of the information in the application, hold down the **Ctrl** key and drag the selected information to the WordPerfect button on the taskbar. When the WordPerfect window opens, drop the information into the WordPerfect document. If you want to remove the information in the other application, click and drag without the Ctrl key.

Creating a New OLE Object

You might decide to create a new object that you can insert into a document. Luckily, you don't even have to switch to another application; you can create it from within WordPerfect. For example, you can create a Quattro Pro notebook or a PowerPoint slide inside a WordPerfect document.

To create a new OLE object:

1. Choose **Insert**, **Object** to display the Insert Object dialog box.

2. Select the object type from the list. Only the OLE-capable programs, also called *OLE servers*, which are installed on your system appear on the list (refer to Figure 13.3).

3. Click **OK**. The OLE server application starts and takes control of WordPerfect's menus and toolbars. It also opens an editing window in which you can use all the application's procedures to create the object (see Figure 13.5). This is called *in-place editing*.

4. Close the OLE editing window by clicking in the document. WordPerfect takes control of menus and toolbars again.

note

Some OLE server applications do not support in-place editing. Instead, they open a completely separate application window where you create or edit the object. You have to exit the application to return to WordPerfect. Make sure that you save your changes in the application before you return to WordPerfect.

PowerPoint menus   PowerPoint toolbar

FIGURE 13.5

You can create
or edit, in place,
OLE objects such
as PowerPoint
slides.

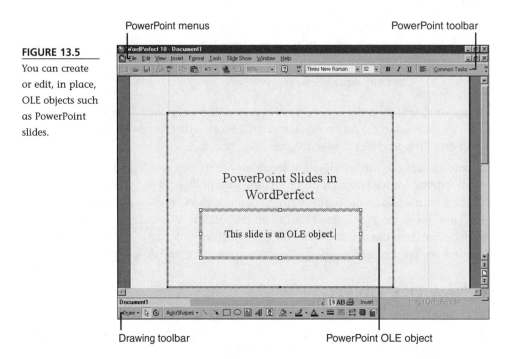

Drawing toolbar   PowerPoint OLE object

Opening (or Importing) Files from Other Programs

When you open a file that isn't in WordPerfect format, the file is automatically converted before it is opened. You may or may not see a message box that indicates a
file is being converted—it depends on how fast the conversion process is. The more
memory your machine has, the less likely you are to see this message.

WordPerfect supports the conversion of many modern formats, including the following:

- ANSI/ASCII (Windows and DOS)
- HTML (Hypertext Markup Language)
- Microsoft Word 4.0, 5.0, 5.5 for DOS
- Microsoft Word 1.0, 1.1, 1.1a, 1.2, 1.2a, 2.0, 2.0a, 2.0b, 2.0c, 5.0, 6.0/7.0 for
  Windows
- Microsoft Word 97/2000, Microsoft Word 2002
- Rich Text Format (RTF), RTF Japanese

- SGML
- Unicode
- WordPerfect for Macintosh 2.0, 2.1, 3.0, 3.1/3.5
- WordPerfect 4.2, 5.0, 5.1/5.2, 6/7/8/9/10
- WordStar 2000 1.0/2.0/3.0
- WordStar 3.3, 3.31, 3.4, 4.0, 5.0, 5.5, 7.0
- XML (Extensible Markup Language; UTF-8, UTF-16 Big Endian and Little Endian)

A complete list of conversion filters appears in the Help topics. In the Help Index, type **import**, select **Import and export file formats for WordPerfect 10**, and then click **Display**.

Saving (or Exporting) to Other File Formats

Even though many of your friends use Microsoft Word, you stubbornly refuse to give up WordPerfect. And you don't have to! WordPerfect Office 2002 has the cleanest, most accurate set of conversion filters for Microsoft Word available anywhere. You can save your documents in Word format, and no one will even know the difference.

To save a document in a different format:

1. Choose **File**, **Save As**. WordPerfect opens the Save As dialog box.
2. Type the name of the file you want to use, unless you intend to use the same name.
3. Click the **File type** drop-down menu and select the file format you want to convert to (see Figure 13.6).

FIGURE 13.6

Select a file format from the File type drop-down list to save the file in that format.

List of file formats

4. Click **Save**. WordPerfect converts the document into the selected format and assigns the proper extension. For example, if you save a document in Microsoft Word 97/2000/2002 format, WordPerfect automatically assigns a .doc extension.

If you continue to work on the document and save it again, WordPerfect prompts you with the Save Format dialog box (see Figure 13.7). Unless you want to change back to the WordPerfect format, select the conversion format (for example, Microsoft Word 97/2000/2002) and click **OK**.

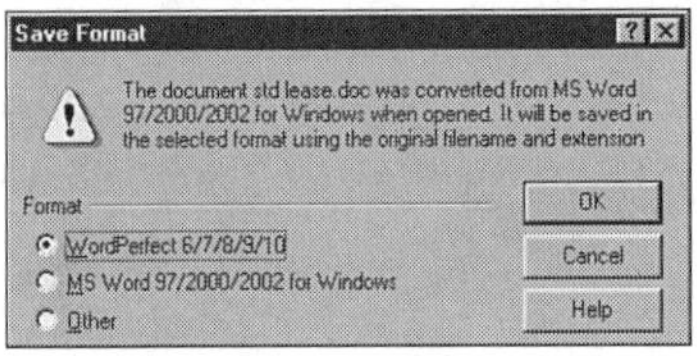

FIGURE 13.7

When you save a non-WP document, WordPerfect asks which format you want to save it to.

Installing Additional Conversion Filters

If you try to open a file and WordPerfect tells you the format of the document is not supported, don't despair. A regular WordPerfect installation installs only a limited number of conversion filters. You can easily install the other conversion filters from the WordPerfect Office 2002 CD. You will be amazed at how many formats WordPerfect converts—lots more than any other word processing program.

To install the additional conversion filters:

1. Insert the WordPerfect Office 2002 CD to start the Setup program.

2. Choose **Add New Components**.

3. Click the **Next** button to move past the list of components. The next screen is for the conversion files.

4. Click the **plus sign** (+) next to Conversion File Types to open the list of different conversion files.

5. Place a check mark next to the filters you want to install.

6. Click **Next** to move past the Writing Tools screen.

7. Click **Next** to move past the destination screen.

8. Click **Install**.

9. Click **OK** when the installation is complete. The new filters have been installed, and they are ready for use.

Using Data from Unsupported Formats

Creative minds working together are a great thing, but incompatible file formats are not. At some point, you're going to run into a file that WordPerfect can't open. When you try to open such a file, WordPerfect displays the Convert File Format dialog box (see Figure 13.8), with Unsupported Format listed in the Convert file format from field. There are a few methods for dealing with this problem:

- If you have access to the program used to create the file, open the document in that program and see whether you can save it to an intermediate format that WordPerfect understands. For example, Rich Text Format (.rtf). You might lose formatting in the translation, but at least you'll preserve the content.

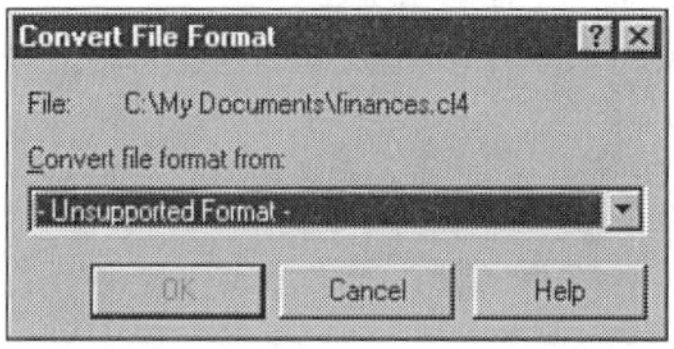

FIGURE 13.8

You can choose an alternative conversion format in the Convert File Format dialog box.

- If you know the source of the document (for example, Microsoft Word 6.0), be sure you have the necessary conversion filters installed.
- If you think you know which program was used to create the file, but not the exact version, try selecting different versions of the program.
- When all else fails, you can usually open the file as an ASCII file. Try the CR/LF to SRt option first because it converts the hard returns at the end of ASCII lines to soft returns, which preserves the paragraph structure. You will lose all document formatting with this option. ASCII imports also usually require extensive editing to clean up the resulting conversion.

The Absolute Minimum

This chapter explained how to incorporate information from other sources into WordPerfect.

- You learned how to use the Copy and Paste features to copy data from another program into WordPerfect.

- You learned how to use the Clipbook to save multiple clips for pasting.

- OLE allows you to create links to data so that any changes made to the data are automatically reflected in WordPerfect.

- You learned how WordPerfect easily converts files from other formats.

- You saw how WordPerfect can save a file in another format.

- Additional conversion filters can be installed from the Corel WordPerfect Office 2002 CD.

- If the data is in an unsupported format, there are still a couple of things you can try, such as saving the file in another format that WordPerfect can understand.

In the next section of the book, you'll learn how to use WordPerfect's tools to make your job easier and faster. You'll learn how to use the Merge feature, how to fill in a template, and how to create and play macros.

PART V

AUTOMATING YOUR WORK

IN THIS CHAPTER

- Learn how to create a data file and enter information to be used in a merge

- Create form files from scratch or from an existing document, and then merge the data file with the form file.

- Create envelopes and labels with information from the data file.

- Build a fill-in-the-blanks form that prompts the user for information.

14

USING THE MERGE FEATURE

Most people think of anything using the Merge feature as a *mail merge*, but you can realistically pull together *any* type of information to produce *any* type of document. You might hear more about using the Merge feature to produce personalized letters, envelopes, and labels, but it's also a very powerful tool for organizing key pieces of information.

This chapter explains how to use the Merge feature to set up a typical mail merge with letters and envelopes. You'll also learn how to create fill-in-the-blanks forms.

Working with Data Files

A *merge* is a combination of information from two different sources. Typically, you have a *form* file, which is the document, and a *data* file, which contains the information that you want to insert. The form file is just a regular document with merge codes in it. The merge codes act as markers for the information from the data file.

A data file is organized into records, which contain fields for every piece of information. Using the mail merge example, the data file is a list of names and addresses, and the form file is the letter. Each person, client, or event has a *record* that is divided into *fields*, such as name, company, address, and phone.

It's easier to build a data file first, so you can use the field names that you create, in the form document. Field names are used to identify the merge field codes that you create. For example, a typical data file might contain these fields: Name, Company, Address, City, State, Zip, Phone, Fax, and Email. Field names are optional, though—you can use Field1, Field2, Field3, and so on, if you prefer.

The main thing to keep in mind when you're creating the data file is that more fields mean more flexibility. For example, if you have three separate fields (instead of one field) for the city, state, and Zip code, you can sort the list by Zip code. The same goes for the name—if you use one field for first name and one field for last name, you can arrange the records by the last name, and you can break out the first name for a personalized salutation. Each field can be acted on individually.

Creating a Data File

It's easy to create a data file from scratch, but before you do, be sure you don't already have the information stored somewhere else. You can transfer information from other sources into a merge data file in several ways. You might have a little cleanup to do, but at least you aren't entering the information all over again. If you already have a file to work with, you can skip to the next section, "Importing Data into Merge Data Files," which contains information on importing data into merge data files.

Follow these steps to create a data file from scratch:

1. Choose **Tools**, **Merge** (**Shift+F9**) to display the Merge dialog box (see Figure 14.1).

2. Click **Data source** to open the list of data sources that can be used in a merge.

3. Click **Create Data File** at the bottom of the list of data sources to display the Create Data File dialog box (see Figure 14.2). This is where you create the field names.

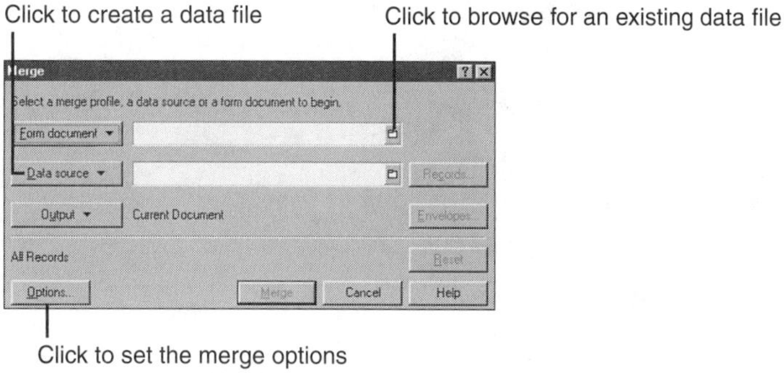

Click to create a data file   Click to browse for an existing data file

FIGURE 14.1

Use the Merge
dialog box to set
up a data file
and a form doc-
ument, and then
merge the two.

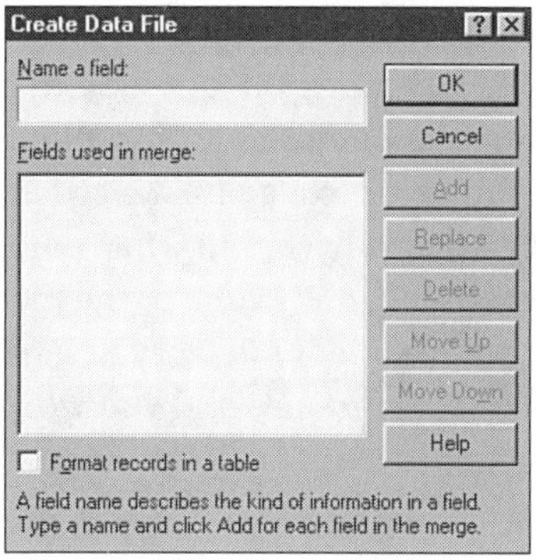

Click to set the merge options

FIGURE 14.2

In the Create
Data File dialog
box, you can
create and edit
the field names
for the data file.

4. Type the first field name in the **Name a field** text box. A field name can be up to 40 characters long, and it can contain spaces.

5. Press **Enter** or click **Add** to insert the field name in the **Fields used in merge** list box.

6. Repeat steps 3 and 4 until you've entered all the field names. If you misspell a field name or change your mind, select the field, and then choose **Delete**. The order of the field names is important because this is the order in which you'll type the information. If you need to rearrange the field names, select a name and click **Move Up** or **Move Down**. Figure 14.3 shows a typical list of field names.

7. If you want the records formatted into a table, click the **Format records in a table** check box.

FIGURE 14.3

Here is a list of field names that you might use for a merge data file.

Formatting a data file in a table has many advantages. In a table, each field has its own column, and each row is one record. Data files that aren't formatted as a table contain special codes, called merge codes, that separate the fields and records. You must be especially careful when editing this type of data file so that you don't accidentally delete one of the merge codes. The one disadvantage is that if you have a lot of fields, you'll get a table with lots of columns, so it's harder to navigate around, and you won't be able to see all the information on one screen.

8. Click **OK** when you're finished. The Quick Data Entry dialog box appears (see Figure 14.4). You can use this dialog box to enter and edit records in the data file.

FIGURE 14.4

Most people prefer using the Quick Data Entry dialog box for creating and editing records in the data file.

When you are ready to enter data into a merge date file, the Quick Data Entry dialog box is definitely the way to go. It simplifies the process of getting the information into the right fields and makes it easy for you to move back and forth between the records. As you enter the data, remember not to use extra spaces or punctuation.

All the formatting, punctuation, and placement of the information is done in the form file.

1. Type the data for the first field. Don't include extra spaces or punctuation marks when you enter the data; for example, don't type a comma after the city. All formatting and punctuation marks should be in the form document.

2. Press **Enter** or **Tab** (or choose **Ne_x_t Field**) to move down to the next field. Press **Shift+Tab** (or choose **Pre_v_ious Field**) to move back up a field.

3. Continue entering the information in each field. When you press **Enter** in the last field, a new record is created. You also can choose **New _R_ecord** from any field to create a blank record.

4. Click **_C_lose** when you're finished entering data.

5. Click **Yes** to save the data file to disk. The Save File dialog box appears.

6. Type a name for the data file in the **File _n_ame** text box, and then click **_S_ave**.

When the Save File dialog box closes, you can see the data that you've entered so far. Figure 14.5 shows the data in table format. Notice that the Merge feature bar has been added to the top of the screen. The generic property bar has also morphed into the table property bar with lots of buttons for working with tables.

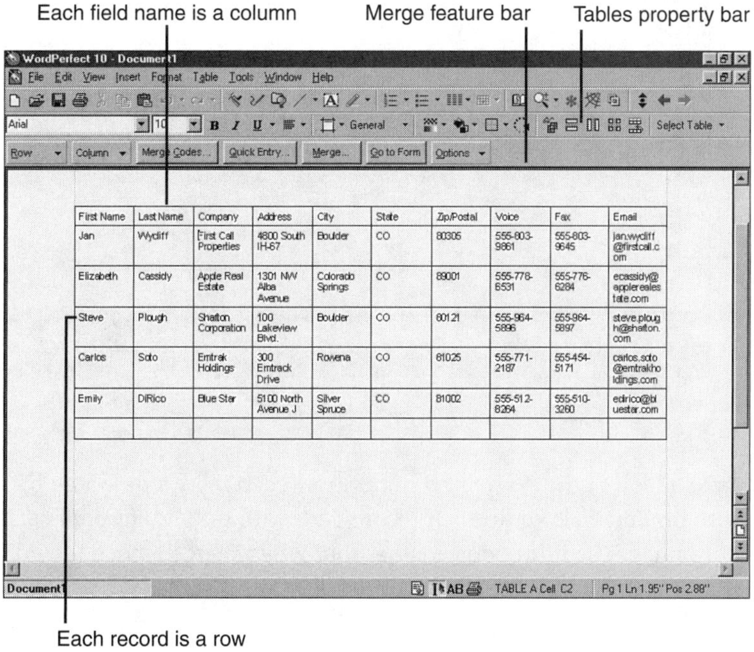

Each field name is a column   Merge feature bar   Tables property bar

FIGURE 14.5

Formatting the records in a table has many advantages. Not only is it easier to read the information in table format, but you can easily manipulate the data with the buttons on the table property bar.

Each record is a row

After you've finished entering the information, you can always go back and edit it later. You can add and edit records directly (in the table), or you can click the **Quick Entry** button on the Merge feature bar to open the Quick Data Entry dialog box.

If you need to edit the field names, you have to do so from the Quick Data Entry dialog box (refer to Figure 14.4). Click the **Field Names** button to open the Edit Field Names dialog box, where you can add, rename, and delete field names.

Importing Data into Merge Data Files

You can use files from other applications as data files, and in some cases, you won't need to convert them before the merge. In addition to files from other word processing programs, WordPerfect supports the import of data files created in spreadsheet and database programs. If field names were used in the source application, they are recognized and used by WordPerfect (see Figure 14.6).

Field name record   Records are separated by a hard page

FIGURE 14.6

This text data file has a field name record, so the fields can be identified by name rather than by number.

Each record ends with an End Record code

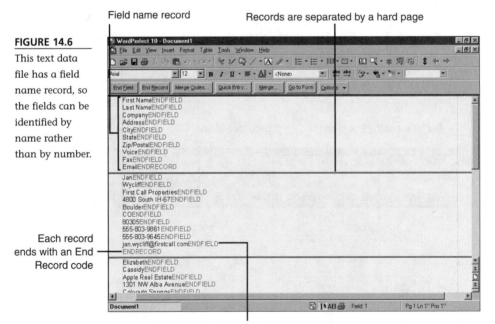

Each field ends with an End Field code

Take a look at the figure and notice how each field is on a line by itself and ends with an End Field code. Each record ends with an End Record code, followed by a hard page. The hard page ensures that when merged, each record is on a page by itself.

For detailed information on importing data from other word processors, personal information managers, and spreadsheet and database programs, open the Help Topics dialog box and click the Contents tab. Scroll down and open the **Merging documents** category. Open the **Converting merge files** category. Double-click the **Converting merge files** topic.

Creating Form Files

If you've gotten this far, take heart—you're in the home stretch! Creating the form file is the easy part, and if you've already typed the document, you're almost finished. An existing document can be turned into a form file in seconds. You just insert the merge codes and save the document. Voilà! It's ready for a merge.

If you create the form file from scratch, this is the where you want to set up all the formatting for the merged documents. You definitely don't want to put punctuation or formatting codes in the data file; otherwise, it is duplicated over and over again.

If you want to convert an existing document to a form document, open it now. Otherwise, create a new document and type any text that you need to precede the information that will be inserted during the merge.

To create a form file:

1. Choose **Tools**, **Merge** (**Shift+F9**) to open the Merge dialog box (refer to Figure 14.1).

2. Click **Form document** to open a drop-down list of options (see Figure 14.7).

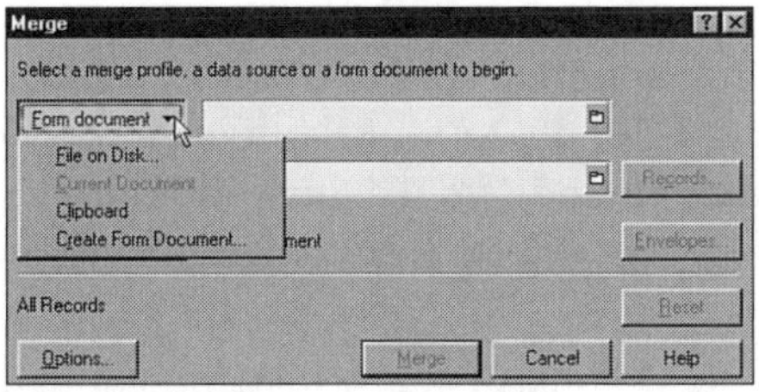

FIGURE 14.7

You can convert the current document into a form document, or you can create a form document from scratch.

3. Choose **Create Form Document**. If you already have a document open, you'll have to click **Use File in Active Window** in the Data File Source dialog box. The Associate Form and Data dialog box appears (see Figure 14.8).

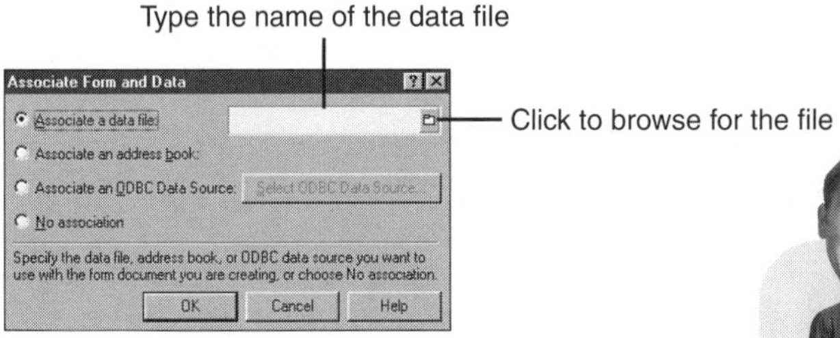

Type the name of the data file

FIGURE 14.8

You can specify a data file or other data source to use with this form document in the Associate Form and Data dialog box.

Click to browse for the file

4. Type the name of the data file in the **Associate a data file** text box, or click the **Files** icon to search for the file. If you haven't created the data file yet, or you don't know where it is, choose **No association**.

5. Click **OK**. WordPerfect adds the Merge feature bar at the top of the document (see Figure 14.9). This document is now marked as a form document.

note

If you associated a data file in step 4, that file is now tied to this one. Whenever you need to edit the data, just click the **Go to Data** button on the Merge feature bar. WordPerfect opens the data file in another window and switches you to that window. To go back to the form document, click the **Go to Form** button in the data file window.

The only difference between a form document and a regular document is that a form document contains merge codes. A merge code acts as a placeholder for the information that will come in from the data file. For example, you insert a merge field code for the Name field into a form document. When you merge the form document with the data file, the data from the Name field replaces the Name merge code. The result is a personalized letter, not a document full of merge field codes.

Remember that punctuation marks, spaces, blank lines, and any formatting that you want applied to the text is done in the form file. If you added commas, periods, or extra spaces to the data in the form file and in the data file, you'll get duplicates in the merge results.

1. Position the insertion point where you want to insert the first piece of information. For example, in a typical mail merge, you insert the name and address information at the top of the letter.

2. Click the **Insert Field** button on the Merge feature bar. The Insert Field Name or Number dialog box appears (see Figure 14.10). The field names (or numbers) in the associated data file appear in the Field Names list box.

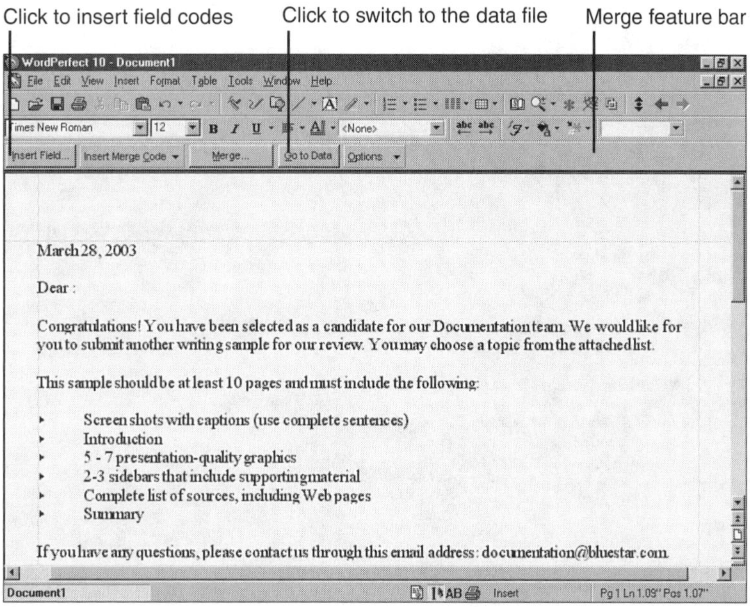

Click to insert field codes   Click to switch to the data file   Merge feature bar

FIGURE 14.9

The Merge fea-
ture bar is
included in
every form docu-
ment and data
file that you
create.

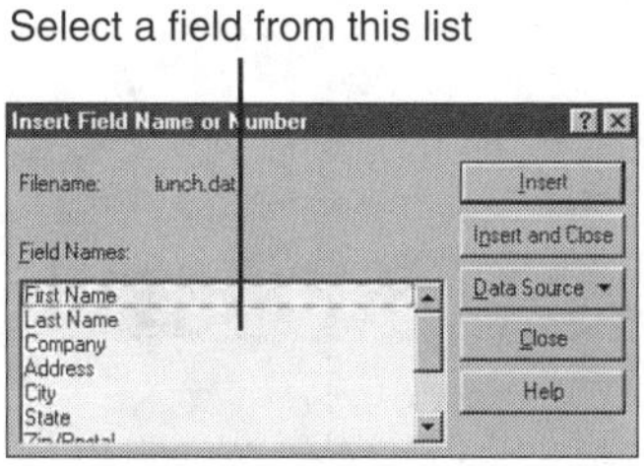

Select a field from this list

FIGURE 14.10

Select a field
name to insert
in the Insert
Field Name or
Number
dialog box.

3. Double-click a field name to insert it in the document at the location of the insertion point. WordPerfect inserts the field name (or number) in parentheses, preceded by FIELD (see Figure 14.11).

4. Continue inserting field names until you complete the form document. Be sure to include the necessary spaces, commas, or other punctuation between field names.

5. Click **Close** to close the Insert Field Name or Number dialog box. Figure 14.12 shows a sample letter with the mailing address and salutation field codes.

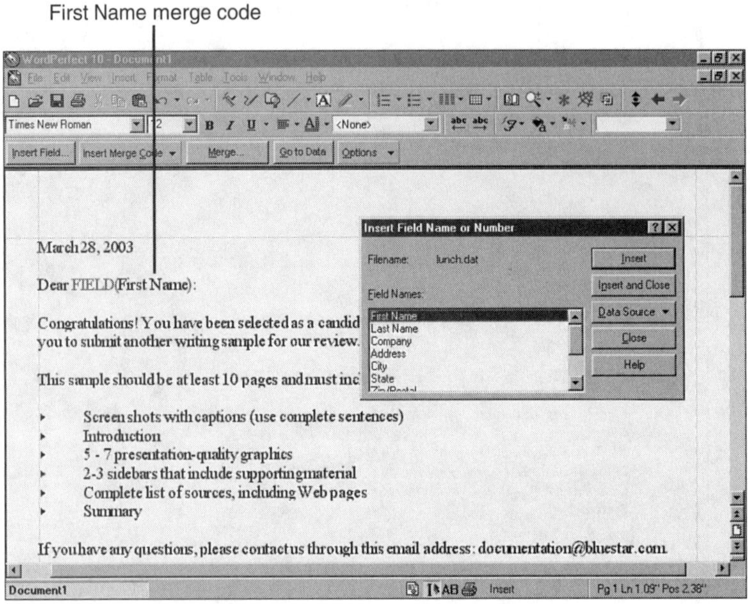

First Name merge code

FIGURE 14.11

Merge codes are displayed in a different color to make them easier to see in the text.

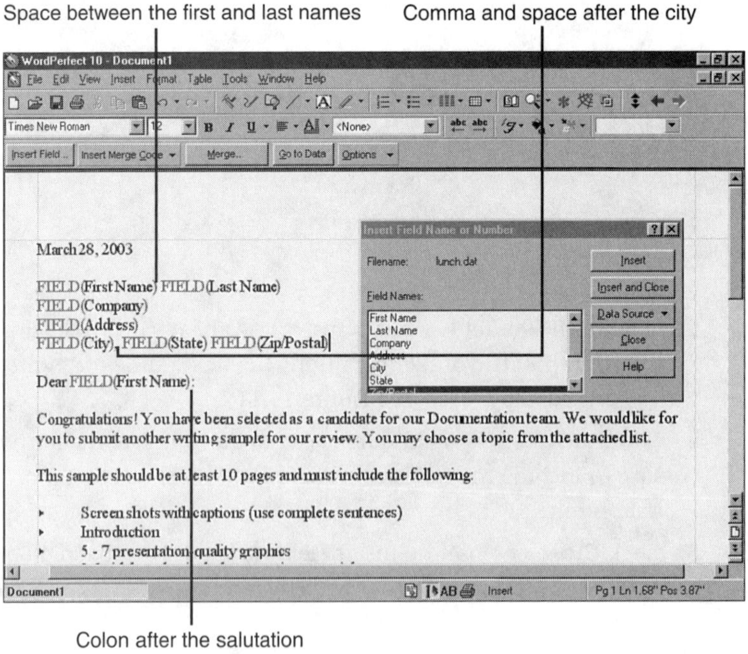

Space between the first and last names   Comma and space after the city

FIGURE 14.12

The mailing address block and salutation will be filled in with information from the data file.

Colon after the salutation

The most straightforward use of the Merge feature is to set up a mail merge, where you are merging a letter with a list of addresses. It's important to emphasize that the Merge feature can be used for much more. An invoice or billing statement could be merged with a database file. A loan application, where the same information is plugged into a thousand different places, could be generated in a merge with spreadsheet data as a data source. Or maybe someday you'll need to create 300 "Hello...My Name Is" labels for your high-school reunion. There are infinite possibilities.

> **tip**
>
> Instead of typing in the date, you can insert a merge code that inserts the date for you when you run the merge. Click the **Insert Merge Code** button then select **Date**.

Merging the Data and Form Files Together

Now that you've got a form document and a data file, you're ready to go! If the form document or data file is open, you can click the **Merge** button on the Merge feature bar. Otherwise, choose **Tools**, **Merge**, **Merge** to open the Merge dialog box (see Figure 14.13).

FIGURE 14.13

You can select a form document, a data file, and the output location in the Merge dialog box.

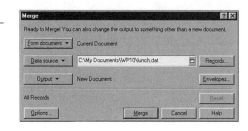

Your dialog box selections will vary depending on what files you have open:

- ▓ If you click the Merge button from the form document, the Form document button is set to Current Document.
- ▓ If you associated the form document with a data file, the name of that file appears next to the Data source button.
- ▓ If you click the Merge button from the data file, the name of the file appears next to the Data source button.
- ▓ If the data file is already associated with a form document, the name of that document appears next to the Form document button. Otherwise, you'll need to type the filename next to Form document or click the Files icon to search for the file.

■ If you aren't running the merge from either document, you see a blank text box next to <u>F</u>orm document and <u>D</u>ata source.

In any case, you need to fill in the blanks by typing the names of the files or clicking the **Files** icon to search for them. By default, O<u>u</u>tput is set to New Document. You can also set the merge to create the results in the <u>C</u>urrent Document.

To change the output setting, click the **O<u>u</u>tput** drop-down list arrow to see the other three options:

■ **Printer**—Sends the output directly to the printer.

■ **File on Disk**—Creates a file and places the output in the file.

■ **Email**—Sends the output via electronic mail. See the section "Merging to Email," later in this chapter, for more information.

When you have everything filled in, click **<u>Merge</u>**. WordPerfect matches up the field names/numbers in the form file and the field names/numbers in the data file and inserts the information into the form. When a merge is complete, the insertion point is always on the last line of the last page, so don't panic if you don't see the letters right away. Figure 14.14 shows the results of a mail merge.

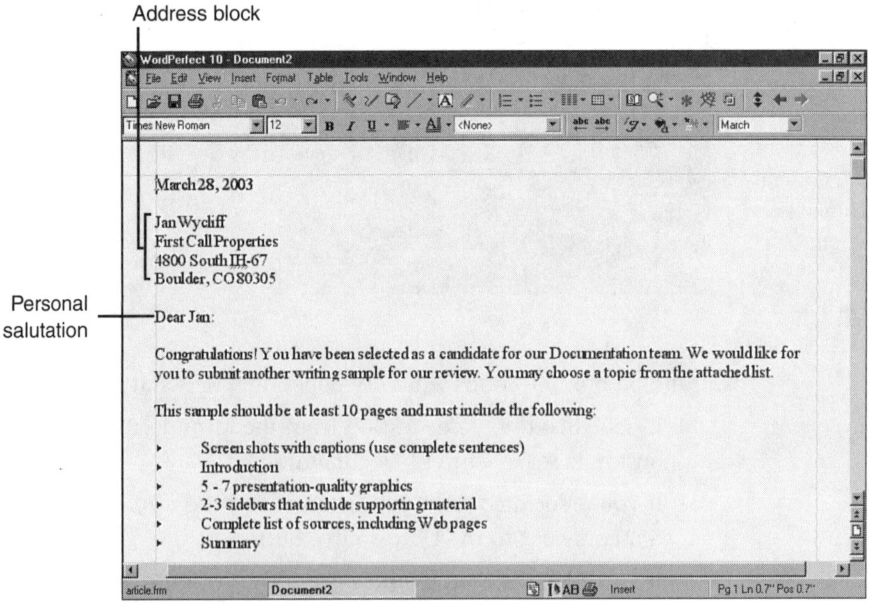

FIGURE 14.14
WordPerfect pulls information from the data file, inserts it into the form document, and creates a new set of documents.

Address block

Personal salutation

Congratulations! You just completed a merge! It might seem like a lot of work at first, but if you consider how much time you would spend creating a separate document for each individual, it's time well spent. I should also point out that you can reuse the data file over and over again, so once you've created that file, you don't have to repeat those steps.

Unfortunately, the results of a merge might not turn out the way you had planned. Don't worry, with just a few minor adjustments, you can sort things out. First, take a good look at the results and see whether you can detect a pattern. Is the state where the city should be? Are all the last names missing, or just one or two? When you're ready to proceed, close the merge results document without saving.

If you're having the same problem over and over, start with the form document. Make sure you have the right field codes in the right places. If you need to change a field code, select and delete the code, and then reinsert it. Save your changes and try the merge again.

If the problem occurs just in one or two entries, go straight to the data file and take a look at the records giving you trouble. Make sure the right information is in the right field. You might have actually typed the state in the city field by accident. Save your changes and try the merge again.

Creating Envelopes

If you are working on a group of letters, you'll need envelopes or labels for them. Envelopes can be created during a merge so that everything is generated together. For labels, you'll need to create a label form document and merge that form with the data file in separate merge.

To generate envelopes during a merge:

1. Open the form document for the merge.
2. Choose **Tools**, **Merge** to open the Merge dialog box.
3. Click **Envelopes**. WordPerfect opens an envelope form document. If necessary, type the return address (or leave it out if your envelopes are preprinted).
4. Press **Ctrl+End** to move down to the mailing address block. If necessary, delete the text in the mailing address block.
5. Click the **Insert Field** button to open the Insert Field Name or Number dialog box.
6. Double-click a field name (or number) to insert the field code. Include all the necessary spacing and punctuation between the fields (see Figure 14.15).

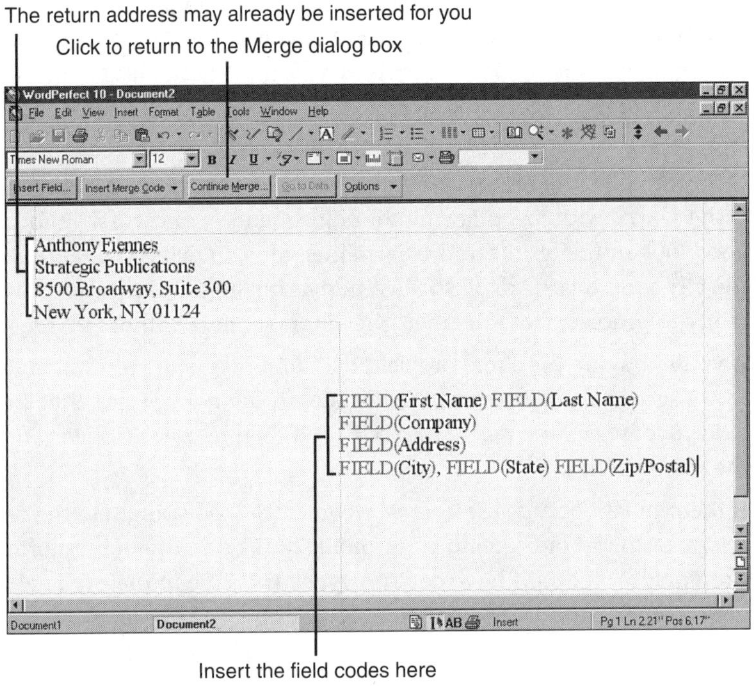

The return address may already be inserted for you

Click to return to the Merge dialog box

FIGURE 14.15

Creating the envelope during a merge has an advantage: WordPerfect creates the envelope form document and integrates it into the merge process.

Insert the field codes here

7. Click **Continue Merge** when you're finished. The Merge dialog box appears.

8. If necessary, specify a form document, a data file, and an output location.

9. Click **Merge**.

Creating Labels

Creating labels isn't integrated in the merge process, so you'll need to create a labels form to use with the data file. It doesn't take long—just a few minutes to locate the correct label definition.

To create labels during a merge:

1. If you've already defined the label form, you can skip to step 4. Otherwise, in a blank document, choose **Format**, **Labels** to open the Labels dialog box (see Figure 14.16).

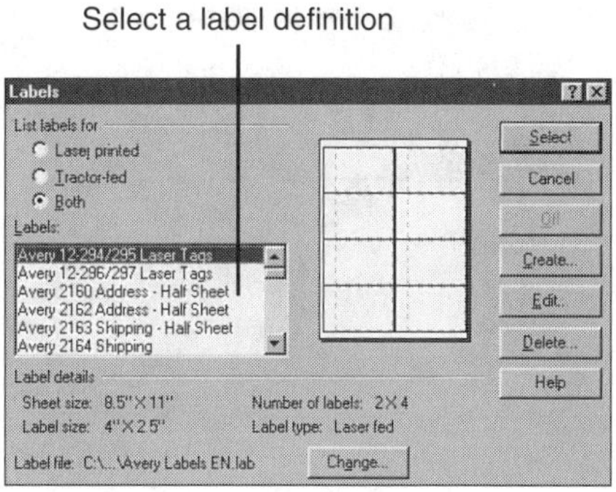

Select a label definition

FIGURE 14.16

You can choose label definitions for both laser-printed and tractor-fed printers in the Labels dialog box.

2. Click **Laser printed** or **Tractor-fed** to narrow down the list, and then select the label definition that matches your labels.

3. Click **Select** to insert the definition in the document.

4. Choose **Tools**, **Merge** to open the Merge dialog box.

5. Choose **Form Document**, **Create Form Document**, **Use File in Active Window** to display the Associate Form and Data dialog box.

6. Specify a data source and then click **OK**. The Merge feature bar appears in the label document.

7. Click the **Insert Field** button to open the Insert Field Name or Number dialog box.

8. Double-click a field name to insert it in the label. Be sure you include all the spacing and punctuation between the fields.

9. When you're finished inserting field codes, click **Close** to close the Insert Field Name or Number dialog box. Figure 14.17 shows a completed label form.

10. Click the **Merge** button on the feature bar to open the Merge dialog box.

11. Verify the data source and output location, and then click **Merge** to create the labels.

note

Just because your label isn't listed in the Labels box doesn't mean the definition doesn't exist. Check the layout (such as 3 columns by 10 rows) or the dimensions, and compare them to the definitions in the list. You'll probably find an exact match (or at least a close approximation).

caution

If every other label is blank, there is an extra page break at the bottom of the label in the form file. Close this document without saving and switch back to the label form document. Position the insertion point at the end of the address and press **Delete** until only one label is displayed. Try the merge again.

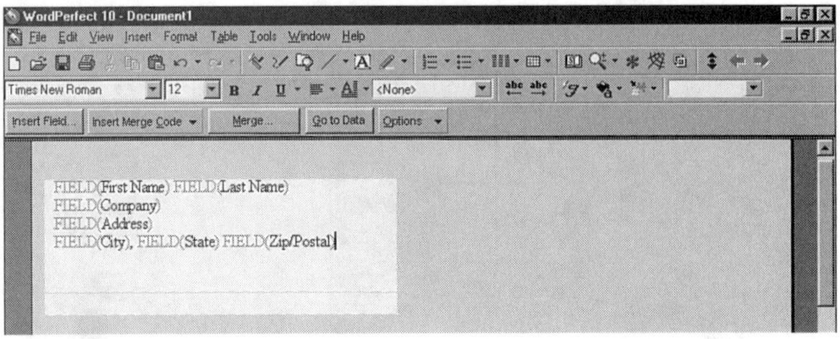

FIGURE 14.17

This form document is actually a sheet of labels, which will be filled in during the merge.

Creating Fill-in-the-Blank Forms

A typical form has a series of blanks that you need to fill in. The blanks are labeled so you know what should be entered. Electronic forms work the same way. The items that don't change are the titles and labels so they are "fixed." The rest of the form is set aside for individual responses, which are variable.

A form document can be designed with merge codes that stop and wait for the user to type in the variable information. You can even create a message that explains what the user should be typing at this point. After the information has been entered, the merge moves on to the next code.

The Merge feature is used to fill in the form. The difference is that you merge data using the keyboard rather than a data file. Existing documents can be converted into fill-in-the-blank merge forms in just minutes.

To create a fill-in-the-blank form:

1. If you've already created the document, open it now. Otherwise, type the titles and labels that won't change. Figure 14.18 shows a fax cover sheet with the labels and the company name typed in. This is the information that doesn't change.

tip

You can create a sheet of identical labels with the Merge feature. Create the label form and type the text of the label. Choose **Tools**, **Merge**. In the Merge dialog box, be sure Form document is set to Current Document and Data source is set to None. Click **Options**. Type the number of labels on the page in the Number of copies for each record text box. Click **Merge**.

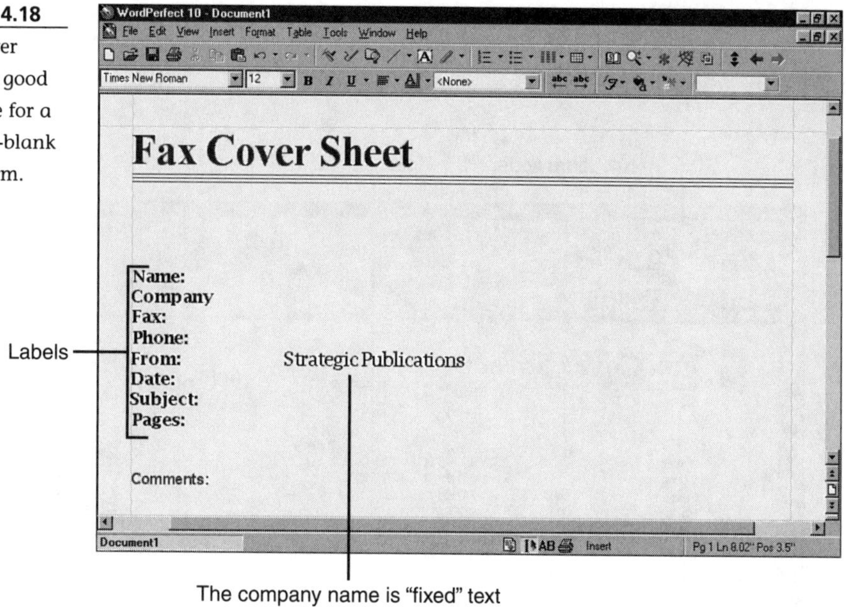

FIGURE 14.18

A fax cover sheet is a good candidate for a fill-in-the-blank merge form.

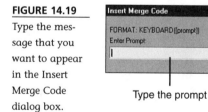

Labels ─────

The company name is "fixed" text

2. Choose **Tools**, **Merge** to open the Merge dialog box.

3. Click the **Form Document** button and choose **Create Form Document** from the drop-down list.

4. Click **Use File in Active** Window in the Data Source dialog box.

5. In the Associate Form and Data dialog box, click **No Association**.

6. Click in the document where you want to insert the Keyboard code.

7. Click the **Insert Merge Code** button and then choose **Keyboard** to open the Insert Merge Code dialog box (see Figure 14.19).

FIGURE 14.19

Type the message that you want to appear in the Insert Merge Code dialog box.

Type the prompt

8. Type the prompt text that you want to appear, and then click **OK** to insert the Keyboard code in the form.

9. Repeat steps 4–6 to insert any other prompts for this form document. Figure 14.20 shows a form document with five Keyboard codes that prompt for the heading information.

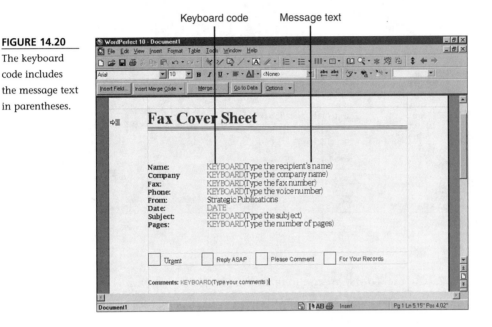

FIGURE 14.20

The keyboard code includes the message text in parentheses.

10. When you're ready to fill in the form, click the **Merge** button on the Merge feature bar.

11. Verify the location of the data file (if there is one), the form document, and the output; then click **Merge**. When a keyboard command is encountered, the merge pauses and displays the prompt message (see Figure 14.21). When the message box is displayed, the insertion point is positioned right where the keyboard code was, so this is where you will enter the information. You'll enter the text directly into the document, not into the message box.

12. Type the requested information, and then click the **Continue** button on the Merge feature bar to continue the merge.

tip

You can get the best of both worlds by combining a typical merge of a data file and form document with the flexibility of a fill-in-the-blank form. Just include keyboard codes in the form document where you want the user to type the information. The rest of the fields can be filled in from the data file.

Click to continue the merge   Click to halt the merge

FIGURE 14.21

The prompt message that you type is displayed in a window at the bottom of the screen.

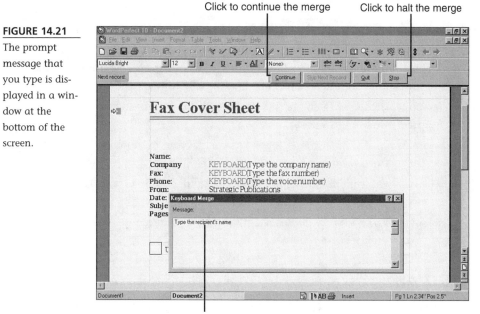

Message text

When you are finished entering information for all the keyboard codes, the merge process stops. The message box and the merge toolbar are cleared off the screen. At this point, you can either save or print the document.

THE ABSOLUTE MINIMUM

This chapter is the first in a section of chapters that explain how to use some of WordPerfect's automation tools. The chapter explains how to use the Merge feature to generate a batch of letters, envelopes, labels, and forms.

- You learned how to create a data file with the information that you want to insert into the form document.

- You learned how to create form documents from existing documents and from scratch.

- When you were finished creating the data file and the form document, you merged the two.

- Envelopes can be created as a part of the original merge operation; labels are created in a separate merge.

- The Keyboard merge code can be used to create fill-in-the-blank forms, complete with messages to prompt the user.

In the next chapter, you'll learn how to use Corel's Address Book to keep track of names, addresses, and other personal information. You'll also learn how to use the Address Book as the data source in a merge.

IN THIS CHAPTER

- Learn how to create address books and add and delete entries.

- Learn how to move and copy address book entries between address books.

- Discover how to import and export address books and edit address books created in other applications.

- Learn how to organize address book entries to make it easier to locate information.

- Understand the role of an address book as a data source in a merge operation.

15

USING THE ADDRESS BOOK

Everyone I know has an address book of some sort. Mine is battered and torn from years of use. Instead of buying a new book and rewriting all the information, I decided to create my address books in CorelCENTRAL. It's much easier to edit an electronic address book than it is a written copy. Plus, you can use the address book information in a merge, so you can have WordPerfect print the labels for your holiday cards.

Address books created in other applications can be opened and edited in CorelCENTRAL so that you can bring all your information together in one place. Entries can be freely moved and copied between books, so you'll never type an entry twice.

The CorelCENTRAL Address Book

The Address Book is one of the programs in the CorelCENTRAL "mini-suite" of applications. CorelCENTRAL is the PIM (Personal Information Manager) application included in the Corel WordPerfect Office 2002 Academic, Standard, or Professional version. CorelCENTRAL can be used to plan your schedule, maintain contact and reference information, write daily reminders, and send and receive email.

The CorelCENTRAL Address Book is tightly integrated with WordPerfect. You can keep track of any type of information: phone and fax numbers, addresses, email addresses, birthdays, personal greetings, job titles, assistant and supervisor names, and so on. You can then use this information with the Merge feature to broadcast documents and email messages.

If you have other address books on your system, you can open them in the CorelCENTRAL Address Book window so you can maintain a centralized database of contact information and still use the other address books on your system.

Starting the CorelCENTRAL Address Book

When you start CorelCENTRAL Address Book for the first time, you'll have to either open an existing address book or create a new address book, before you can actually get into the program. For this reason, you'll have a take a few more steps the first time. After you've opened an existing address book or created a new address book, you'll get straight into the CorelCENTRAL Address Book application window. For the sake of keeping things simple, you'll create a personal address book rather than a shared address book in the following steps.

To start the CorelCENTRAL Address Book:

1. Start WordPerfect.

2. Choose **Tools**, **Address Book**. The first time you open the CorelCENTRAL Address Book, a welcome message box appears (see Figure 15.1).

> **note**
>
> If you received a copy of the WordPerfect Productivity Pack with your new computer, you might not have access to CorelCENTRAL. If the computer is a Sony, it comes with the standard version of WordPerfect Office 2002, so you have access to CorelCENTRAL and the Address Book. If you purchased a system from Hewlett-Packard, Dell, or Gateway, your free copy of the Productivity Pack does not include CorelCENTRAL. If you are interested in getting CorelCENTRAL, you can upgrade to the Standard or Professional version of Corel WordPerfect Suite 2002. Contact Corel at 800-77COREL for more information.

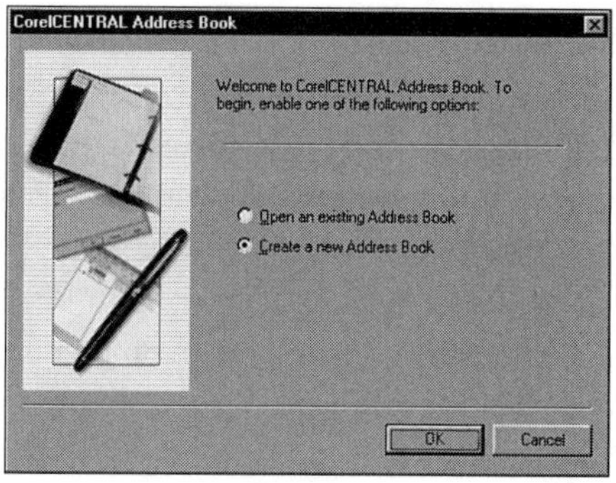

FIGURE 15.1

The first time you open the CorelCENTRAL Address Book, you'll have to create a new address book or open an existing address book.

3. Select one of the following options:

■ **Create a new Address Book**—This option takes you through the steps to create a new address book. Click **Next** to move to the next screen. Select **Personal**; then click **Next**. Type a name in the **Address Book Name** text box; then click **Finish**. Click **Yes** to create a directory for the new address book.

■ **Open an existing Address Book**—This option allows you to select an existing address book on your system. Select **Personal** or **Shared With Others**, depending on how the address book was set up; then click **Next**. If you selected Personal, you'll see a list of available address books on your system. Select an address book, and then click **Finish**. If you selected Shared With Others, you'll have to specify a location and name for the book that you want to open (your system administrator will have this information). After you locate the book, click **Finish**.

The CorelCENTRAL Address Book application window opens with the newly created address book selected (see Figure 15.2).

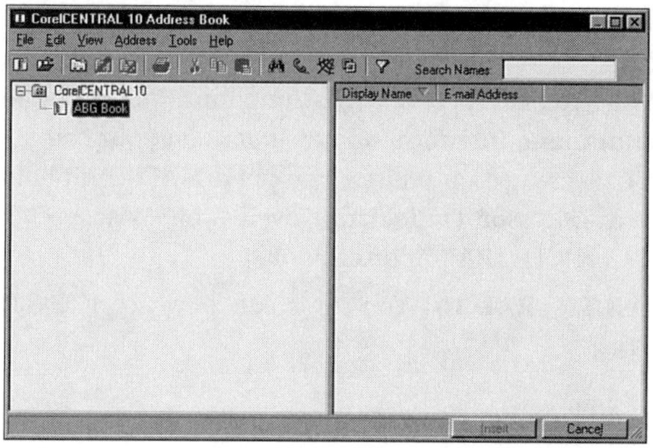

FIGURE 15.2

A newly created address book is selected in the left pane.

Creating New Address Books

The Address Book is designed to store a wide variety of information on individuals, organizations, resources, and groups. You can create books with contact names for each project you are involved in. Another address book might be created for your holiday greetings address list, yet another for the names of the children in your child's classroom. The possibilities are as varied as the people who use it.

After you've created (or opened) that first address book, you'll go straight into the CorelCENTRAL Address Book application window. You can create more address books from there.

To create new address books in the CorelCENTRAL Address Book application window:

 1. Click the **Create a New Address Book** button (**Ctrl+N**) on the CorelCENTRAL toolbar. The New Address Book dialog box opens (see Figure 15.3).

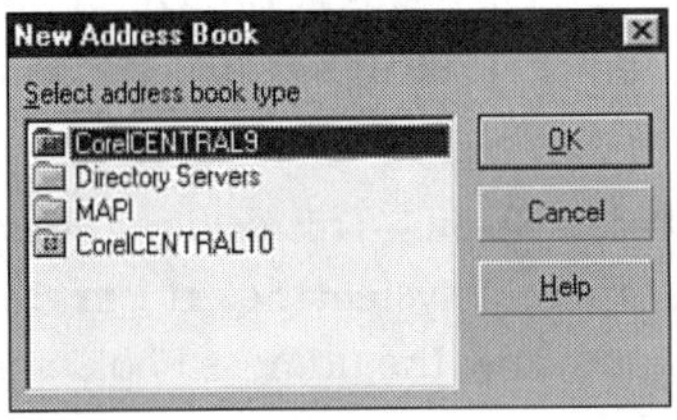

FIGURE 15.3

You can choose the type of address book you want to create in the New Address Book dialog box.

2. Select the type of address book that you want to create:

- **CorelCENTRAL 9**—You can create an address book that can be opened and edited in CorelCENTRAL 9, which was included with Corel WordPerfect Suite 2000.

- **Directory Servers**—CorelCENTRAL Address Book lets you connect to and open directory server address books using Lightweight Direct Access Protocol (LDAP).

- **MAPI**—You can access MAPI-compliant (Messaging Application Programming Interface) address books on your computer. For example, if you've created an address book in a MAPI-compliant application, such as Microsoft Outlook or Novell GroupWise, you can open and edit it in CorelCENTRAL Address Book.

- **CorelCENTRAL 10**—You can create new CorelCENTRAL 10 address books.

Depending on the type of address book you select, you'll see other dialog boxes where you can specify a name and other properties for the new address book. When you are finished, the new address book is created, and the name appears in the left pane.

Adding Entries to an Address Book

After you create an address book, you can start adding entries to it. You can create four different types of address book entries: person, organization, resource, and group.

To add an entry to an address book:

1. Choose **Tools**, **Address Book** to open the CorelCENTRAL Address Book application window. Figure 15.4 shows several different types of address books and different types of entries.

Click to create a new address book
Click to create a new address book entry
Address book group

FIGURE 15.4

You can access your CorelCENTRAL address books and other address books on your system in CorelCENTRAL Address Book.

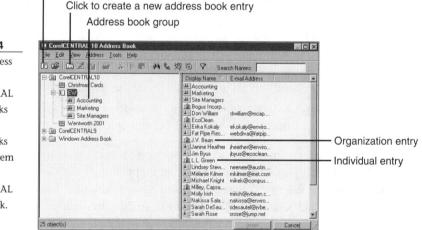

Organization entry
Individual entry

 2. Click the **Create a New Entry** button on the toolbar. The New dialog box appears (see Figure 15.5).

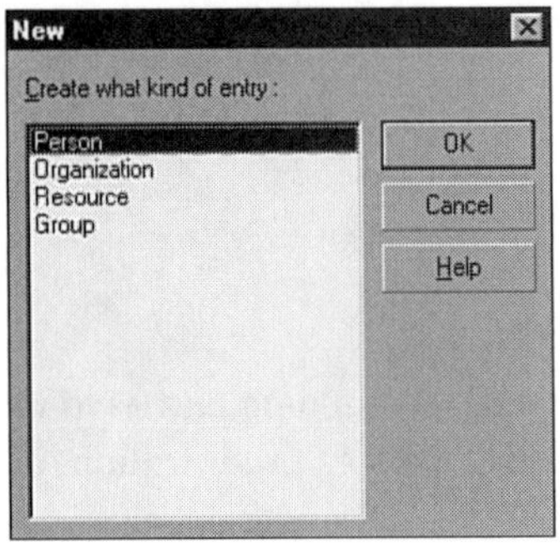

FIGURE 15.5

Select the type of
entry you want
to create from
the New dialog
box.

FIGURE 15.5

Select the type of
entry you want
to create from
the New dialog
box.

3. In the New dialog box, select a type of entry to create:

- **Person**—This is the most comprehensive entry you can create. There are seven tabs where you can organize the information: General, Personal, Address, Phone/Fax, Business, Certificate, and Security.

- **Organization**—This is a subset of the Person record, with four tabs: General, Address, Phone/Fax, and Security.

- **Resource**—You can maintain records on your company resources by identifying the name and type of the resource, the owner, the main phone number, the category, and comments. A resource might be a conference room, projection unit, videoconferencing equipment, or laptop.

- **Group**—You can create a group of address book records to make it easier to broadcast messages and general correspondence.

Depending on the type of entry you select, a blank record opens up for you to fill in. Figure 15.6 shows an entry form for the Person category on the General tab. Type the information in the fields, pressing **Tab** to move to the next field and **Shift+Tab** to move back a field. Click the other tabs to enter data in additional fields.

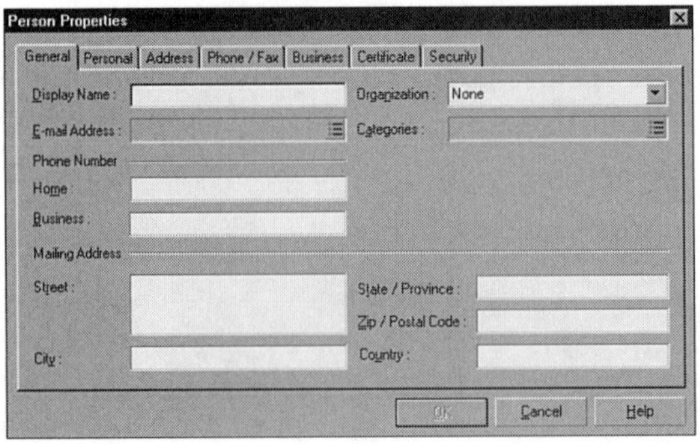

FIGURE 15.6

The Person
Properties dialog
box has seven
tabs to help you
organize data for
an individual.

Working with Address Book Entries

Creating an address book and typing in the entries is only half the battle. Someone has to maintain the information, right? Those pesky clients keep changing their cell phone numbers and email addresses, so you have to stay on top of things to keep your information current. Thankfully, working with address book entries is a breeze in CorelCENTRAL. You have many options for editing, deleting (be careful here), moving and copying records between books, printing entries, and searching for information.

To edit an address book entry:

1. Double-click the person, organization, or resource entry in the list to edit the information, or select the entry and then click the **Edit an Address Entry** button.

2. Make your changes.

3. Click **OK** to save the changes or **Cancel** to discard the changes.

If you don't need an address book, or a single address book entry, you can delete it. To delete an address book entry:

1. Select one or more entries. Use the **Shift** key to select consecutive entries, or the **Ctrl** key to select entries scattered throughout the list.

2. Click the **Delete an Address Entry** button, or press **Delete** on the keyboard. You can also right-click the selection and choose **Delete**.

3. Click **Yes** to confirm the deletion, or **No** to bail out and keep the entry.

To move entries to another address book:

1. Select the entries in the list.

2. Click and drag the selected entries over to an address book in the left pane, as seen in Figure 15.7.

3. When the correct address book is high-lighted, release the mouse button to move the entries.

caution

Be very, very careful when you delete records in an address book. No Undo feature can restore an entry that you've deleted in error. The same is true for deleting an entire address book. The only way to recover an accidentally deleted address book is if you can restore the files from a backup. Consider this one more reason to back up regularly so that a recent copy of your address book is secure.

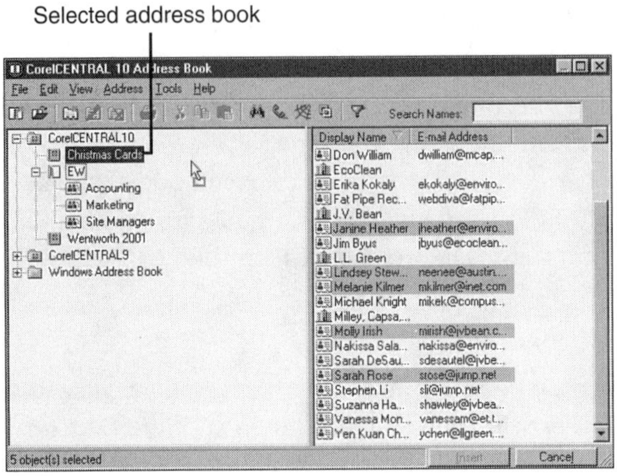

FIGURE 15.7

Clicking and
dragging
address book
entries is a quick
way to move
entries to
another book.

Selected address book

To copy entries to another address book:

1. Select the entries.

2. Choose **Edit**, **Copy**, or right-click the selection and choose **Copy**.

3. Open the other address book.

4. Choose **Edit**, **Paste**, or right-click in the right pane and choose **Paste**.

You can print the current record, selected records, or all the records. The records will print with the same fields displayed in the CorelCENTRAL Address Book window. If you want to print something else, you need to customize the columns in the right pane and then print.

To print address book entries:

1. Select one or more records.

2. Click the **Print** button on the toolbar (**Ctrl+P**) to open the Print dialog box.

3. Make the necessary selections; then click **Print**.

To search for text in address book entries:

1. Click the **Search for Specified Text** button, or choose **Edit**, **Find** (Ctrl+F) to open the Find dialog box.

2. Type the text you want to search for.

3. Click **OK**. If records are found that contain the search text, the dialog box expands and the records are listed below the Find text box (see Figure 15.8).

Text to search for

FIGURE 15.8

Type the text
you want to
search for in the
address book
entries in the
Find dialog box.

Search results

To send an email message to a contact:

1. Select an address book entry.

2. Choose **Tools**, **Mail** to start composing a
   mail message. If there is an email address
   in the selected record, it's automatically
   inserted into the message.

3. Finish creating the message, and then
   send it as you normally would.

Opening Other Address Books

The nice thing about CorelCENTRAL is that you
can access other address books created in other
programs. You have equal access to these address
books, so you can work with them in the same way that you work with the
CorelCENTRAL 10 address books. You can add your other address books to the list by
opening them in CorelCENTRAL 10 Address Book. If, for some reason, you aren't
able to open the address book in CorelCENTRAL 10, you might be able to export it
to a common file format and import it into CorelCENTRAL.

To open an existing address book:

1. Click the **Open an Existing Address Book** button, or choose **File**, **Open**
   (**Ctrl+O**) to display the Open Address Book dialog box (see Figure 15.9).

2. Choose which type of address book you want to open. The list of address
   types varies depending on what applications you have installed on your
   system.

3. Select from the list of available address books, or browse for the address
   books.

> **tip**
>
> CorelCENTRAL 10 Address
> Book includes Net2Phone
> Pro Version 10.4, a suite of
> utilities that let you place a
> call from your computer to
> another computer, to a fax,
> or to a phone. You can
> also send voice mail messages. For
> more information, look up the
> help topic "net2phone."

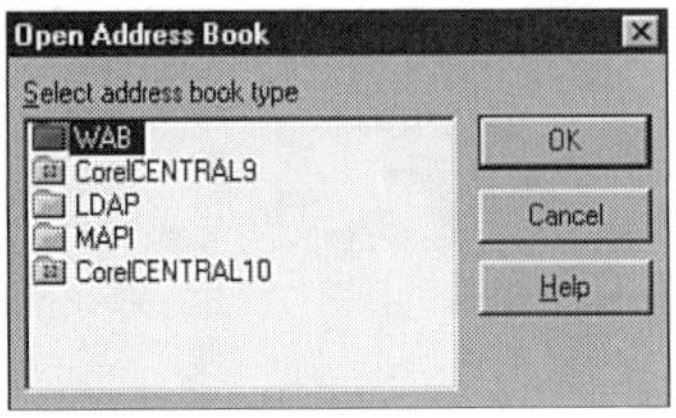

FIGURE 15.9

Choose which type of address book you want to open in the CorelCENTRAL 10 Address Book in the Open Address Book dialog box.

Importing and Exporting Address Books

If you're having trouble opening an existing address book in CorelCENTRAL 10, you might need to export the book into a common file format, such as ASCII, and then import it into CorelCENTRAL. You can use several different techniques to get the information into CorelCENTRAL 10. You also might want to export your address books from CorelCENTRAL 10 so that you can use them in another program.

- **Using the Import/Export Expert**—Corel designed this expert to walk you through the process of importing and exporting information. You can import address books from Corel Address Book 8 (.abx), text file format (.csv, .txt), Outlook 97/98/2000, and vcard (.vcf). You can export to text file format (.csv, .txt) and Outlook 97/98/2000.

- **Importing a merge data file**—If you want to add names and addresses that you have stored in a merge data file to an address book, you can convert the merge data file into a text file and import the text file into an address book. If you created the data file as a table, you can open and save the file as text without making any changes. Open the data file; then choose **File**, **Save As**. In the Save As dialog box, choose **ASCII (DOS) Delimited Text** from the **File type** drop-down list, and then save the file. Now, you can import this .txt file directly into the address book. See Chapter 14, "Using the Merge Feature," for more information on creating data files.

- **Importing spreadsheet and database files**—You can use information from spreadsheet programs, such as Quattro Pro or Excel, or database programs, such as Paradox or Access in CorelCENTRAL. First, save the file as an ASCII text file, which you can import directly into the Address Book. During the import process, you'll be able to "map," or match up, the field names from the ASCII text file with the Address Book field names, so you can be sure that the information from the text file is inserted in the right places.

- **Importing other address books**—If you can save the file to ASCII, you should be able to import it directly into the CorelCENTRAL 10 Address Book. During the import process, the field names used in the other address book will be listed next to the fields in the Corel Address Book. After you've matched up the field names, you can import the data.

- **Exporting to an ASCII text file**—If you want to use CorelCENTRAL address book data in another program, the universally accepted format is ASCII. After you've exported an address book to a text file (*.csv, *.txt), you can open, or import, the .txt file in another application.

OPENING EXISTING ADDRESS BOOKS AFTER A REINSTALL

In early releases of WordPerfect 10 (including Service Packs 1 and 2), there was a problem with opening existing CorelCENTRAL 10 address books after reinstalling WordPerfect 10. For example, after the initial install of WordPerfect 10, you create several CC10 address books. Service Pack 2 becomes available, so you uninstall WordPerfect and reinstall it with the service pack. When you try to open your CC10 address books, they don't show up. The folders are there under \my documents\ccwin10\addrbk, but when you try to open a CC10 address book, there are no personal address books in the list.

The workaround is to open the address books as shared Paradox address books. When prompted for the user ID and password, type **Administrator** for both items (with a capital "A"). After you've successfully opened the address books as shared, they should appear in the list and work just fine.

This issue was resolved in Service Pack 3. Call 800-77COREL to order SP3 on CD. The CD is free; the shipping and handling is about $10. You can download the English version from Corel's FTP site here: ftp://ftp.corel.com/pub/WordPerfect/wpwin/10/english/ WP02002SP3.exe. The file is approximately 85MB to download and approximately 192MB when extracted. As of this writing, SP3 wasn't available in other languages. Check the main WPWin 10 page to see whether other versions of SP3 are now available: ftp://ftp.corel.com/pub/WordPerfect/wpwin/10/.

Customizing the CorelCENTRAL Address Book Window

The default display settings in the CorelCENTRAL Address Book window might not be very useful to you, so you might be looking for a way to alter the display to make it easier to locate information. You can do this in several ways: You can change the column headings and display different fields, or you can sort the records to group certain records together. You can also set a filter and specify what criteria must be met for a record to be displayed.

To change the fields (columns) displayed in the records list:

1. Right-click a column heading to display the Columns dialog box. A list of all the fields (see Figure 15.10) appears. These settings can vary among address books.

2. Place a check mark next to each of the fields that you want to see listed. These settings "stick" with the address book, so you can customize the display of fields for each address book.

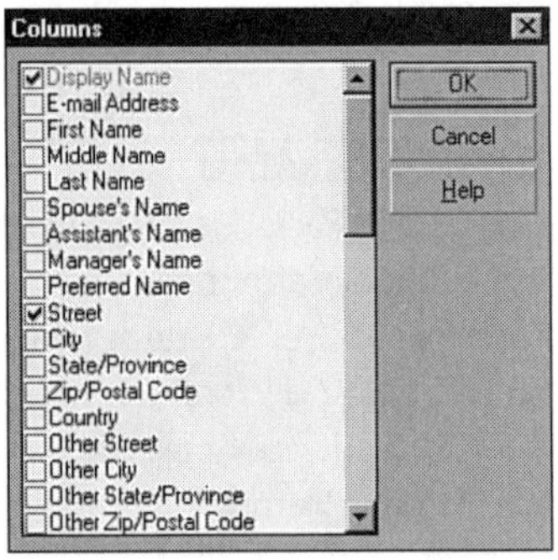

FIGURE 15.10

Mark the fields that you want displayed in the record list in the Columns dialog box.

Sorting address book records is one way to group related records together. After they are grouped together, you can quickly select them and work with the records as a group. For example, you might want to work with only those records in a certain state. Sorting in Zip code order can help you organize your records for a bulk mailing.

To sort the address book records:

1. Click the column heading for the field by which you want to sort. You can now select the sorted records for printing, email, or merging. For example, you can print labels in Zip code order if you sort the records by Zip code before selecting them.

2. Click the column heading again to reverse the sort (ascending to descending and vice versa). The arrow on the column heading shows you which direction the sort is done.

If you have an especially large address book and you want to be able to view only a certain group of entries, such as everyone at CompanyABC, you need to filter the entries. *Filtering* means that you tell the address book to show only the entries that include a specific criteria, such as a company name like CompanyABC. The rest of the entries in your address book seem to "disappear" when the entries are filtered; however, they are all still in the address book. They are just not being displayed. After you finish viewing the specific entries for CompanyABC, you can remove the filter, and all your entries will be visible again."

To set a filter for address book records:

1. Choose **View**, **Filter** or click the **Filter the Address Book** button to display the Filter dialog box (see Figure 15.11).

FIGURE 15.11

Specify the criteria that must be met for the record to be displayed in the list in the Filter dialog box.

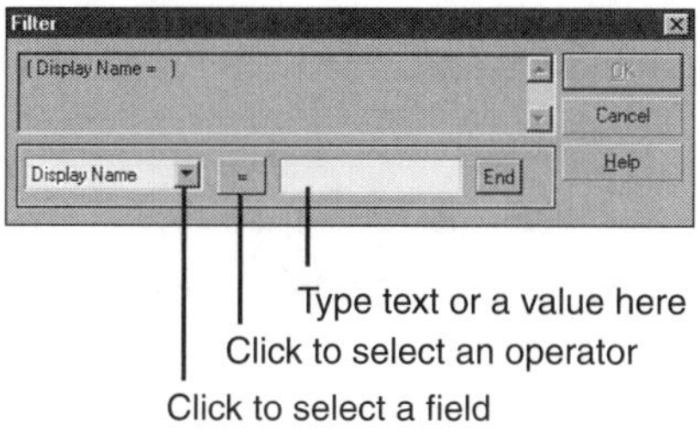

Type text or a value here
Click to select an operator
Click to select a field

2. Click the first drop-down list arrow and choose a field. These fields are the column heading names, and you are choosing the one that you want the entries to be filtered by.

3. Click the operator button between the list box and the text box. Until you change it, the button has an equal sign on it.

4. Select an operator from the list. The operators are used to narrow down the list. For example, you can filter out all the records with a ZIP Code of Greater Than 53600.

5. Type the text or value that you want to use as a filter in the text box, and then click **OK**. To continue the example in step 4, you would enter **53600** as the ZIP Code value. CorelCENTRAL refreshes the list and displays only those records that meet the criteria.

After you apply a filter, it stays there until you remove it. If you apply a filter and then close the CorelCENTRAL Address Book, when you reopen it, the filter is still in place. You won't see a full list of records until you remove the filter. To switch back to the full list, choose **View**, **Remove Filter**.

Merging with the Address Book

Corel's Address Book is tightly integrated into WordPerfect 10 (and other suite applications), and it's well suited for tracking all sorts of contact information. When you use the Merge feature to produce personalized letters, you can select records directly from the Address Book. So, if you maintain a comprehensive Address Book, you might never create a data file again.

Associate a Form File with an Address Book

When you create a form document, you can associate the form with an address book rather than a data file. See Chapter 14 for more information on creating form documents and data files.

To associate a form file with an address book:

1. Choose **Tools**, **Merge**.

2. Click **Data source**, and then select **Address Book**.

3. Click the drop-down list arrow to display a list of available address books (see Figure 15.12).

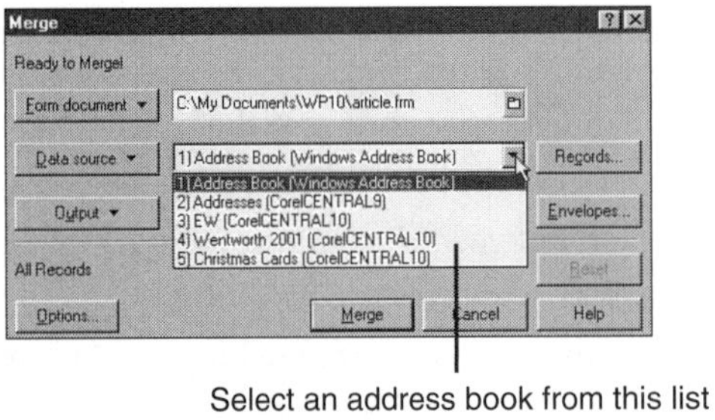

FIGURE 15.12

Select an address book to merge with a form file from the list of address books on your system.

Select an address book from this list

Edit an Association to an Address Book

If you need to switch to another address book, or if you created the form document with a different association, you can edit the association.

To edit an association to an address book:

1. Open the form file.

2. Click the **Insert Field** button on the **Merge** feature bar.

3. Click the **Data source** drop-down arrow and choose one of the address books from the list.

4. Click **Close**. You should see an updated list of field names in the Insert Field list so that you can revise the field names in the form file.

THE ABSOLUTE MINIMUM

In this chapter, you learned how to use the CorelCENTRAL Address Book application to keep track of contact information.

- You learned how to create an address book and how to add entries to it.

- You saw how easy it is to edit and delete entries and to move and copy entries between address books.

- Other address books can be opened in CorelCENTRAL, so you have access to all the contact information on your system.

- Techniques for importing and exporting address books were covered so you can bring everything in to CorelCENTRAL.

- You learned how to sort and filter the address book entries to locate exactly what you need.

- Address books can be used as a data source for a merge, so you learned how to associate a form file with an address book.

In the next chapter, you'll learn how to use templates to automate document production and to ensure consistency throughout company documents.

- Learn how to open a template and how to customize the WordPerfect default template.

- Understand how important it is to back up your default template before you make any changes.

- Download and install bonus template files from a Corel WordPerfect Web site.

- Convert existing documents into templates to automate your document production.

16

Working with Templates

Every document in WordPerfect is based on a template. Until now, you've been using the `wp10us.wpt` template (for the U.S. version of WordPerfect), which is the default template in WordPerfect and contains all the default settings for new documents. The default template is blank except for the initial settings. A template that you might use would be created as a fill-in-the-blanks document containing formatting, layout, and standard blocks of text, so all you have to do is provide the content.

Using WordPerfect's Templates

Only a handful of templates are included with WordPerfect Suite 2002, but plenty more are available for a free download at www.officecommunity.com. You might not have to create your own for quite a while, if ever. When you do venture out and create your own template, you'll be able to convert any of your existing documents into templates.

Each template has a companion PerfectExpert project that guides you through the process of filling in the template. Rather than opening a template just as you would any other document, you select the project that you want to work on. The template is opened in the document window, and the PerfectExpert panel opens on the left side of the screen. You simply click the project buttons and choose from a list of options to alter the style, add other elements, and fill in the important text.

To create a new document based on a WordPerfect template:

1. Choose **File**, **New from Project** (**Ctrl+Shift+N**). The Corel PerfectExpert dialog box appears (see Figure 16.1).

Recently used projects Click to choose a different category.

FIGURE 16.1

You choose the PerfectExpert project that you want to use in the Corel PerfectExpert dialog box.

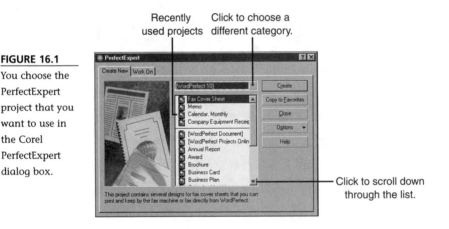

Click to scroll down through the list.

2. If necessary, click the **Create New** tab to display the list of templates.
3. Scroll through the list of projects and double-click the one you want to run. You'll see a PerfectScript message box asking if you want to disable macros in this document.
4. Click the **No** button to run the macros in the template.

If you don't see the project you want, click the category drop-down list arrow at the top of the project template list and choose another category. Select WordPerfect 10 for a list of all the WordPerfect Office 2002 templates.

Some of WordPerfect's templates require personal information. If you, or anyone else, haven't filled that in yet, you'll be prompted for it the first time you open a project template that uses the personal information.

Filling in Personal Information

Many project templates require personal information (such as a name, company, address, and fax number), which you can type in once and have WordPerfect insert for you whenever it's necessary. If this information hasn't been created yet, you are prompted for it when you open a template that uses it (see Figure 16.2).

When you click **OK**, the CorelCENTRAL Address Book dialog box opens, with a list of available address books. You need to be able to select an address book entry that contains your personal information. If you haven't already created this record, do it now. Refer to the section titled "Creating a New Address Book Entry" in Chapter 15, "Using the Address Book," for the steps to create a new, personal information entry.

> ## caution
>
> In this case, you're using a template that came with the WordPerfect Office suite, so you can be relatively sure that it's safe. If you get this message when you are using a template that didn't come from a trusted source, you should choose **Yes** to disable the macros. The template will probably not work correctly—this is to be expected. You should check into the sender of that template and assure yourself that it came from a respected source before you run the macros in it. The reason for extreme caution is that viruses can hide themselves in macros. By disabling the macros in a template, you are protecting yourself and your system from marauding macro viruses.

FIGURE 16.2

If you haven't filled in the personal information, you will be prompted for it.

Select the entry in the list, and then click **Insert**. That's it—you're done. This entry becomes the default for all the templates. In many offices, computers are shared, so users need to select their own personal information entry in the Address Book.

To select a different personal information entry:

1. Choose **File**, **New from Project** to open the PerfectExpert dialog box.
2. Click the **Options** button.
3. Choose **Personal Information**. A message box appears and identifies the current personal information entry.
4. Click **OK** to open the CorelCENTRAL Address Book dialog box, where you can select another personal information entry.

The Disable Macro Message

Before the project template opens, you might see a PerfectScript macros message box that explains there are macros in the document, and if you don't know the source of the document, you might want to disable the macros. A macro is like a small program that you can create to repeat your actions. Some macros are malicious because they contain computer viruses, which can wreak havoc on your computer system. For this reason, it's a good idea to disable macros in documents that do not come from trusted sources.

If you're using one of the templates that shipped with WordPerfect, or a template from a trusted source, you can click **No**; you don't want to disable the macros. However, if you are unsure of the source, it's best to click **Yes** to disable the macros. Granted, the results won't be the same, but it's better to be safe than sorry.

> **caution**
>
> Under no circumstances should you enable the check box that turns off the PerfectScript macros message box. In the battle against computer viruses, the capability to disable macros in a document is a fundamental tool. Turning off this message box removes your ability to choose to disable or enable the PerfectScript macros.

Using the PerfectExpert Panel

When you open a template, the PerfectExpert panel opens next to the template (see Figure 16.3). The buttons in the PerfectExpert panel give you options for customizing the template by choosing from the available variations.

Click to fill in the To and From information.
PerfectExpert panel

FIGURE 16.3

PerfectExpert projects combine templates and a PerfectExpert to guide you through the process of creating the document.

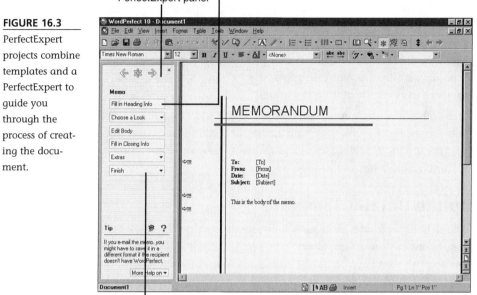

Click to check spelling, print, fax, or save.

Now you can start building the document by clicking the buttons in the PerfectExpert panel. For example, in the Memo project shown in Figure 16.3, click the **Fill in Heading Info** button to open the Memo Heading dialog box, where you can type all the To and From information (see Figure 16.4). Remove the check mark next to any item that you don't want on the memo. Click the drop-down list arrows to choose items that you've already used in these fields. Otherwise, type the information in the text boxes.

Remove the check mark if
you don't want to use the element.

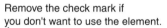

FIGURE 16.4

After you type the information in the Memo Heading dialog box, WordPerfect places it in the proper place in the template.

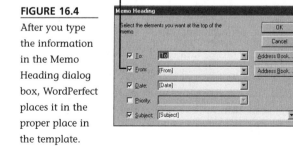

Click to select an address
book entry for the To section.

Click to select an address book
entry for the From section.

Customizing WordPerfect's Templates

Every document that you create from scratch is based on the default template. Some of the default settings are listed in Table 2.1 in Chapter 2, "Creating and Editing Documents." The default template can be customized to suit your preferences. For example, if you want 1.25-inch margins, specific tab settings, and Century Schoolbook 12 point, you can make these changes to the default template so that they are in place for all new documents.

The WordPerfect templates can also be edited and customized to your preferences. If you like everything about the fax cover sheet template except the small footer line, edit the template and take it out. Add your company logo to the templates for instant business forms!

Backing Up the Default Template

The default template contains a lot more than initial settings. It contains the majority of your customization efforts (such as Quickwords, custom toolbars, menus, and keyboards), so it is particularly important that you make a backup copy of the file before you make changes.

To make a backup copy of your default template:

1. Search for the default template file—wp10us.wpt—for the U.S. version. Change the "us" to the two-letter abbreviation for your language.

2. When you find the file, rename it to wp10us.old.

If the changes that you make to the default template cause any problems, you can go back to using the original default template by renaming or deleting the new template and renaming the old template back to its original filename. In other words, you delete the wp10us.wpt that you have created and then rename your original default template, wp10usold.wpt, back to wp10us.wpt. This would "reinstate" the original default template. Before you start renaming template files, be sure you close WordPerfect. When you are finished renaming, start WordPerfect again. The original template is back in place so everything should be in place again.

Editing the Default Template

If you routinely use settings other than the defaults, you can place these settings in the default template. The next time you create a new document, the new default settings will be in place. Be sure to make a backup copy of the default template before you make any editing changes to it. If something goes wrong, you can revert to the previous copy.

Follow these steps to edit the default template:

1. Choose **View**, **Reveal Codes** to turn on Reveal Codes.

2. Find the **DocumentStyle** code at the top of the document.

3. Double-click the code to open the Styles Editor (see Figure 16.5).

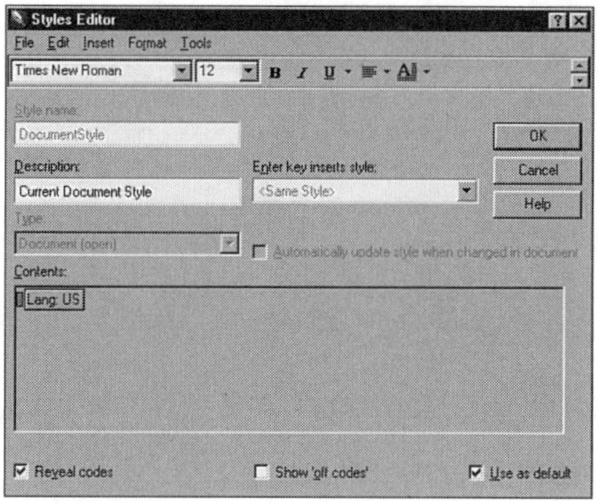

FIGURE 16.5

Use the Styles Editor menus and toolbars to customize the document initial style, and then save them to the default template.

4. Make the necessary changes, and then place a check in the **Use as default** check box.

5. Click **OK**. You'll see a message box asking whether you want to apply the Document Style to new documents as they are created.

6. Click **Yes** to save your changes to the default template.

If you find that your changes haven't worked out the way you wanted, and you made a backup copy of the template before you started editing, you can revert to the previous copy of the default template. Refer to the previous section, "Backing Up the Default Template," for more information.

Editing the WordPerfect Templates

WordPerfect's project templates are designed so that you can use them right away. They are generic enough to work in most situations, especially when time is more important than personalization. However, when you're ready to customize the templates, you can revise a template as easily as you revise any other document.

To edit a template:

1. Choose **File**, **New from Project**. If necessary, click the **Create New** tab.

2. Select a template from the list.

3. Click the **Options** button and select **Edit WP Template** from the list. The template opens in a document window, and the Template toolbar is displayed on top of the property bar (see Figure 16.6).

Fax Cover Sheet

Name: [To]
Organization: [Of]
Fax: [Fax]
Phone: [Phone]
From: [From]
Date: [Date]
Subject: [Subject]
Pages: 1

☐ Urgent   ☐ Reply ASAP   ☐ Please Comment   ☐ For Your Records

Comments: [Comments]

4. Revise the template as you would any other document.

5. When you're finished, click the **Close** button to close the Template Editor. A confirmation message box appears.

6. Click **Yes** to save the template.

Earlier in the chapter, you learned how to edit the default template by modifying the DocumentStyle in the Styles Editor and saving the changes to the default template. This method works smoothly for items that you want to add to the template, but if there is something that you want to remove, or if you want to make some adjustments, you're better off editing the default template through the PerfectExpert dialog box.

To edit the default template:

1. Choose **File**, **New From Project** to open the PerfectExpert dialog box.

2. Click the category drop-down list arrow and select **Custom WP Templates**. A list of customized templates appears in the list box (see Figure 16.7).

Select the category here

FIGURE 16.7

The templates
that you create
are stored in the
Custom WP
Templates folder.

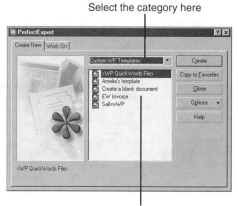

Edit the default template

3. Select **Create a Blank Document**.

4. Click the **Options** button and select **Edit WP Template**.

5. Use the menus, toolbars, and property bars to make your changes.

Here's an example for you: If you want all your new documents to start out with a 12-point Century Schoolbook font and .75-inch margins on all sides, you can make those selections here and save them to the default template. Bear in mind that any changes you make here will affect all new documents, so be careful of the formatting and codes that you add.

Downloading and Installing Templates

Shortly after the release of WordPerfect 2002, Corel announced that it would be making additional templates and projects available in a free download. This news is especially welcome to users of Academic and OEM products, which do not contain the same set of templates as the Standard and Professional versions. Academic products are discounted, and OEM products are included free with computer systems from companies such as HP, Dell, Gateway, and Sony. Because the customer doesn't pay the retail price, some of the goodies are left out.

These templates and projects can be downloaded from http://www.officecommunity.com in the Download Gallery section (see Figure 16.8) and from Corel's FTP site at ftp://ftp.corel.com/pub/WordPerfect/wpwin/10/english/templates. On the FTP site, a Zip file called WP 10 Temp contains all the template files so that you can download the whole collection at one time. Also on the FTP site, within each template category folder is a README file with instructions for installing. There is a thumbnail folder in each category, containing a GIF file that shows you what each created project form might look like.

If you downloaded a Zip file, unzip it first. Extract the template files (`.wpt` and `.ast`) to the …`\program files\corel\wordperfect office 2002\template` folder. (The ellipsis (…) represents the drive letter where you installed WordPerfect on your computer.) Now, you're ready to add them into WordPerfect.

FIGURE 16.8

Office Community's Download Gallery has a complete set of downloadable templates for WordPerfect 9 and 10.

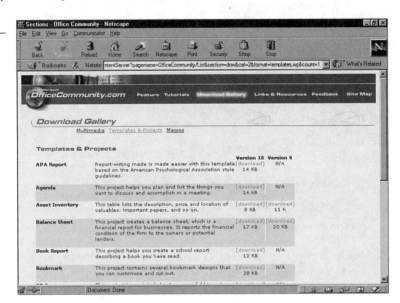

To install downloaded templates:

1. Choose **File**, **New from Project** to open the PerfectExpert dialog box.
2. Click the **Options** button, and then select **Refresh Projects** from the list. Click **Yes** to confirm.

The default template folder shown in Settings (**Tools**, **Settings**, **Files**, on the **Templates** tab) is where the default template is stored. Any custom templates that you create are also saved to this folder. The templates that ship with WordPerfect are stored in a different location. They are copied to the `\program files\corel\wordperfect office 2002\template` folder.

Converting an Existing Document to a Template

Creating a template from scratch is definitely a last resort. Other options are much faster. First, you can convert an existing document into a template. You're bound to have a handful of "form" documents that you use over and over. Fax cover sheets come to mind, but so do supply requests, time sheets, network maintenance bulletins, expense reports, newsletters, equipment checkout sheets, and so on.

Second, you can revise an existing template and then save your changes as a new template. You can use as your starting point one of your own templates or one of the templates that comes with WordPerfect, and then just make the necessary adjustments. Refer to the section "Editing the WordPerfect Templates" earlier in the chapter for the steps.

To create a template from an existing document:

1. In a blank document, choose **File**, **New from Project**.

2. Click the **Options** button and select **Create WP Template** from the list. A blank template opens in the document window, and the Template toolbar is displayed at the top of the screen.

3. Click the **Insert File** button (or choose **Insert**, **File**) to display the Insert File dialog box.

4. Select the filename for the existing document, and then click **Insert**.

5. Delete all the text that varies for each document. In other words, turn the document into a form, where there are blank spaces for the information that changes. The text that stays the same stays in the document. Make any other necessary revisions.

6. Click the **Close** button when you're finished.

7. Click **Yes** when you're asked whether you want to save the template. The Save Template dialog box appears (see Figure 16.9).

Type a descriptive name here.

FIGURE 16.9

In addition to naming the templates, you can create a description for the template and choose a category to store the template in.

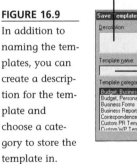

Type a filename here.

Choose a category.

8. In the **Description** text box, type a descriptive name to appear in the template list.

9. Type a filename in the **Template name** text box. Don't type an extension—WordPerfect assigns the .wpt extension to templates so that they can be recognized as templates and not as documents.

10. Choose the category where you want the template stored in the **Template category** list box.

11. Click **OK** to save and close the template.

ABSOLUTE MINIMUM

In this chapter, you learned how to use templates to speed up the creation of frequently used documents. Templates are extremely popular in settings where consistency across documents is particularly important.

- You learned how to use the WordPerfect templates to create frequently used documents.

- The default template, which contains all the initial settings for new documents, can be edited and adjusted for your preferences.

- Any WordPerfect template can be edited so you can add your company logo or any other customization to personalize them for your business.

- Additional template projects are available online. You learned where to download them and how to add them to the list of templates in the PerfectExpert dialog box.

- Existing documents make the best templates because most of the work is already done. You saw how easy it is to convert a document into a template.

In the next chapter, you'll learn how write your own macros to speed up repetitive tasks. You'll also learn how to play the macros that come with WordPerfect.

- Learn how to play macros that someone else has written.

- Create your own macros and edit them to make minor changes.

- Create three sample macros that you can use right away.

17

CREATING AND PLAYING MACROS

Macros are different from the other automation features in WordPerfect. The macro language is powerful. With a few exceptions, anything you can do in a document can be done in a macro. The nice thing about macros is that you don't have to learn the macro language to write your own macros. And one more thing: You might have heard about macro viruses infecting computers and causing all sorts of problems. Rest assured that WordPerfect macros are more secure and less vulnerable to viruses than Microsoft products.

What Is a Macro?

Stop and think for a minute—how much of your time is spent doing repetitive tasks? Do you create the same types of documents every week? Do you type the same address block all day long? Do you repeat the same series of steps over and over again, setting up formatting for your documents? Are you responsible for maintaining a consistent appearance in company documents? If you answered "yes" to any of these questions, you will *love* the Macro feature.

A macro can be created to perform a series of steps. Those steps might take you several minutes to complete manually, but when you play the macro, the process takes only seconds. And equally important, every time you play the macro, the exact same steps are done. That means the results are consistent and accurate.

Let me use a popular analogy to try to explain how a macro works. A camcorder records video and sound on a videotape. You can turn on the recorder, record the video, and then turn off the recorder. The video that you recorded is there for you to access when you play back the tape. The same is true for creating a macro, except instead of recording video, you record actions taken on a document. You turn on the Macro Recorder, record your actions, and then turn off the Macro Recorder. Whatever you do between turning on the Macro Recorder and turning it back off is recorded in a macro.

Don't skip this chapter because you think only techies write macros. A macro can be simple: Type a signature block, insert a page number, change to a different font, and so on. A macro can also be complex. Some macros ask questions and assemble documents based on the answers.

If you're lucky, your firm maintains a standard set of macros for everyone's use. If this is the case, all you need to know is how to run them; so let's start there. I'll explain how to create your own macros later in the chapter.

Playing Macros

If someone else has written macros for you, you'll need to know where they are stored so that you can play them. Actually, you don't have to know *exactly* where they are because you will have an opportunity to browse for them. The macros that come with WordPerfect are stored in the default macro folder.

The locations of the default macro folder and the supplemental macro folder are specified in Settings. Choose **Tools**, **Settings** (**Alt+F12**). Click **Files**, and then click the **Merge/Macro** tab. If you need to change the location, click the **Files** icon at the end of the text box to browse for the folder. The supplemental macro folder is generally used as a method for gaining access to macros stored on a network. Your network administrator will be able to give you the location of the folder.

Before you play a macro, be sure everything is in place first. If you are running a macro to add page numbers to a document, for example, you need to open the document first. Likewise, if the macro acts on selected text, select the text before you run the macro. Finally, if the macro creates a new document, you should start in a blank document.

To play a macro:

1. Choose **Tools**, **Macro**, **Play** (**Alt+F10**) to open the Play Macro dialog box (see Figure 17.1).

2. Double-click a macro, or select it and click **Play**.

If the macro "hangs," you'll have to cancel it manually. Press the **Esc** key to cancel the macro. A message box appears stating that the user canceled the macro.

note

When you open the Play Macro dialog box, the contents of the default macro folder are displayed by default. If the macro you are looking for is stored in another folder, you'll need to navigate to that folder. The name of the default macro folder can be found in **Tools**, **Settings**, **Files**, on the Merge/Macro tab.

FIGURE 17.1

The shipping macros are stored in a `WordPerfect` subfolder of the `PerfectScript` folder.

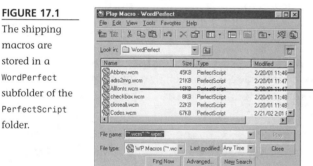

Double-click a macro file to play it.

Running WordPerfect's Shipping Macros

WordPerfect ships with a collection of macros that are helpful both to use and to examine if you want to become familiar with the PerfectScript macro language. In a later section, I'll show you how to edit macros, so you can open any of the shipping macros and see how they were written.

- `Abbrev.wcm`—Opens an Abbreviations dialog box where you can select a QuickWord and expand it in a document. The dialog box stays open so that you can expand multiple QuickWords without opening the QuickCorrect dialog box each time.

- adrs2mrg.wcm—Opens an Address Book to Merge dialog box, where you can choose an Address Book and then create a merge data file from the entire Address Book or just from selected records. This macro creates a text data file with a field name record at the top of the file.

- Allfonts.wcm—Searches for all the fonts installed for the current printer and generates a list of the fonts along with a short sample of text. Depending on the number of fonts you have installed, it might take a few minutes to generate the list. Also, your printer might not have enough memory to be able to print the list.

- checkbox.wcm—Creates a check box that you can click to insert an "x" in the box and click again to remove the "x." The check box is created as hypertext, so it will show up underlined and blue.

- closeall.wcm—Displays a Close All Documents dialog box, where you can selectively save open documents before they are closed. If documents are unnamed, you can specify a name for the documents in the dialog box. A Save check box lets you decide which documents should be saved before they are closed.

- ctrlm.wcm—Displays the PerfectScript Command dialog box, where you can select, edit, and insert macro commands in a macro. You don't have to open the Play Macro dialog box to select this macro. Just press **Ctrl+M** in the document window.

- cvtdocs10.wcm—Opens the WordPerfect Conversion Expert dialog box, where you can choose to convert a single file, a folder, or a folder and its subfolders to several different WordPerfect formats. You can choose from WordPerfect 10, 9, 8, 7, 6, 5.1, and HTML.

- DCConvert.wcm—Converts WordPerfect drop cap characters (that is, the first whole word is a drop cap) to a drop cap character that is Microsoft Word compatible (that is, a number of characters drop cap).

- endfoot.wcm—Converts the all the endnotes in a document (or just those in selected text) to footnotes. You must be outside the footnote/endnote area to run this macro.

- Expndall.wcm—Expands all the QuickWords in the document. You might use this if you work with documents with complex QuickWords. You might decide to turn off Expand QuickWords as you type them and then expand them all at once with this macro.

- Filestmp.wcm—Opens the File Stamp Options dialog box, where you can choose to insert the filename or the filename and path into a header or footer.

If the document has not been named when you run this macro, a filename code is placed in the header or footer. When you save and name the file, the filename (and the path) shows up in the header or footer. If you select Change Font, a Font Properties dialog box appears so that you can select the font (or font size) that you want to use for the file stamp.

▓ `flipenv.wcm`—Displays an Envelope Addresses dialog box, where you can type the return address (unless you've already selected a personal information entry in the Address Book) and a mailing address. You also can select a mailing address from the Address Book. After you fill in the address information, you can choose an envelope size. The macro creates the envelope, only it flips it 180 degrees so that it is upside-down. This macro was created because some printers have trouble printing text within 1/4 inch of the top-left corner of an envelope, but they don't have a problem printing it within 1/4 inch of the lower-right corner. If you have one of these printers, this macro allows you to print the return address closer to the edge of the envelope.

▓ `Fontdn.wcm`—Reduces the font size by two points. If you select text before running the macro, only the selected text is affected. Otherwise, the change takes place at the insertion point and remains in effect until you change the size again.

▓ `Fontup.wcm`—Increases the font size by two points. If you select text before running the macro, only the selected text is affected. Otherwise, the change takes place at the insertion point and remains in effect until you change the size again.

▓ `footend.wcm`—Converts the footnotes in the entire document (or just in selected text) to endnotes. You must be outside the footnote/endnote area to run this macro.

▓ `Longname.wcm`—This macro is for everyone who got around the DOS 8.3 filename by creating descriptive names in document summaries. This macro converts those descriptive filenames into long filenames, which can have up to 255 characters. When you run this macro, a Convert to Long Filenames dialog box appears. You can either type the name of the drive and folder where the files are stored, or you can click the **Files** icon to open the Select Folder dialog box. Select the file(s) that you want to convert in the Select Files to Rename list, and then click **OK**. When the macro is finished, a record of the changes is created in a blank document.

▓ `Parabrk.wcm`—Displays a Paragraph Break dialog box, where you can choose a symbol or graphic to display at every paragraph break. The symbol or graphic is centered on the blank line between paragraphs.

- `pleading.wcm`—Displays the Pleading Paper dialog box, where you can choose from a variety of options to generate a legal pleading paper.

- `prompts.wcm`—Opens Prompt Builder, which helps you create prompts for your templates. You can create messages that help guide the user along in using the template. You must be editing a template (other than your default template) before you can run this macro.

- `reverse.wcm`—Displays the Reverse Text Options dialog box, where you can choose a color for the text and a color for the fill (or background). If you've selected text, you can place the reverse text in a text box. If you've selected table cells, the dialog box is a little different. You choose from three table-oriented options: Center Text, Lock Cell, and Header Row.

- `saveall.wcm`—Displays the Save Open Documents dialog box, which is similar to the Close All Documents dialog box. It works the same way: If you want to save a document, place a check mark next to the filename. If necessary, you can change the filename and path before saving the file.

- `Savetoa.wcm`—Saves the current document and then copies the file to a disk in drive A. If you haven't named the document yet, you will get the opportunity to do so. When you name the file, don't worry about switching to drive A or typing `a:` in the path—all you need to do is name the file—the macro saves it to drive A.

- `tconvert.wcm`—Displays the Convert Template dialog box, where you can type the name of a template that you want to convert for use in WordPerfect 10. If you can't remember the name (or the location) of the template file, click the **Files** icon to search for it.

- `uawp10en.wcm`—According to the documentation, this macro is used by the PerfectExpert. You must not delete this file from the macros folder, so don't even think about getting rid of it!

- `wp_org.wcm`—Creates a basic organization chart that you can start filling in immediately. You get the same results that you would if you chose **Insert**, **Graphics**, **Draw Picture** to open the Presentations/Draw editing screen and then chose **Insert**, **Organization Chart** and selected the first **Single** option in the Layout dialog box.

- `wp_pr.wcm`—Opens an outline from a WordPerfect document in Presentations as a slide show. You can run the macro whether you have an outline in the document or not, but Presentations will have a hard time figuring out what to put on the slides with a regular document. The document is saved as `pr_outln.wpd`.

Creating Macros

When you create your first macro, try to remember that you don't have to do it perfectly the first time. You can keep recording the macro over and over until you get it right. You can also edit a macro and make some adjustments to it rather than re-recording.

Before you get started, grab a pen and jot down a rough sequence of events that you need to go through so you don't forget anything. For example, if you want to create a macro to insert a signature block, write down the closing that you prefer, make a note about the number of blank lines you want to allow room for a signature, and then jot down all the elements that you want to include beneath the written signature.

You can record a macro in a blank document or in an existing document. It's more efficient to create the macro the next time you need to perform a certain series of steps because you can create the macro and accomplish your task at the same time.

To record a macro:

1. Choose **Tools**, **Macro**, **Record** (**Ctrl+F10**).

2. Type a name for the macro in the **File name** text box. A macro is automatically saved with the .wcm extension, which identifies it as a macro file. By default, new macros are created in the default macro folder.

3. If necessary, choose a location for your macro from the **Save in** drop-down list.

4. Click **Record**. The Macro feature bar is displayed underneath the property bar (see Figure 17.2). The recorder is now on, so you're ready to start recording your actions.

5. Type the text, use the menus and toolbars, go through the dialog boxes, and make your selections. The macro records all your actions, whether you use the keyboard or the mouse. The only exception is that you have to use the keyboard to position the insertion point in the document window.

6. When you're finished, click the **Stop the macro play or record** button. The Macro feature bar disappears, and you are returned to a normal document window. The actions that you took while you created the macro have been performed on the document, so you might or might not want to save those changes.

To run the macro, follow the steps detailed previously in the "Playing Macros" section.

FIGURE 17.2

The Macro tool-
bar has buttons
to help you
record and edit
macros.

Click to stop recording.　　　　　　　　　　　Macro feature bar

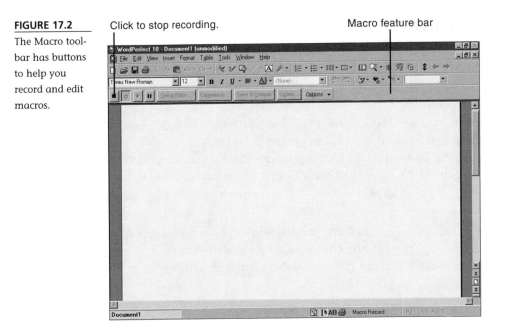

FIGURE 17.2

The Macro tool-
bar has buttons
to help you
record and edit
macros.

You can insert a pause in a macro so that someone can type something in. When you are at the point in your macro where you are ready for user input, click the **Pause while recording/executing a macro** button (on the Macro tool-bar). At this point, you can either type something and click the button again, or just click the button again to move past the pause. When you run the macro, the macro pauses and waits for input. When you press **Enter**, the macro resumes.

The Pause feature is powerful and easy to use. It greatly extends the power of a macro to automate any number of tasks. For example, you could pause to type in a new margin setting or to type an author name in a header.

Editing Macros

This book is written for those who have very little experience with word processors. You might be thinking, "Editing macros doesn't exactly sound like something a beginner would do, does it?" What if I told you that for simple changes, it isn't much different from editing a document, would you be interested?

You can open a macro file just as you would any other document. If all you want to do is delete an extra blank line or revise some of the text, you open the macro file and make your changes in the document window using the same techniques that you use in documents. In most cases, it's faster to edit a macro than it is to create it again.

To edit a macro:

1. Choose **Tools**, **Macro Edit**.

2. Double-click the macro to open it in the document window (see Figure 17.3). The macro shown in the figure inserts a signature block.

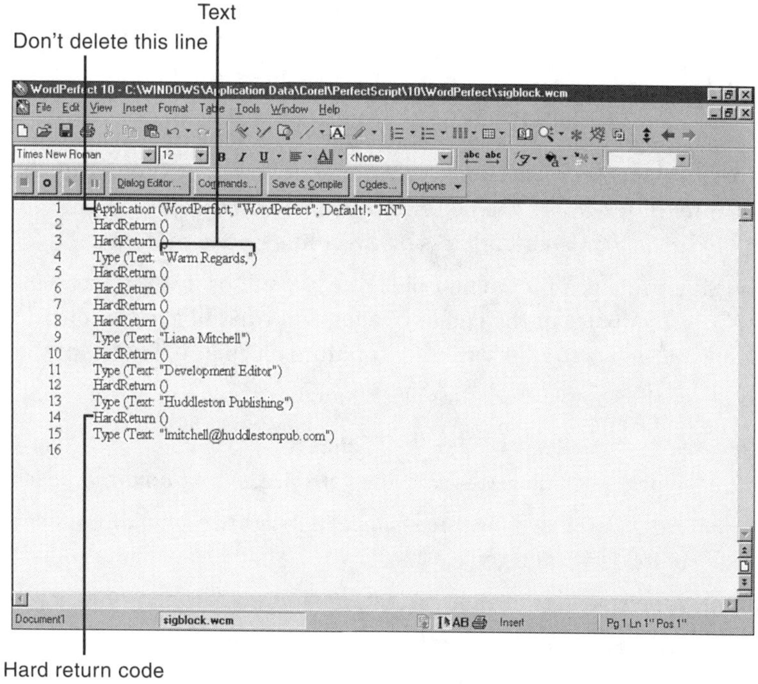

FIGURE 17.3
You can edit macro files in the document window.

Take care not to delete the first line—it is important information for the macro to run correctly. Here are some basic editing tricks:

- To delete a blank line (hard return), select `HardReturn ()`; then press **Delete**.

- To insert an extra blank line, type `HardReturn ()` on a blank line. If you press Enter, you'll just insert a blank line in the macro; you won't insert a Hard Return code.

■ When revising the text, be sure you don't delete the quote marks on either side of the text. If you accidentally delete one, type it back in.

When you're finished making changes, click the **Save & Compile** button to save your changes. Click the document **Close** button to close the macro file.

Recording Several Sample Macros

The best way for you to learn how to write macros is "just do it." So, the following sections contain the steps to create three sample macros. Even if you don't think you'll ever use the macros, take a few minutes and create them anyway. You'll learn a lot about the way macros work.

Creating a Signature Block Macro

A typical signature block is two lines down from the last line of a letter. A signature block generally contains a person's name, followed by four blank lines (or enough room for a signature), the person's title, and other identifying information. This might include an email address or direct line phone number.

You can create this macro in a blank document, or if you prefer, you can position the insertion point at the end of a letter. You can kill two birds with one stone by creating your macro and inserting a signature block in the letter, at the same time.

To create the sample signature block macro:

1. Choose **Tools**, **Macro**, **Record**.
2. Type the name `sigblock` in the **File name** text box; then click **Record**.
3. Press **Enter** two (or three) times to insert two blank lines between the last line of the letter and the closing.
4. Type `Sincerely` or `Warm regards`, or whatever closing phrase you prefer.
5. Press **Enter** four (or five) times to insert four blank lines.
6. Type your name; then press **Enter**.
7. Type your title; then press **Enter**.
8. Type your email address; then press **Enter**.
9. Click the **Stop macro play or record** button (**Ctrl+F10**) to stop recording the macro.

When you stop recording, the macro file is saved. Refer to Figure 17.3 to see what a typical signature block macro looks like when you open it for editing.

Now, open a blank document and run the macro you just created. Don't blink, because if you do, you might miss seeing the macro run. Some macros run so quickly that it might seem as though the results appear out of thin air.

Creating a Document Identification Footer Macro

This sample macro creates a footer that appears on every page of the document. The filename and location will be inserted against the left margin of the footer, in an 8-point type. This type of document identification is popular, especially when you share documents on a company network. Anyone who receives a copy of the document knows where it can be found on the network.

To create a document identification footer:

1. Choose **Tools**, **Macro**, **Record**.
2. Type the name `idfooter` in the **File name** text box; then click **Record**.
3. Choose **Insert**, **Header/Footer**.
4. Choose **Footer A**; then click **Create**.
5. Click the **Font Size** drop-down list arrow and choose **8**. If you want, change the font as well by clicking the **Font** drop-down list arrow and choosing a new font.
6. Choose **Insert**, **Other**, **Path and Filename**.
7. Click the **Close** button on the Header/Footer toolbar.
8. Click the **Stop macro play or record** button on the Macro feature bar. Figure 17.4 shows the `idfooter` macro.

The idfooter macro

FIGURE 17.4

This macro inserts a footer with the filename and path in 8-point text.

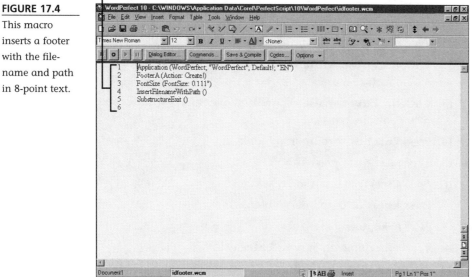

Now, open a document that you have already created. Run the `idfooter` macro to add a footer with the path and filename for the document. Don't worry—you don't have to save the changes—this is just so that you can test your new macro.

Creating a Fax Cover Sheet Macro

This sample macro creates a fax cover sheet with the headings and the date automatically inserted. This macro pauses for user input when appropriate. A horizontal graphic line is inserted between the headings and the comment area.

To create the fax cover sheet macro:

1. Choose **Tools**, **Macro**, **Record**.
2. Type `faxcover` in the **File name** text box; then click **Record**.
3. Change the font size to `36` point. If you want, change the font as well by clicking the **Font** drop-down list arrow and selecting a new font.
4. Type `Fax Cover Sheet`.
5. Change the font size to **12**. If necessary, choose a different font as well.
6. Press **Enter** five or six times to insert blank lines.
7. Type `To:`; then press the **Tab** key once.
8. Click the **Pause while recording/executing a macro** button on the Macro feature bar.
9. Click the **Pause while recording/executing a macro** button again to move past the pause.
10. Press **Enter** twice to insert a blank line.
11. Type `Fax:`; then press the **Tab** key once.
12. Click the **Pause while recording/executing a macro** button on the Macro feature bar.
13. Click the **Pause while recording/executing a macro** button again to move past the pause.
14. Press **Enter** twice to insert a blank line.
15. Type `Date:`; then press **Tab**.
16. Press **Ctrl+D** to insert today's date.
17. Press **Enter** twice to insert a blank line.
18. Type `From:`; then press **Tab**.
19. Type your name; then press **Enter** twice.
20. Type `Fax:`; then press **Tab**.
21. Type your fax phone number; then press **Enter** four times.
22. Choose **Insert**, **Line**, **Horizontal Line**.

23. Press **Enter** three times.

24. Type `Comments:`; then press **Enter** twice.

 25. Click the **Stop macro play or record** button on the Macro feature bar. Figure 17.5 shows the `faxcover` macro.

FIGURE 17.5

This macro uses the Pause command to create a fill-in-the-blanks fax cover sheet.

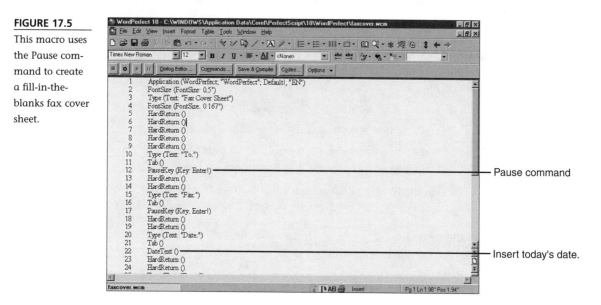

This macro creates the fax cover sheet shown in Figure 17.6.

FIGURE 17.6

This fax cover sheet was created with the `faxcover` macro.

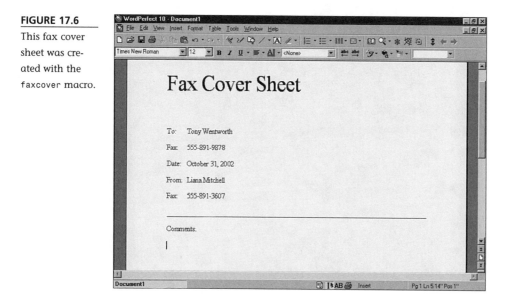

As you can see from these three examples, macros can help make you more efficient. They can also improve consistency in companywide documents. Any task that you can do in WordPerfect can be re-created in a macro, so the possibilities are endless. The next time you find yourself repeating the same series of steps for the second or third time, ask yourself if this is a good candidate for a macro.

THE ABSOLUTE MINIMUM

In this chapter, you learned how to use the Macro feature to create macros for your repetitive tasks.

- You learned how to play macros that someone else has written.
- You saw how simple it is to create your own macros.
- You also learned some basic editing techniques so that you can make minor changes instead of recording the macro all over again.
- Finally, you created three sample macros to give you an idea of how quick and easy it can be to create powerful macros for everyday use.

In the next chapter, you'll learn how use the Task Manager that comes with the Productivity Packs and Family Packs.

In This Chapter

- Learn how to launch the Task Manager from a desktop shortcut and from the Start menu.

- Understand how to select projects from the Task Manager categories.

- Discover how to view the User Guide and how to access support sites on the Web.

18

Using the Task Manager

Think of the Task Manager as a launching pad from which all the tasks and projects included in the Productivity Pack and Family Pack can be started. WordPerfect 10, Quattro Pro 10, and the other applications can also be started from Task Manager. The projects are grouped by category: projects for home finances, communication projects, projects for home and family. When you select a task, the Task Manager launches it and opens the appropriate application.

The Task Manager also has some helpful links to the WordPerfect 10 and Quattro Pro 10 help files and user guides. There are also links to Corel support sites where you can get help on the Web. If you bought an HP computer, you will have some additional links to special software offers, exclusively for HP customers.

Launching the Task Manager

The Task Manager is included in Corel's Family Pack 4 and the Productivity Packs bundled with new Hewlett-Packard and Gateway computer systems. The Task Manager included in the Family Pack looks a little different from the Productivity Pack Task Manager, so I'll show you how both of them work.

There are two ways to launch the Task Manager: from a shortcut on the desktop or from the Start menu. If you have a Task Manager shortcut on your desktop, double-click the icon to start the Task Manager. Otherwise, use the Start menu:

1. Click the **Start** button.

2. Choose **Programs**, **WordPerfect Productivity Pack or WordPerfect Family Pack 4**.

3. Click **WordPerfect Task Manager**. The Task Manager for the Productivity Pack appears in Figure 18.1. The Task Manager for the Family Pack appears in Figure 18.2.

The categories for the Productivity Pack and the Family Pack are not quite the same. The Task Managers have a unique style, so the categories are organized differently.

FIGURE 18.1

The WordPerfect Productivity Pack Task Manager displays a list of categories you can choose from.

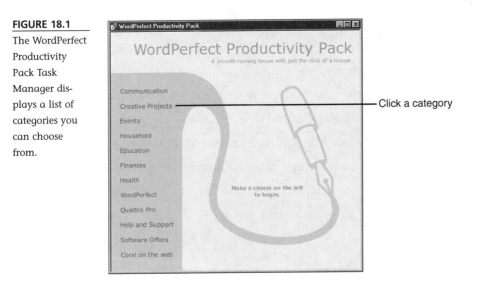

Selecting a Project from the Task Manager

To select a project:

1. Click a category to open a list of tasks. Figure 18.2 shows the list of tasks under the Creative Projects category in the Family Pack; Figure 18.3 shows the list of tasks for Creative Projects in the Productivity Pack.

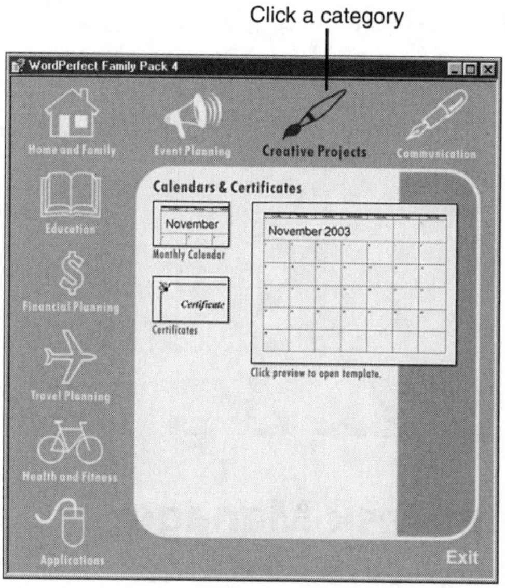

Click a category

FIGURE 18.2

The WordPerfect Family Pack Task Manager displays a list of categories you can choose from.

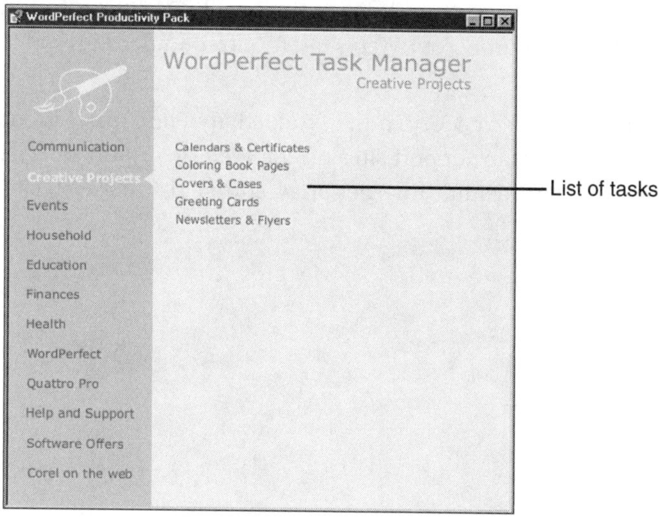

FIGURE 18.3

When you click a category, a list of projects appears.

List of tasks

2. Click a task to launch the application and start the project. Figure 18.4 shows the Calendar project in WordPerfect.

FIGURE 18.4

When you choose a project, Task Manager takes care of starting the application and guiding you through the project.

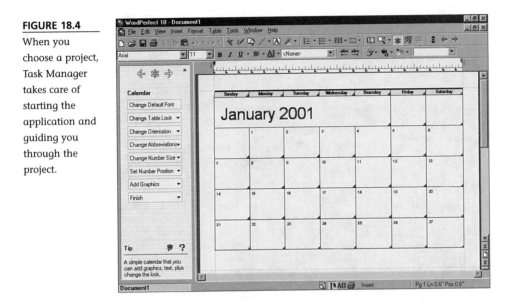

Getting Help Through Task Manager

The Productivity Pack Task Manager has a Help & Support category with links to WordPerfect Help, Quattro Pro Help, and the User Guide (see Figure 18.5). The Task Manager for Family Pack 4 has links to the Family Pack User Guide, Corel's Web site, and the OfficeCommunity.com Web site organized under the Application category (see Figure 18.6).

The Corel on the Web category in the Productivity Pack Task Manager (refer to Figure 18.5) has links to support sites on the Web (see Figure 18.7). Click one of the items to launch your default Internet browser and visit the Web site.

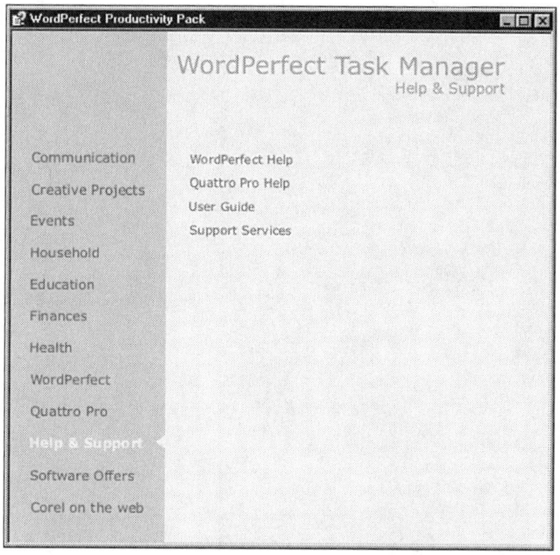

FIGURE 18.5

You can open the Productivity Pack User Guide and the help files for WordPerfect and Quattro Pro from the Task Manager.

FIGURE 18.6

You can view the Family Pack 4 User Guide from the Task Manager.

FIGURE 18.7

The OfficeCommunity .com site has a huge collection of articles, tips and tricks, templates, macros, and plenty of other resources.

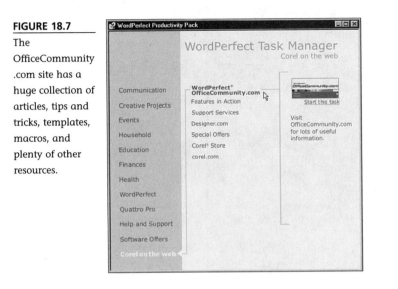

THE ABSOLUTE MINIMUM

In this chapter, you learned how to use the Task Manager to start the tasks and projects that come with Corel's Productivity Pack and Family Pack 4.

- You learned how to launch Task Manager.
- You discovered how to look through the categories to find the project that you want.
- You saw how to open the User Guide and how to visit support sites on the Web.

This is the last chapter. You made it all the way through! Congratulations! You are now a confident, successful WordPerfect user.

PART VI

APPENDIXES

A

LEARNING QUATTRO PRO BASICS

Quattro Pro is a full-featured spreadsheet program, equally as powerful and functional as Microsoft Excel. It is included, along with WordPerfect 10, in the Productivity Packs being bundled with major name computers. HP, Dell, Gateway, and Sony have all replaced Microsoft products with Corel's Productivity Pack. If you've purchased Family Pack 4, an upgrade to, or the full version of Corel WordPerfect Office 2002, you will also have Quattro Pro on your CD.

The Quattro Pro Screen

The first part of this appendix covers the basics of using a spreadsheet. I'm assuming that you have zero experience with a spreadsheet application, so I want to start at the very beginning. If you've already used another spreadsheet program, you might just want to glance at Figure A.1 to get familiar with the Quattro Pro screen, and then skip ahead to the section that interests you.

Starting Quattro Pro

f you already have a shortcut on your desktop, double-click it to start Quattro Pro. If not, you'll have to use the Start menu to launch Quattro Pro. I'll show you how to create a shortcut on your desktop so that you don't have to use the Start menu every time.

To start Quattro Pro from the Start menu:

1. Click **Start**.

2. Select **Programs, WordPerfect Office 2002**.

3. Click **Quattro Pro 10**. The Quattro Pro program starts and opens the Quattro Pro screen, shown in Figure A.1.

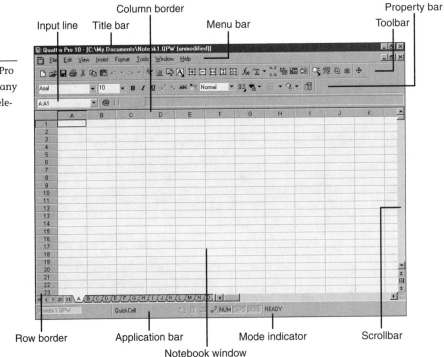

FIGURE A.1

The Quattro Pro screen has many of the same elements as the WordPerfect screen.

The Quattro Pro Interface

Let's focus on the areas of the screen that are similar to WordPerfect and then move on to what is different. These elements are common, although they might have a different function in Quattro Pro:

- **Menu bar**—For access to features.
- **Toolbar**—Contains buttons for frequently used features.
- **Property bar**—Has buttons and drop-down lists for frequently used features. This bar changes depending on what you are working on.
- **Application bar**—Displays the open notebooks and status indicators.
- **Scrollbar**—Works exactly the same as the scrollbar in WordPerfect. Notice the Browse by button on the scrollbar.

Now, get ready for the new stuff! These elements might be new to you:

- **Notebook window**—Has all the same controls as a WordPerfect document window, but it's laid out in a grid. The columns are labeled with letters; the rows are numbered.
- **Row border**—Identifies the row number. Clicking a row number selects the entire row.
- **Column border**—Identifies the column letter. Click a column letter to select an entire column.
- **Input line**—Shows the current cell's address and contents.
- **Mode indicator**—Pay attention to the mode indicator that shows READY for input, VALUE if the entry is a number, and TEXT if the entry is text.

Entering Data

Data is entered into individual cells. The currently selected cell is the active cell, so you can enter or edit the data in it. A cell address is a combination of the row number and column letter. For example, the cell in the top-left corner of the notebook is in column A, on row 1, so the cell address would be A1. The input line (see Figure A.1) displays the cell address for the currently selected cell(s).

Entering Values and Labels

Entering the information into a spreadsheet is most of the work. After you've typed in the titles and figures, you can move, copy, format, and perform calculations to your heart's content.

There are two types of data in Quattro Pro:

- **Label**—An entry that you won't be using for calculations. For example, "February", "MP3", and "2-1-05" are all labels. A label can begin with any letter or punctuation mark *except* the following: +, -, /, $, (, @, #, ., or =. If you type one of those symbols, Quattro Pro treats the information as a formula or a value.

- **Value**—A numeric entry or calculated result. Numbers can begin with leading plus or minus signs; an equal sign, currency symbols, numerals, commas, or periods; a trailing percent sign or an E for scientific notation. As you enter the values, don't include currency symbols, decimal points, commas, or spaces. You'll set that up with cell formatting later.

To enter labels:

1. Click in the cell where you want the label to appear.
2. Type the label.

If you are typing a label that begins with a number, type a quotation mark and then the number. The quotation mark tells Quattro Pro that the information is a label, not a value.

To enter values:

1. Click in the cell where you want the value to appear.
2. Type one of the symbols that indicate a value (+ - / $ (@ # . % =).
3. Type the value.

Most people use the plus sign (+) to start a value. After all, if you are using the numeric keypad to enter values, the plus sign is nearby.

Navigating Around the Notebook Window

The fastest way to move around in a notebook is to use the mouse to click in a cell. You can also use some other keyboard shortcuts to move around:

- **Home**—Move to cell A1.
- **Tab/Shift+Tab**—Move one cell to the right; move one cell to the left.
- **Arrow keys**—Move up, down, left, or right one cell.
- **PgUp/PgDn**—Move one screen up; move one screen down.
- **Ctrl+Left/Right Arrow**—Move one screen to the left; move one screen to the right.
- **GoTo(F5)**—Move to a specified cell.

Working with Cells

It's a rare day if you can create an entire spreadsheet and not need to go back and make changes to it. Whether you have typed in an incorrect value or you need to rearrange some columns, you can make these changes using the same techniques that you learned for editing text in WordPerfect.

Editing Cell Entries

Data in a cell can be edited as easily as you would edit text in WordPerfect. You get several different options for editing the contents of a cell:

- Click in the cell and retype the entire entry.
- Double-click in the cell and edit the entry.
- Click in the cell, and then click in the Input box to edit the entry in the Input box (see Figure A.2).

When you are finished, press **Enter**, **Tab**, or one of the arrow keys to apply the change.

FIGURE A.2

The input box is white when active.

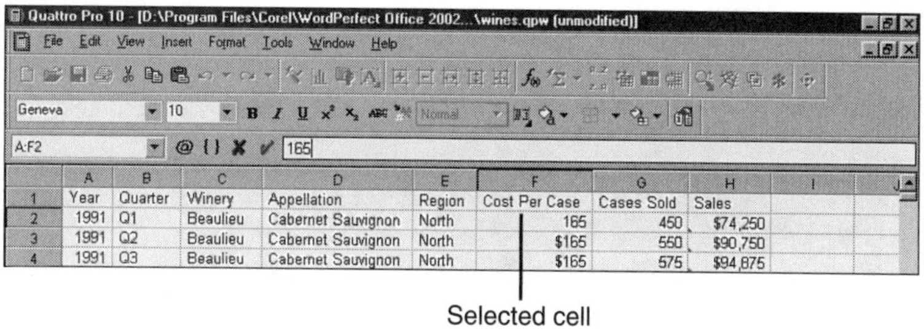

Selected cell

Selecting Cells

If you want to work with more than one cell at a time, you need to select the cells. Here are some tricks to quickly select a group of cells:

- Click in the cell that marks the upper-left corner of your selection. Hold down the **Shift** key and click in the cell that marks the lower-right corner of the selection (see Figure A.3).
- Click the first cell. Hold down the **Ctrl** key to click other cells. This technique also works in combination with clicking and dragging to select a group of cells.
- Click the row number on the row border to select a row. Click and drag to select multiple rows.
- Click the column letter on the row border to select a column. Click and drag to select multiple columns (see Figure A.4).

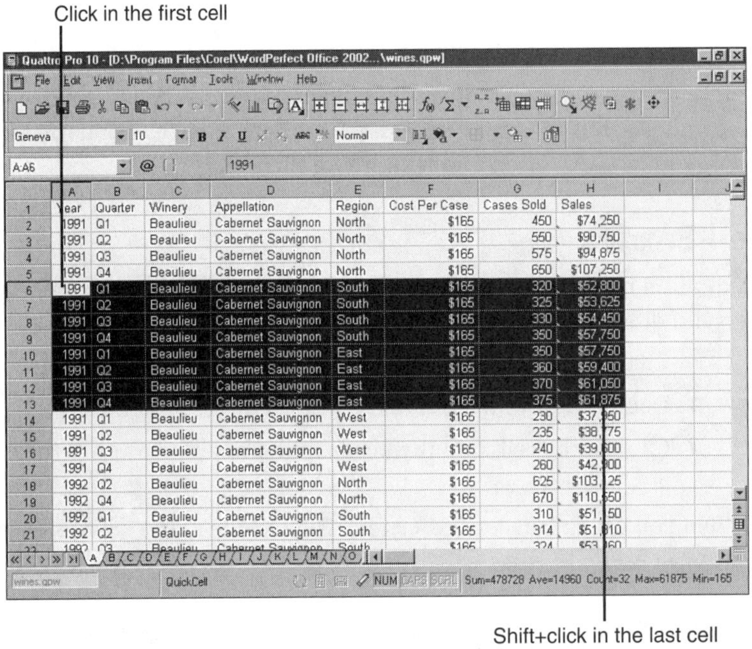

Click in the first cell

FIGURE A.3

A block of contiguous cells can be quickly selected in just two clicks.

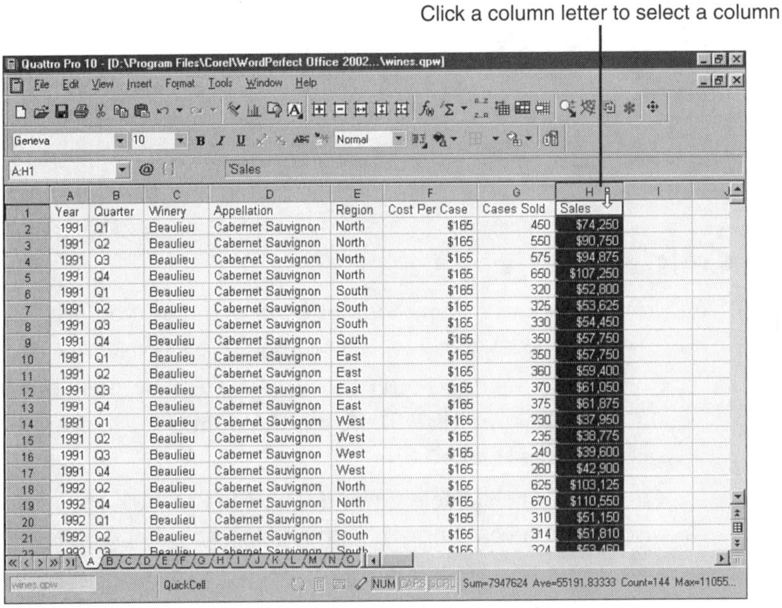

Shift+click in the last cell

Click a column letter to select a column

FIGURE A.4

An entire column or row can be selected by clicking the row number or column letter.

Moving and Copying Information

You can move and copy data in cells using the same techniques that you learned for WordPerfect. In Quattro Pro, you can move or copy data with drag-and-drop, or with the Cut, Copy, and Paste commands.

To move or copy selected cells with drag-and-drop:

1. Select the cell(s).

2. Point to the edge of the selection and wait for a four-sided arrow (see Figure A.5). This is the move pointer.

FIGURE A.5

Drag-and-drop is a quick method to move or copy text.

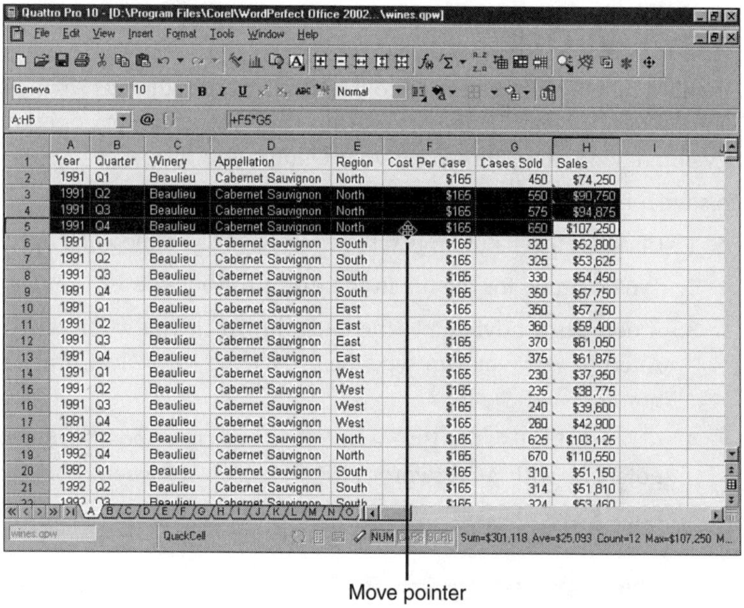

Move pointer

3. Drag the selection to the new location and do one of the following:

    ■ Release the mouse button to move the selection.

    ■ Hold down the **Ctrl** key as you release the mouse button to copy the selection.

    ■ Press **Esc** to cancel the move or copy.

If the move or copy operation will replace existing data, you'll get a warning message. Think carefully before responding Yes or No. If you opt to replace the existing data and then change your mind, you can use **Undo** to reverse your action and recover the data.

To move or copy selected cells with cut, copy, or paste:

1. Select the cell(s).

2. Click the **Cut** button (**Ctrl+X**) to move the selection; click the **Copy** button (**Ctrl+C**) to copy the selection.

3. Click in the upper-left cell of the new location.

4. Click the **Paste** button (**Ctrl+V**) to paste the data. Be careful where you paste because, unlike drag-and-drop, you won't get a warning message before replacing existing data.

Saving Your Work

Saving a notebook in Quattro Pro is essentially the same as saving a document in WordPerfect. It's equally important that you save your work often and that you develop a good filing system for your Quattro Pro files.

To save a new notebook:

1. Click the **Save** button (**Ctrl+S**). The Save File dialog box opens (see Figure A.6).

2. Type a name for the file in the **File name** text box.

3. If necessary, navigate to the folder in which you want to save this notebook. Alternatively, you can type the drive letter and folder name with the file-name.

4. (Optional) Click the **Password Protect** check box if you want to save the notebook with a password. Type the password when prompted.

5. Click **Save**.

FIGURE A.6

In the Save File dialog box, you can give a notebook a name and a location.

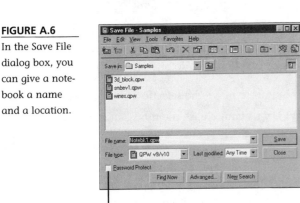

Click to save the file with a password

To save a notebook that is already named, click the **Save** button (**Ctrl+S**). Because you've already named the notebook, you don't have to enter the name again. Quattro Pro automatically saves over the existing file.

Importing and Exporting Data

Quattro Pro has superior importing and exporting capabilities, so it won't matter what program your friends or business associates are using. You can open notebooks created in other applications—Lotus 1-2-3 and Microsoft Excel, for example—with relatively few conversion problems.

For Microsoft Excel users, you can open Microsoft Excel versions 3, 5, 7, and 97 workbooks in Quattro Pro. You can also save a Quattro Pro notebook as a Microsoft Excel file, although some file format features unique to Quattro Pro might be lost. For a list of conversion considerations, see "Moving Between Microsoft Excel and Quattro Pro" in the Contents tab of the Help Topics dialog box."

Lotus 1-2-3 users can open Lotus 1-2-3 files (version 2 and 3) in Quattro Pro. After you have opened and worked on a file, you can save it as a Quattro Pro notebook. For a list of conversion considerations, see "Moving Between Lotus 1-2-3 and Quattro Pro" in the Contents tab of the Help Topics dialog box.

You can use spreadsheet files from a variety of applications with Quattro Pro. A table in Help identifies the Quattro Pro conversion filters available to convert files created in other applications. Look in the Help Index under "importing, file formats." Note that you will also be able to save a Quattro Pro file in most of the formats in the list.

Exporting data from Quattro Pro is as easy as saving the notebook to a different file format. Selected portions of a notebook can also be saved to a separate file. The Save File dialog box has a File type drop-down list that displays a list of file formats you can save to (see Figure A.7). Similarly, the Open File dialog box has a File type drop-down list that lists the names of the file formats that you can open.

note

To make the transition even easier, Quattro Pro allows you to choose a Microsoft Excel workspace for a similar command arrangement, a Lotus 1-2-3 workspace for a similar menu arrangement, or a Quattro Pro 7 workspace for similar menu arrangement. This lets you work in a familiar environment until you are accustomed to the Quattro Pro 10 interface. Choose **Tools**, **Settings**. Click **Workspaces** (in the left pane), place a check mark next to the workspace you want to use, and then click **OK**.

FIGURE A.7

In the Save File dialog box, click the File type drop-down arrow to display a list of file formats.

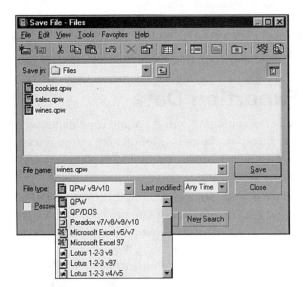

Getting Expert Assistance

If you have ever used Help in WordPerfect, you already know how to use it in Quattro Pro. In fact, the Help feature in Windows applications works essentially the same way. A section for Help topics is organized by category or project, and an index can be searched with keywords. In Corel products, there is also a page that allows you to search the knowledge base, provided you have an Internet connection. See the section titled "Getting Help" in Chapter 1, "Getting Around and Getting Help in WordPerfect," for more information on the Help topics.

For those making the transition from Microsoft Excel, Quattro Pro has a special help section just for you. Choose **Help**, **Microsoft Excel Help**. A help topic titled "Moving between Microsoft Excel and Quattro Pro" appears (see Figure A.8). This topic and the topics linked to it have information on how to make the transition easier.

FIGURE A.8

Click the green underlined text to jump to another help topic.

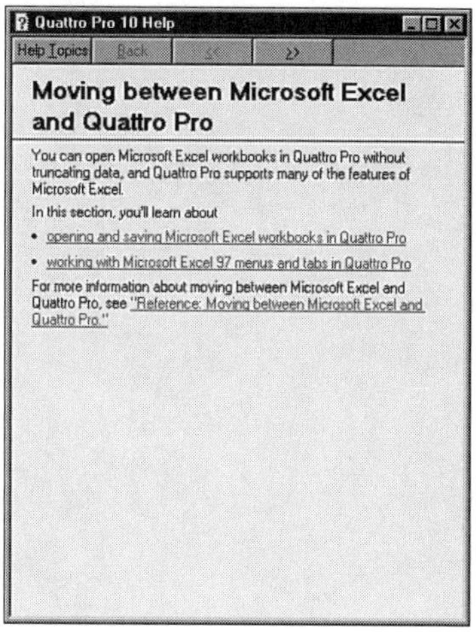

Quattro Pro 10 Help

Help Topics | Back | << | >>

Moving between Microsoft Excel and Quattro Pro

You can open Microsoft Excel workbooks in Quattro Pro without truncating data, and Quattro Pro supports many of the features of Microsoft Excel.

In this section, you'll learn about

- opening and saving Microsoft Excel workbooks in Quattro Pro
- working with Microsoft Excel 97 menus and tabs in Quattro Pro

For more information about moving between Microsoft Excel and Quattro Pro, see "Reference: Moving between Microsoft Excel and Quattro Pro."

B

Working with Formulas and Functions in Quattro Pro

In Chapter 10, "Creating and Formatting Tables," you learned how to build formulas that performed calculations within a WordPerfect table. The same principles apply in Quattro Pro. You can build simple formulas with operators such as the plus sign (+), the minus sign (–), the division symbol (/), and the multiplication (*) symbol. Most of your formulas will contain cell addresses, so you'll be pleased to know that you can click a cell to add it to a formula, rather than typing the cell address.

Understanding Formulas

Every calculation is considered a formula, even something as simple as 3+3. To build a formula, you have to start it with one of the following symbols: =, -, (, @, ., #, or =. A formula might contain numbers, cell addresses, cell names, and operators. If a formula starts with a cell address, such as C4*D8, you must put a symbol in front of it or Quattro Pro will treat it like a label.

When you create a formula in a cell, the result of the formula is displayed in the cell, not the formula itself. If you select a cell with a formula, the formula is displayed in the input line where you can edit it. You cannot edit the result of a formula—you can only edit the formula itself.

Understanding the order of operations is essential for the calculations to be performed the way you want them to be. The use of parentheses alters the order of precedence so that you can force calculations to be performed in a certain order.

Order of Operations

A formula uses mathematical operators to perform calculations on values. There are operators for addition, subtraction, multiplication, division, and exponentiation. Operations are performed according to their *order of precedence*. To help you remember the correct order, remember the phrase "My Dear Aunt Sally," which stands for Multiplication, Division, Addition, Subtraction.

To put it another way, if you build a formula like this one: D3*4-A7/12+9, the problem will be calculated in the following order:

1. Contents of cell D3 multiplied by 4.
2. Result of A7 divided by 12.
3. Result of step 2 added to 9.
4. Result of step 3 minus (subtract) A7.

If the order of precedence doesn't match the calculation that you need to perform, you can use parentheses to alter the order. Consider the results of the following calculations:

- 5 + 3 * 7 = 26
- (5 + 3) * 7 = 56

In the first example, you would multiply 3 by 7 and then add the results (21) to 5. In the second example, you use parentheses to make sure that 5 is added to 3, and the result is multiplied by 7. The key to having a calculation done exactly the way you want it is to use parentheses. This is a fundamental concept when you work with spreadsheets.

Entering Formulas

As mentioned earlier, instead of typing a cell address into a formula, you can click a cell to insert the cell address. This is especially nice when you want to use a range of cells in a calculation. For example, instead of typing **A3:A31**, you can click and drag across cells A3 through A31.

When you create a formula, you must begin with a symbol that tells Quattro Pro you are creating a formula, not typing in a label. Most people use the plus sign (+) to begin a formula, but you can also use any of the following: /, $, (, @, #, ., %, or =.

To create a mathematical formula:

1. Click in the cell where you want the result of the formula to appear.
2. Type a plus sign (+).
3. Type the formula.
4. Press **Enter** to enter the formula and display the results in the selected cell (see Figure B.1).

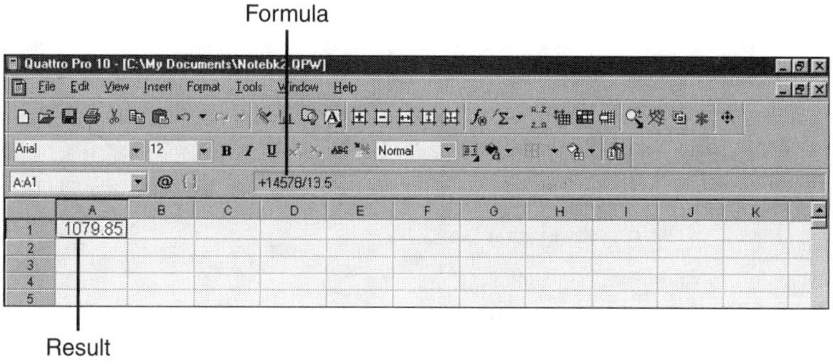

Formula

FIGURE B.1

When you enter a formula, the results of that formula are displayed in the cell.

Result

To create a formula with a cell address:

1. Click in the cell where you want the result of the formula to appear.
2. Type a plus sign (+).
3. Click in the first cell that you want to include in the formula. Quattro Pro inserts the cell address in the formula, as shown in Figure B.2. (The letter in front of the cell address is the name of the sheet.)
4. Click after the cell address (in the formula editing field) and type a mathematical operator.
5. Repeat steps 3 and 4 to continue entering the formula as necessary.
6. Press **Enter** to add the formula and display the result (see Figure B.3).

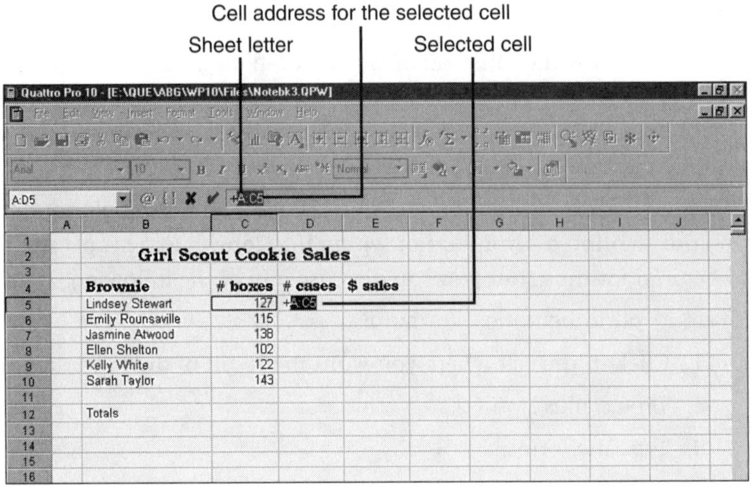

FIGURE B.2

Clicking a cell is much easier than figuring out the cell address and typing it in.

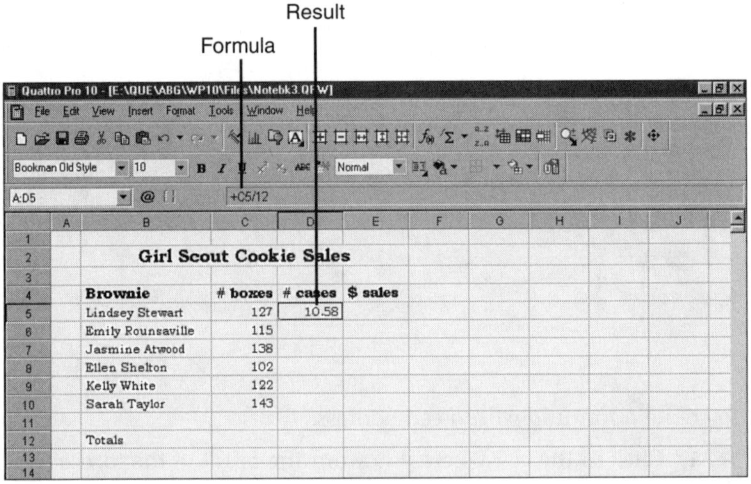

Cell address for the selected cell

Sheet letter

Selected cell

FIGURE B.3

The results of the calculation are displayed in the cell.

Result

Formula

Editing Formulas

It seems as though you no sooner create a formula than you have to turn around and revise it. No problem—you can edit a formula as quickly as you can create one, maybe even quicker. For example, if you find that a formula isn't delivering the result that you need, you can edit it and change the order of precedence.

To edit the contents of a cell:

1. Double-click the cell. This opens the cell and places the contents in the input line where you can edit it (see Figure B.4). You are now in Edit mode.

2. Make the necessary changes.

3. Press **Enter** to save your changes and switch back to Ready mode.

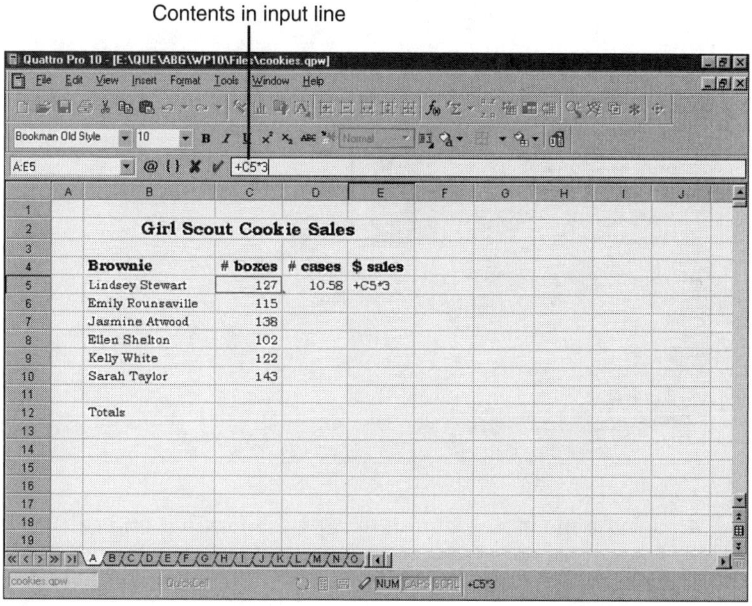

Contents in input line

FIGURE B.4

Double-click a cell to place the contents in the input line for editing.

Copying Formulas

In many cases when you create a formula, you need to use it more than once. You might be totaling the contents of a column, and you need to do the same thing for another 10 columns. Rather than re-creating the formula each time, you can copy the first formula across to the other 10 columns. Through the magic of Quattro Pro, the formulas are automatically adjusted for the new cell addresses in each column.

To copy a formula:

1. Click in the cell that contains the formula you want to copy.

2. Point to the lower-right corner of the cell and wait for a crosshair pointer to appear. The crosshair pointer has very thin lines with no arrowheads, so don't mistake it for the thicker four-sided arrow.

3. Click and drag across the cells where you want the formula copied (see Figure B.5).

Crosshair pointer

FIGURE B.5

Instead of re-creating the same formula over and over, you can copy it to adjacent cells.

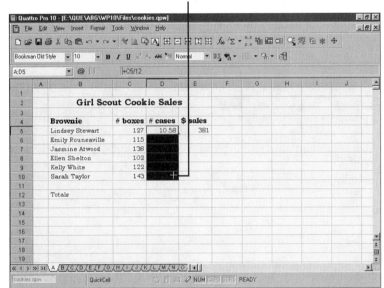

4. Release the mouse button to copy the formula and calculate the results (see Figure B.6).

Notice that after you selected the cells to copy the formula to, some helpful statistics popped up on the application bar (refer to Figure B.6). At a glance, you can see the total of the selected cells, the average, the number of selected cells, the biggest number, and the smallest number. Think about this for a minute—you can calculate statistics on any range of cells in a spreadsheet *without* having to create the formulas in the spreadsheet. Select any group of cells, and you get instant statistics—that's pretty cool.

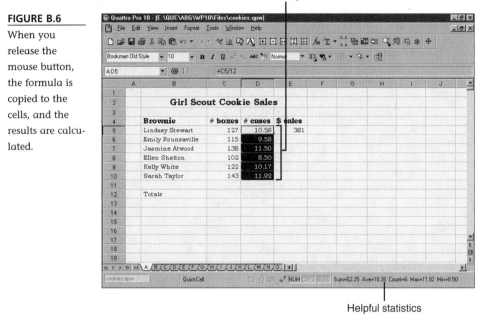

Results of the copied formula

FIGURE B.6

When you release the mouse button, the formula is copied to the cells, and the results are calculated.

Helpful statistics

Using QuickSum

The most frequently used function is the SUM function, which adds together the values in the cell range. For example, typing @sum(C3..C7) is the same as typing +C3+C4+C5+C6+C7. As mentioned earlier, you can click and drag across the cells that you want to add together so that you don't even have to type the cell addresses.

Wouldn't you know it—there is an even quicker way to add together the values in a series of cells. You can click and drag through the cells that you want to add together, and if you include a blank cell at the end of the selection, QuickSum places the total in that cell.

To use QuickSum to total a series of cells:

1. Click in the first cell of the series.

2. Click and drag through the series, making sure that you select a blank cell at the end of the row, or at the bottom of the column. You can have several blank cells between the last cell with a value and the cell where you want the total. Quattro Pro places the total in the last cell of the selection.

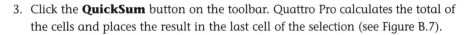

3. Click the **QuickSum** button on the toolbar. Quattro Pro calculates the total of the cells and places the result in the last cell of the selection (see Figure B.7).

QuickSum button

FIGURE B.7

QuickSum is a convenient shortcut when you need to add the values in selected cells.

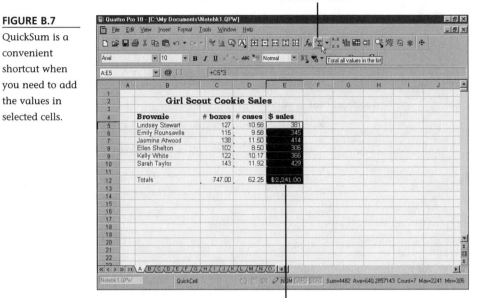

Result of sum

Understanding Functions

Quattro Pro has more than 500 built-in functions that cover a wide variety of calculations. Not only do the functions save you time in creating formulas from scratch, but they also allow you to perform calculations that would be almost impossible to create. You'll find a complete list of formulas in the Help Index. In the Index tab, search for "functions, list" and then select Quattro Pro Function Help from the list of Help topics (see Figure B.8). You can also type the function name such as @PAYMT in the Help Index to open a help topic devoted to that function.

The rules for creating a function are as follows:

- A leading at symbol (@), a plus sign (+), or an equal sign (=) must be entered first.

- The function can be typed in upper- or lowercase letters. There cannot be a space between the @ symbol and the function name.

- Arguments are the values, cells, or text strings on which operations are performed. They must be typed in the correct order.

- Multiple arguments are separated by a semicolon (;).

- Optional arguments must be typed within angle brackets, <>.

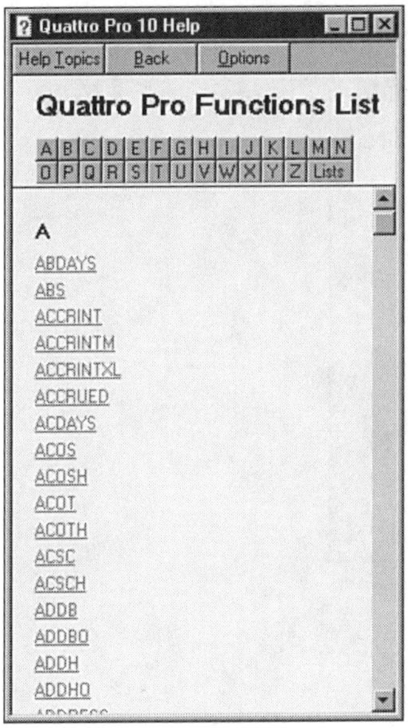

FIGURE B.8

Click a function to display a description.

Quattro Pro 10 Help

Help Topics | Back | Options

Quattro Pro Functions List

A B C D E F G H I J K L M N
O P Q R S T U V W X Y Z Lists

A

ABDAYS
ABS
ACCRINT
ACCRINTM
ACCRINTXL
ACCRUED
ACDAYS
ACOS
ACOSH
ACOT
ACOTH
ACSC
ACSCH
ADDB
ADDBO
ADDH
ADDHO
ADDRESS

Using the Formula Composer

If you don't care to remember the exact function names or the required arguments, you can select the function from a master list in the Functions dialog box. When you select a function from the Functions dialog box, you are immediately taken into the Formula Composer to finish creating the formula. The Formula Composer helps you build the formula by reminding you which elements are needed and alerting you if there is an error.

To select functions and use the Formula Composer to build the formula:

1. Click (or double-click) in the cell where you want to add the function.

2. Click the **Insert a Pre-existing Formula** button on the input line, or choose **Insert**, **Insert Function** to open the Functions dialog box (see Figure B.9.)

3. Select a function from the list.

4. Click **Next** to open the Formula Composer (see Figure B.10). The Formula Composer helps you build formulas by reminding you of the correct syntax and pointing out errors. In Figure B.10, an error appears because there is no list of cell addresses to sum.

Select a category   Choose a function from this list

FIGURE B.9

Instead of memorizing the syntax for a function, you can select it in the Functions dialog box.

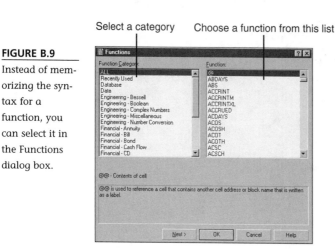

Shows the location
of the error   Insert a function

FIGURE B.10

The Formula Composer helps you create and troubleshoot formulas.

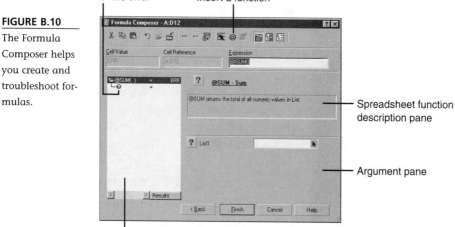

Spreadsheet function description pane

Argument pane

Outline pane

5. Click the arrow next to the **List1** field to minimize the Formula Composer dialog box so that you can see the spreadsheet again.

6. Select the cell or group of cells for the argument.

7. Click the **maximize** button on the Formula Composer title bar to display the Formula Composer dialog box again (see Figure B.11).

Click to display the Formula Composer dialog box

FIGURE B.11

The Formula Composer can be minimized to get it out of your way while you select cells.

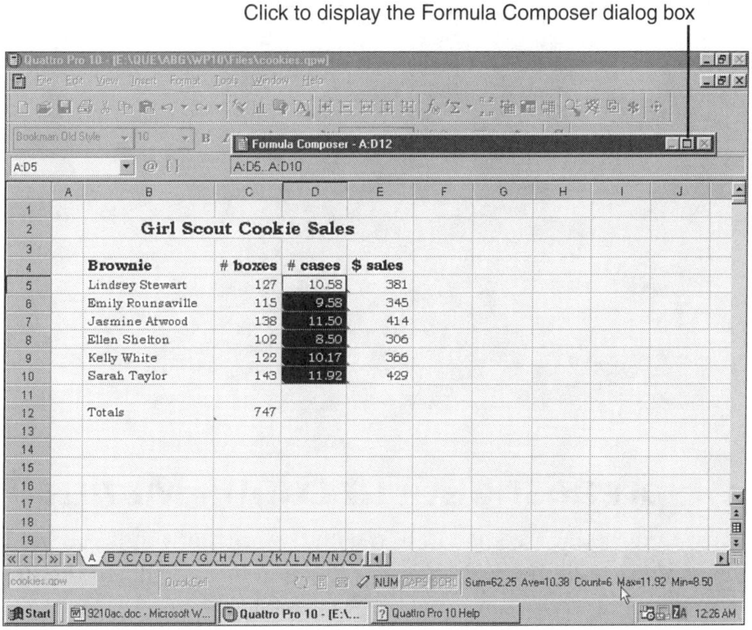

8. To add more cells to your formula, click the arrow next to **List2** and select the cell or group of cells.

9. Continue specifying the necessary arguments, and then click **Finish** when you are done.

10. If there is a problem with the formula, you'll see a message box that indicates a syntax error, and you won't be able to close the Formula Composer dialog box. Click **OK** to clear the message box.

You can use the Formula Composer at any time, not just when you are selecting from the Functions dialog box. The Formula Composer button opens the Formula Composer where you can create and edit formulas in a selected cell.

To open the Formula Composer to create, edit, or debug a formula:

1. Click the **Formula Composer** button on the toolbar to open the Formula Composer dialog box (see Figure B.12).

2. Type or edit the formula in the **Expression** box.

The Formula
Composer can
be used to cre-
ate, edit, and
debug formulas.

Entering Spreadsheet Functions Manually

Over time, you'll become familiar with the functions that you use often. When you do, you may opt to simply type the function into a cell. For the simpler functions, it's probably faster to type it yourself than to select it from a list. The previous section discusses the Formula Composer, which helps you create more complex formulas.

To type a spreadsheet function in a cell:

1. Click (or double-click) the cell that you want to add the function to.
2. Type a plus sign (+) to start the formula.
3. Type the @ symbol and then the name of the function (for example, @sum).
4. Type an opening parenthesis to enter the arguments. Look at the application bar and notice that it shows the syntax, or the rules for entering the formula, next to the mode indicators (see Figure B.13).
5. Either type the arguments, or use the mouse to select a cell or group of cells.
6. Type the closing parenthesis to end that part of the argument.
7. Continue adding the necessary arguments.
8. Press **Enter** to add the formula and calculate the result.

FIGURE B.13

The application bar shows the syntax for a function.

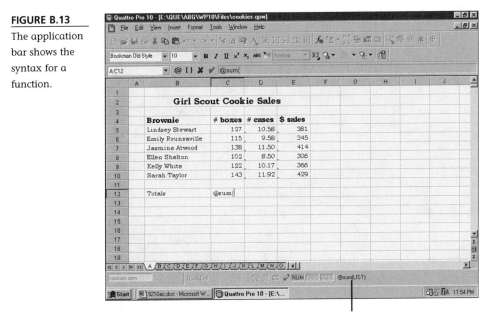

Syntax for the @sum function

FORMATTING YOUR SPREADSHEETS

Now that you've learned how to enter data in a spreadsheet and create formulas to calculate the data, you're ready to get started on making changes to the structure. In this appendix, you'll learn how to add and remove rows and columns when you need to adjust the size of the spreadsheet. You will learn how to combine cells and see how easy it is to lock cells so that the contents are not accidentally deleted or changed. And last but not least, you'll learn how to format a spreadsheet to make it more attractive and easier to read.

Inserting, Clearing, and Deleting Cells, Rows, and Columns

A common situation is to start typing column headings in the first row of a spreadsheet, and after you've typed in all the information, you realize that you didn't leave enough room for a title. No problem—you can insert as many rows as you need right on top. The same thing goes for columns. If, after entering a lot of data, you realize that you need to add a column between two columns full of data, again, no problem.

The same thing is true for clearing the contents of cells, or deleting the cells themselves. When you don't need the information anymore, you can get rid of it quickly.

Inserting Rows and Columns

When you insert new rows and columns in Quattro Pro, the existing data is shifted down or to the right of the notebook to make room. Also, when you add rows and columns, Quattro Pro automatically adjusts formulas to account for the added space. For example, let's say that you have a SUM formula at the bottom of a column that sums rows 2–13. You add three rows to the notebook. Quattro Pro adjusts the formula to include rows 2–16.

To insert rows or columns:

1. Select the number of rows or columns that you want to insert (see Figure C.1). For example, if you select three columns, Quattro Pro inserts three columns. Or, if you select five rows, Quattro Pro inserts five rows.

2. Click the **Insert cells, rows, columns or sheets** button. Quattro Pro inserts the new rows on top of the existing rows, so the existing data is moved down. New columns are inserted to the left of the existing columns, so the existing data is moved to the right.

To insert a cell or block of cells:

1. Select a cell or click and drag to select a group of cells that define the size of the block that you want to insert. For example, if you want to insert three columns and two rows, select the cells in three columns and two rows.

2. Click the **Insert cells, rows, columns, or sheets** button. Select one of the following:

   - **Columns**—To shift to the right
   - **Rows**—To shift down

3. In the Insert Cells dialog box, click **Partial**; then click **OK**.

FIGURE C.1

You can select the number of rows or columns that you want to insert.

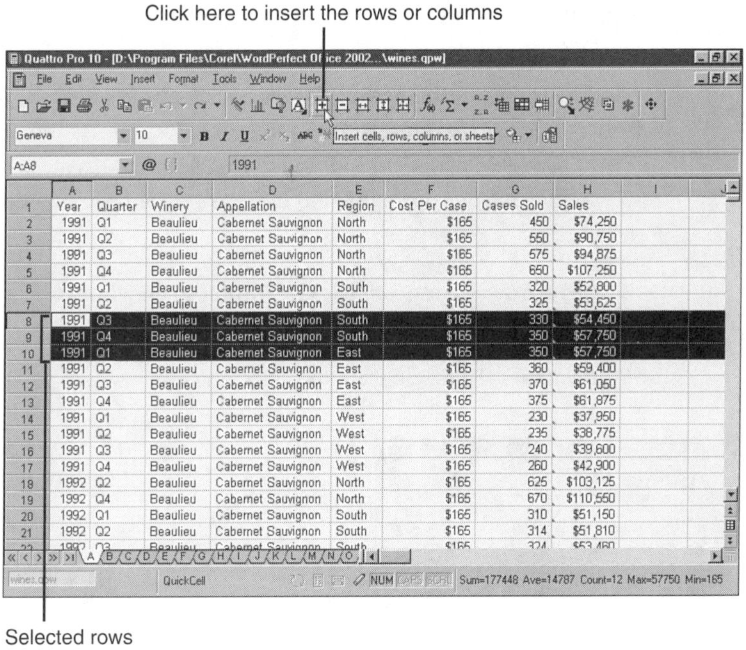

Click here to insert the rows or columns

Selected rows

Clearing the Contents

If you decide that you want to wipe out the contents of a cell, row, or column, you can do that without affecting the rest of the data.

To clear the contents of a cell, row, or column:

1. Select the cell, row, column, or block of cells.

2. Choose from one of the following options:

   ▓ Right-click the selection and choose **Clear** to clear both the contents and the formatting.

   ▓ Press **Delete** to clear just the contents.

   ▓ Choose **Edit**, **Clear**, **Formats** to clear just the formatting.

Deleting Cells, Rows, and Columns

You can delete unnecessary cells, rows, and columns. Deleting a block of cells is not the same thing as clearing their contents. You're deleting the actual space in the spreadsheet, which causes the rows and columns to move up or over to fill the gap.

To delete cells, rows, or columns:

1. Select the number of rows or columns that you want to delete.

2. Click the **Delete cells, rows, columns, or sheets** button, or right-click the selection and choose **Delete Cells**. Quattro Pro inserts the rows on top of the existing rows, so the existing data is moved down. If you're deleting cells, make a choice from the following options in the Delete dialog box (see Figure C.2):

   ■ **Columns, Rows, or Sheets**—To indicate what to delete.

   ■ **Entire**—To delete the selected rows, columns, or sheets entirely.

   ■ **Partial**—To delete only the selected cells.

FIGURE C.2

The location of the cell or series of cells to be deleted is seen in the Cells field.

Adjusting Column Width and Row Height

It often happens that the contents of a cell exceed the size of the cell. In most cases, the width of the column is the problem—you have a long title, for example, and the next column chops it off. To display the full text, you need to expand the column width so that the text fits.

Any changes to column width and row height apply to every cell within that column or row. In either case, you can use the mouse to click and drag a row or column border to adjust the width and height. You also can enter precise measurements in a dialog box. Remember, you can always use Undo to reverse your last action.

Adjusting Column Width

There are several ways to adjust column width. The quickest way is to use the mouse. The disadvantage of the mouse is that you can't be very precise. If you want to select a specific column width, you can type it into a dialog box. I'll touch on this later.

note

Quattro Pro displays a row of asterisks (*******) or scientific notation (E+) if the column isn't wide enough for the contents.

To adjust the column width using the mouse:

1. Position the mouse pointer on the right or left side of a column border (see Figure C.3). The mouse pointer changes to a thick double-sided arrow.

Resize pointer

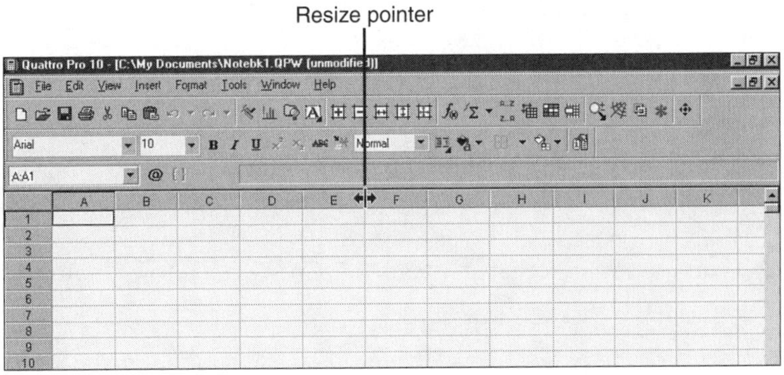

FIGURE C.3

Clicking and dragging the column borders is a fast and easy way to adjust the column widths.

2. Click and drag the column border to the left or right to adjust the column width. Notice that the changes affect the entire column.

There are several shortcuts for adjusting the column width to fit the longest entry:

■ Double-click the column border.

■ Click the **Column QuickFit** button on the toolbar, or choose **Format**, **QuickFit**, **Colu_m_n QuickFit**.

■ Click the **Column/Row QuickFit** button, or choose **Format**, **QuickFit**, **Column/Row QuickFit** to adjust the row height and the column width at the same time.

Adjusting Row Height

You can click and drag a row border to fine-tune the height of a row, or as I mentioned before, you can enter precise measurements in a dialog box.

To adjust the row height using the mouse:

1. Position the cursor on the top or bottom of a row border (see Figure C.4). The cursor changes to a thick double-sided arrow.

2. Click and drag the row border up or down to adjust the row height. Notice that the changes affect the entire row.

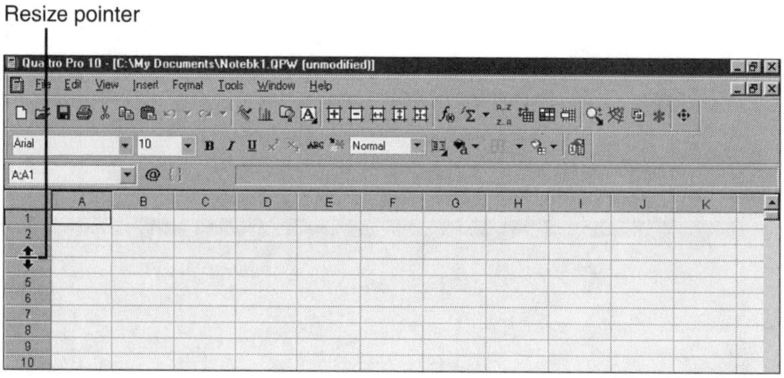

Resize pointer

FIGURE C.4

Using the mouse to click and drag a row border is the quickest way to adjust the row height.

You can use several great shortcuts for adjusting the row height:

■ Double-click the row border.

 ■ Click the **Row QuickFit** button on the toolbar, or choose **Format**, **QuickFit**, **Row QuickFit**.

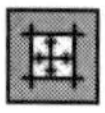

 ■ Click the **Column/Row QuickFit** button, or choose **Format**, **QuickFit**, **Column/Row QuickFit** to adjust the row height and the column width at the same time.

Assigning Precise Dimensions to Columns and Rows

If you need specific widths in your spreadsheet, you can type precise measurements in the Active Cells dialog box. For example, you might need to have three columns that are exactly 1.25-inch wide.

To adjust the column width or row height using measurements:

1. Select the column(s) or row(s) to be resized.

2. Click the **Selection Properties** button, or choose **Format**, **Selection Properties** to open the Active Cell dialog box (see Figure C.5).

3. Click the **Row/Column** tab. Choose from one of the following options:

■ Type the width in the **Set width** text box.

■ Type the height in the **Set height** text box.

■ Click **Reset Width** to switch back to the default width.

■ Click **Reset Height** to switch back to the default height.

4. Click **OK** when you're finished.

Type the column width here

FIGURE C.5

You can enter precise column width and row height measurements in the Active Cells dialog box.

Type the row height here

Formatting Values

By default, the values that you enter are displayed in a General numeric format, which displays the numbers as you have entered them. There are many other types of formats, such as Currency, Percent, Scientific, and Date.

To set the format for values:

1. Select the cell(s) that you want to format.

2. Click the **Selection Properties** button, or choose **Format**, **Selection Properties** to open the Active Cells dialog box.

3. Click the **Numeric Format** tab to display a list of formats.

4. Select a format from the list. The sample box shows you what that format will look like (see Figure C.6).

5. Click **OK** when you're finished.

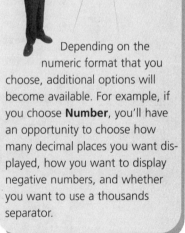

note

Depending on the numeric format that you choose, additional options will become available. For example, if you choose **Number**, you'll have an opportunity to choose how many decimal places you want displayed, how you want to display negative numbers, and whether you want to use a thousands separator.

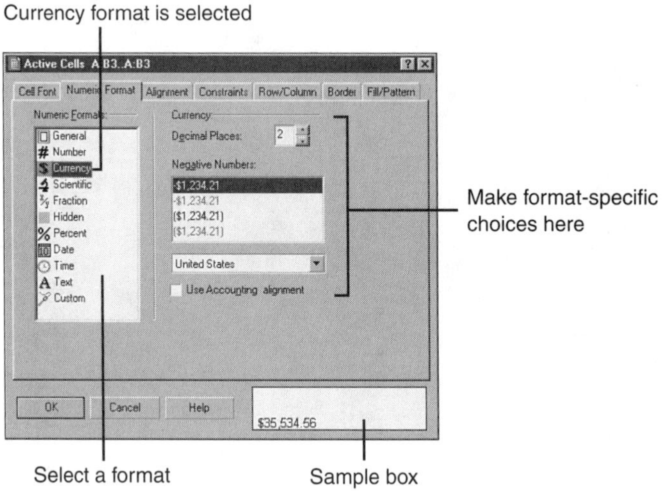

Currency format is selected

FIGURE C.6

In the Numeric Format tab, select one of the many ways to display the values in your spreadsheet.

Make format-specific choices here

Select a format

Sample box

Aligning Entries in Cells

By default, Quattro Pro aligns labels on the left and values on the right side of a cell. You can also center text in a cell or across selected cells, rotate text for column headings, display the text vertically, and more.

To align text in a cell:

1. Select the cell(s) that you want to align.

2. Click the **Selection Properties** button, or choose **Format, Selection Properties** to open the Active Cell dialog box.

3. Click the **Alignment** tab to display the alignment options (see Figure C.7).

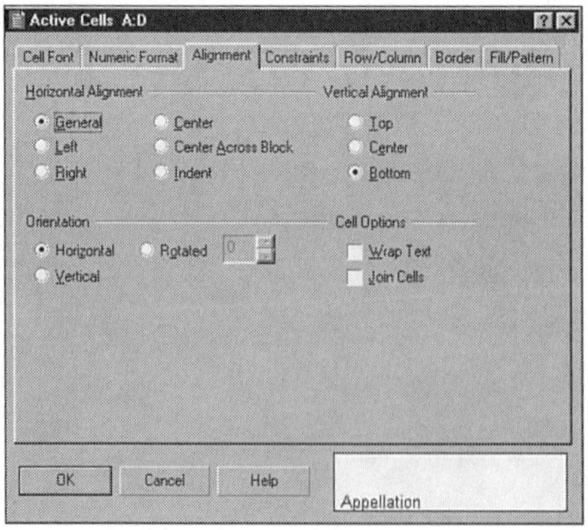

FIGURE C.7

The Alignment tab has options for horizontal alignment, vertical alignment, and orientation.

4. Choose from the following options. The sample box shows you how the text will look with the selected setting:

  - **Left/Center/Right**—Aligns text horizontally in the cell.
  - **Center Across Block**—Centers text in the left cell across the selected cells.
  - **Indent**—Indents the text away from the edge of the cell.
  - **Top/Center/Bottom**—Aligns text vertically in the cell.
  - **Horizontal**—Displays text horizontally in a cell.
  - **Vertical**—Stacks the text vertically in the cell.
  - **Rotated**—Turns the text by degrees (–180° to 180°).

5. Click **OK** when you're finished.

 There is also a button on the toolbar that you can use to quickly align text in a cell. Click the **Horizontal Alignment** button; then choose one of the four alignment options. If you hover over the alignment button, a QuickTip appears with details.

Adding Emphasis to Cells

Text in a Quattro Pro spreadsheet can be formatted using the same techniques that you learned in WordPerfect. Bold, italic, and underline can be applied to selected cells by clicking the button on the toolbar. Another font, or font size, can be applied by selecting from the property bar (see Figure C.8).

To make changes in the Active Cell dialog box:

1. Select the text, a cell, or group of cells.

2. Click the **Selection Properties** button, or choose **Format, Selection Properties**.

3. Click the **Cell Font** tab to display the font options (see Figure C.9).

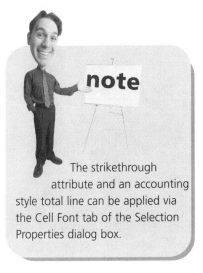

note

The strikethrough attribute and an accounting style total line can be applied via the Cell Font tab of the Selection Properties dialog box.

FIGURE C.8

You format text in Quattro Pro using the same techniques as in WordPerfect.

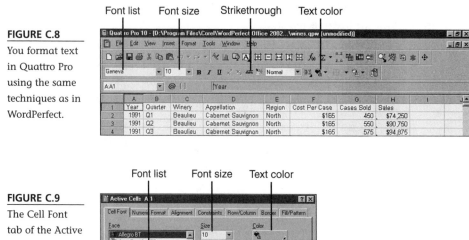

FIGURE C.9

The Cell Font tab of the Active Cells dialog box looks a lot like the Font dialog box in WordPerfect.

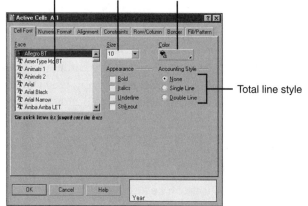

Protecting Cells

You can protect data in a spreadsheet in a number of ways. If you want to make sure that the data is secure, you can protect an entire spreadsheet. You also can selectively unprotect cells in a protected spreadsheet and lock a specific cell or group of cells.

When you lock, or *protect*, a cell or spreadsheet, you are preventing editing, replacement, or deletion of data. Columns and rows that contain protected cells cannot be deleted until you remove the protection.

To protect the entire spreadsheet:

1. Choose **Fo**r**mat**, **S**h**eet Properties** and click the **Protection** tab.

2. Click the **Enable Cell Locking** check box.

To unlock a cell in a protected spreadsheet:

1. Select a cell.

2. Click the **Selection Properties** button, or choose **Fo**r**mat**, **Selection Prope**r**ties**.

3. Click the **Constraints** tab to display the Constraints options (see Figure C.10).

Click to lock a cell   Click to unlock a cell

FIGURE C.10

Use the Data Input Constraints options to limit the type of data that can be entered in a cell.

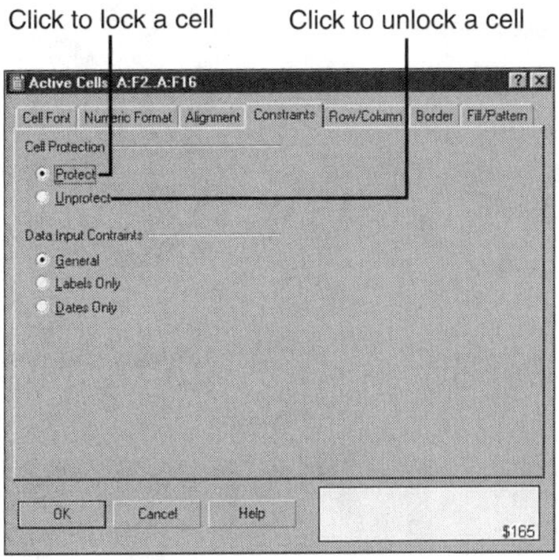

4. Enable the **Unprotect** option.

To selectively lock a cell or group of cells:

1. Select the cell(s) that you want to protect. 
2. Click the **Selection Properties** button, or choose **Format**, **Selection Properties**.
3. Click the **Constraints** tab.
4. Enable the **Protect** option.s

Joining Cells

A series of cells can be joined to create one big cell. This is usually done for a long title, but other situations also might call for joined cells. Remember, you can join cells horizontally or vertically, so you could have a vertically aligned label alongside several rows.

You can join cells in rows, in columns, or in both rows and columns. Data in a joined cell can be used in calculations just like any other cell. The same goes for aligning and formatting—you can format a joined cell just as you would a single cell.

note

You can also constrain the types of entries allowed in a cell or selected cells. Choose **Format**, **Selection Properties.** Click the **Constraints** tab and then choose **Labels Only** or **Dates Only**. The General option removes the constraints and accepts all entries.

To join cells:

1. Select the cells that you want to join.

2. Click the **Selection Properties** button, or choose **Format**, **Selection Properties**.

3. Click the **Alignment** tab.

4. Enable the **Join Cells** option. Quattro Pro joins the selected cells into one big cell (see Figure C.11).

> **tip** 
>
> The Join Cells button on the toolbar joins cells and centers the text, all at the same time.

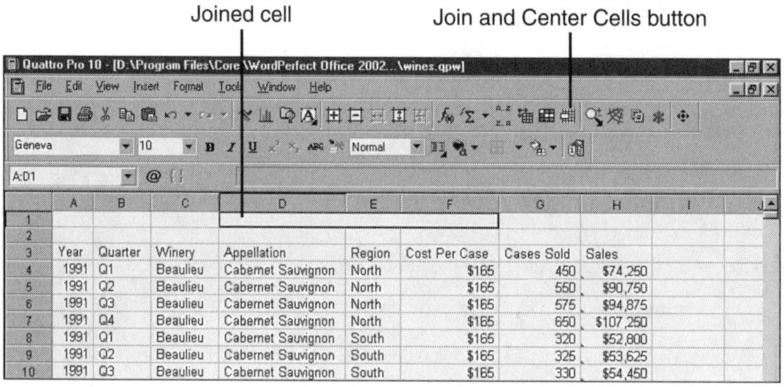

FIGURE C.11

A joined cell can be used in calculations and can be formatted just like you would any single cell.

Joined cell   Join and Center Cells button

Naming Cells

The idea behind naming cells is to be able to reference a cell by name rather than by cell address. This proves useful when building formulas because you don't have to remember the exact cell address, only a name. You can assign a name to a single cell or to a range of cells. This comes in handy if you plan to export portions of your spreadsheet for use in another application. One of the options you'll have is to export a named range. Put simply, it's easier to remember "net profit" or "jan2002 sales" than it is to remember "d123" or "A13:A47."

To name a cell or group of cells:

1. Select the cell(s).

2. Choose **Insert**, **Name**, **Name Cells** to display the Cell Names dialog box (see Figure C.12).

Type

FIGURE C.12

You can name a
single cell or
group of cells in
the Cell Names
dialog box.

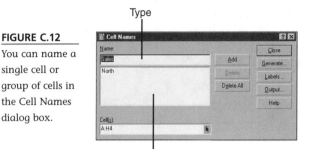

List of existing cell names

3. Type a unique name in the **Name** text box. Be careful not to use a name
   that already appears in the list, or you'll accidentally replace it.

4. Click **Add**.

Cell names can be edited to change the cell address(es). They can also be deleted if
you no longer want to use them. Take a look at the help topic titled "Naming cells"
for more information and a link to a page titled "Guidelines for naming cells."

Using SpeedFormat

You can use a variety of different formatting options to emphasize cells. A simple
application of bold or italic might be enough. Or, you might decide to use a text
color or a fill color to color the background of the cell.

Take my word for it—before you try to do all these things manually, you need to
look at the SpeedFormat feature. There are plenty of different styles to choose from,
and you can format an entire table in just seconds.

To use SpeedFormat on your spreadsheet:

1. Click the **SpeedFormat** button, or choose **Format**, **SpeedFormat** to display the SpeedFormat dialog box (see Figure C.13).

2. Select one of the formats in the **Formats** list box. The Example box shows
   how your spreadsheet will look if you apply that format to it.

3. If necessary, remove the check marks from the options that you don't want to
   apply formatting to. For example, you could skip the text color or shading.

4. Click **OK** to apply the selected SpeedFormat to the spreadsheet.

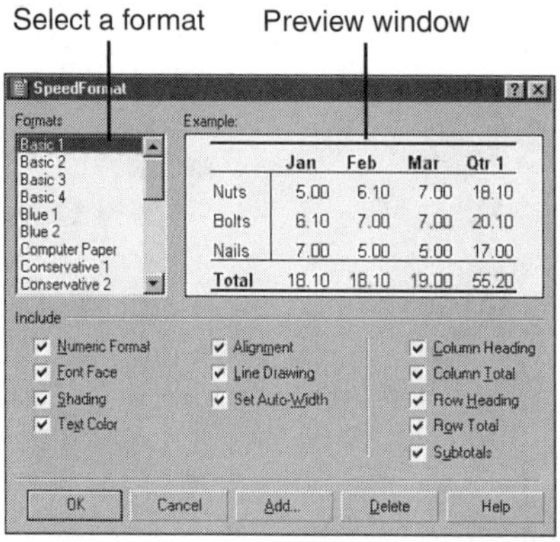

Select a format   Preview window

FIGURE C.13

You can quickly turn a plain-Jane spreadsheet into a presentation-quality spreadsheet with one of the predefined SpeedFormats.

UNDERSTANDING THE WORDPERFECT PRODUCT FAMILY

With so many different flavors of WordPerfect available, figuring out what you have and what you don't have can be confusing. I'll try to sort things out, but please understand that this is the information we had when the book was sent to the printer. Some things might have changed since then.

WordPerfect 10 is a part of the following releases:

- Corel WordPerfect Office 2002 Suite

- Corel Family Pack 4

- Corel Productivity Pack

The Full Suite

The full Corel WordPerfect Office 2002 suite is available in the following releases: Standard, Professional, Academic, and the Trial version.

The Standard Version

The Standard version of the WordPerfect Office 2002 suite includes the following components:

- WordPerfect 10
- Quattro Pro 10
- Presentations 10
- CorelCENTRAL 10
- Language Module
- Microsoft Visual Basic for Applications
- Bitstream Font Navigator
- QuickView Plus
- Net2Phone
- Adobe Acrobat Reader
- Printed Manual

Sony is bundling the full suite with some of its systems. Only a few obscure features are missing: XML authoring, digital signatures, and some rarely used filters.

The Professional Version

The Professional version of the WordPerfect Office 2002 suite includes the components in the Standard suite, plus the following:

- Paradox 10
- Paradox 10 Runtime
- Dragon NaturallySpeaking
- Headset

The Academic Version

The Academic version includes WordPerfect Office 2002 Professional (including Paradox), the Dragon NaturallySpeaking CD, and a headset. It does not include clip art, photos, fonts, and a clip art reference guide or the manuals.

The initial release of the Academic edition contained an OEM CD#1, which did not include QuickView Plus, Internet Explorer, VBA, and the Scrapbook. Corel announced in July 2001, that it would be replacing the OEM CD#1 with the full Professional Edition CD#1. If you purchased an early Academic release, you can call Corel at 800-772-6735 for a new CD. If you're not sure what you have, open the `volinfo.txt` file on CD#1. If you see OEM in the product name, you are eligible for the update.

The Trial Version

A trial version of the WordPerfect Office suite is available. You can order the CD from the Products List on Corel's site (`www.corel.com`), or from the Try It link on the page for the Standard or Professional versions on Corel's site. You can also call Corel directly at 800-772-6735. You can use the trial for 30 days, after which, you need to purchase a license to continue to use the software.

On the Try Before You Buy CD, the following suite items have been removed:

- Microsoft Internet Explorer 5.5
- Microsoft Visual Basic for Applications
- Dragon NaturallySpeaking
- QuickView Plus
- Adobe Acrobat 4.0
- Bitstream Font Navigator
- Writing tools (except English, Spanish, and French)
- Most of the clip art, photos, and other graphics
- Some conversion filters
- WordPerfect 10—digital signatures, Entrust security, XML tools
- Quattro Pro 10—mapping, most charting templates, samples
- Presentations 10—sample slideshow, most masters, Graphicsland
- Paradox 10—Delphi add-in kit, some experts

Templates for all applications and Inso Viewers were not part of the original Try Before You Buy CD, but they were added to the Service Pack 2 version.

Corel Family Pack

The Family Pack is perfect for the home or home office user on a budget. It has plenty of ready-to-use templates, so you can get started right away. You can manage your finances, create personal correspondence and school project materials, and work with your digital photos.

The Family Pack includes

- WordPerfect 10
- Quattro Pro 10
- Task Manager
- Dragon NaturallySpeaking Essentials
- Picture Publisher Digital Camera Edition
- McAfee VirusScan 6
- Brittanica Ready Reference Encyclopedia
- Avery DesignPro

Corel Productivity Pack

Corel's Productivity Pack is essentially WordPerfect 10 and Quattro Pro 10 with a few other goodies thrown in. The Productivity Pack is being bundled with computers from the largest computer manufacturers: Dell, HP, and Gateway. Because the manufacturers can pick what applications they want to include with their systems, there are several different flavors of Productivity Packs.

The Productivity Pack included with Dell systems contains WordPerfect 10, Quattro 10, and the same templates included in the suite.

HP and Gateway systems are shipping with WordPerfect 10, Quattro Pro 10, the Task Manager, and around 100 templates.

Places to Go for Help

The WordPerfect community is a friendly one. Here are a couple of excellent places to go for peer-to-peer support.

Did I say friendly? The volunteer C-Techs on the Corel WordPerfect newsgroups are the friendliest and most knowledgeable people you would ever hope to meet. There is no such thing as a stupid question, so don't hesitate to drop in and get help. Just remember that they are *volunteers*, not employees of Corel. Subscribe to the Corel's newsgroups here: http://www.corel.com/support/newsgroup.htm.

Also visit the discussions at WordPerfect Universe (www.wpuniverse.com), which is where WordPerfect people hang out online. It's a great community of users, trainers, consultants, and those who live, breath, and eat WordPerfect. You can ask questions here too. The group is smaller, so the response may not be as fast, but we do our best to make you feel welcome. The Universe has a great set of links to other sites that offer tips and tricks, macros, tutorials, articles, and many other resources.

Index

C

How can we make this index more useful? Email us at indexes@quepublishing.com

How can we make this index more useful? Email us at indexes@quepublishing.com

Formula Composer, *327-329*
order of operations, *320*
QuickSum, *325*
functions, 326
help, 316
importing/exporting data, 315
navigating, 310
numeric formats, 339
password protecting, 314
rows
clearing, *335*
deleting, *335-336*
inserting, *334*
sizing with Active Cells dialog box, *338*
sizing with Row QuickFit command, *337-338*
saving, 314-315
SpeedFormat, 345
starting, 308
user interface, 309
number of copies (Print dialog box), 54
numbered lists
creating, 180
numbering styles, 182-183
Numbering command (Page menu), 122
numbers
numbered lists
creating, *180*
numbering styles, *182-183*
page numbers
inserting in predefined positions, *122-124*
inserting manually, *124-125*
spreadsheet numeric formats, *339*
Numbers tab (Bullets & Numbering dialog box), 180, 184
Numeric Format command (Table menu), 170
Numeric Format tab (Active Cells dialog box), 339
numeric formats (spreadsheets), 339

O

Object command (Insert menu), 228
OLE (Object Linking and Embedding), 227-228
creating OLE objects, 229
in-place editing, 229
linking data, 228-229
OLE servers, 229
online help, 14-15
Open Address Book dialog box, 265
Open an Existing Address Book button, 265
Open button, 30
open codes, 73
Open command (File menu), 30
Open File dialog box
customizing view, 30-31
displaying, 30
opening files, 30
rearranging file list, 32
open styles, 138
opening
address books, 258-259, 265-267
Clipbook, 225
documents
blank documents, *8-9, 18, 51*
converting on open, *36-37*
multiple documents, *31*
Open File dialog box, *30*
Quattro Pro, 308
QuickCorrect, 93
QuickMenu, 11
Task Manager, 300
WordPerfect, 8
operators, 320. *See also* **formulas**
Options menu commands
Create WP Template, 283
Custom WP Templates, 280
Edit WP Template, 280
Language, 88
order of precedence (formulas), 320
ordinal text, converting to superscript, 96

Organization entries (Address Book), 262
organizing documents in folders
creating folders, 37-38
deleting folders, 40
naming folders, 38
renaming folders, 39
orphans, 115
Outline property bar, 185-186
Outline/Bullets & Numbering command (Insert menu), 178-184, 190
outlines, 183
adding items to, 186-187
collapsing/expanding, 189-190
creating, 184-185
Outline property bar, 185-186
outline styles, 190
promoting/demoting items, 188-189
rearranging items in, 187-188
Oxford English Pocket Dictionary, 85-86

P

Page Border/Fill dialog box, 132-133
page breaks
creating, 118
deleting, 118-119
hard page breaks, 118
soft page breaks, 118
Page command (View menu), 109
Page menu commands
Border/Fill, 132-134
Delay Codes, 130
Insert Page Number, 125
Numbering, 122
Page Setup, 119
Suppress, 130
Page Numbering button, 128
page numbers
inserting in predefined positions, 122-124
inserting manually, 124-125

How can we make this index more useful? Email us at indexes@quepublishing.com